GOOD DEBT CHEAP

Value Investing in Bonds, Preferreds,
and Other Fixed Income Securities

First Edition

KENNETH JEFFREY MARSHALL

JUDICIAL CORPORATION

ISBN 978-1-737-67344-6 (hardcover)

www.gooddebtcheap.com

CONTENTS

PREFACE

Compared to my first book, this one stinks. But it's not my fault. I'll explain.

Good Stocks Cheap—my first book—is about equities. That's a great subject to master. It's a great subject to master because listed equities return better than anything else. Not every day or every year, of course. In the short term, anything can happen. But over time and on average, publicly traded stocks beat everything. Gold, farmland, yen—everything.

One of those everythings is fixed income securities. Bonds, notes, debentures—they just can't do what stocks do. A percentage return that earns a bond fund manager an award could get a stock fund manager fired.

Plus stocks offer bigger outperformance opportunities. The distance between excellent and average is greater with equities than with fixed income. A top stock investor beats a typical stock investor by miles. But a top bond investor barely inches past a typical bond investor. In the rollicking language of statistics, bond returns have a narrower standard deviation.

This is so true that many good institutional money managers just give up. They don't try to pick individual bonds. Instead, they put any capital earmarked for fixed income into bond index funds. They opt for average, knowing that the alternative won't be much better. They choose a *passive* approach over an *active* approach, and for good reason.[1]

So that's the problem with this book: its utility is limited by its subject. Like an instruction manual for a can opener, there's only so much you can do with it.

Nonetheless, fixed income securities are worth mastering. There are six reasons why.

First, the bond market is huge. Very huge. By some estimates it's three times larger than the stock market.[2] So to know your way around fixed income is to know your way around much of the investment universe.

Second, bonds sometimes offer enormous returns. Not often, but sometimes. I've seen occasional high-yield opportunities so great that they impress even championship stock pickers. I'll show them to you.

Third, debt sometimes offers a low-cost route to stock ownership. *Convertible* bonds can become equity via advantageous *conversion ratios*. And some *distressed debt* investors buy fixed income securities without conversion provisions in the hope that a court will exchange them for stock.

Fourth, even pure equity investors can find themselves in fixed income. Like cash, it's an asset class that capital sits in while awaiting more delectable opportunities. For example someone in a *money market fund* owns—albeit indirectly—*T-bills* and *commercial paper*. Those are fixed income securities.

Fifth is *income*. That's payments a security periodically makes to its owner. With stocks it takes the form of dividends. With bonds it takes the form of interest. Generally speaking, stocks pay dividends less reliably than bonds pay interest.

Stocks can pay dividends. But most bonds *must* pay interest. So investors seeking periodic inflows see a special glow in fixed income securities. The cash stream from them is more, well, fixed.

Sixth is *volatility*. Like income, it's a quantitative angle from which bonds look good.

Volatility is how much the price of an asset moves. It's higher with stocks than with bonds. Listed equity prices simply flit around more than do fixed income prices. That matters to some investors.

Bank treasurers, for example. They mind their institutions' coffers. They're required to maintain some minimum portfolio market price. If they dip below that level, their bank could be taken over by regulators. So to them, volatility control is essential.

Or *balanced* fund managers. Some fear spooking their unit holders with a monthly statement written during the depths of a bear market. So they allocate more to fixed income and less to stocks to make their performance look steadier. Sure, returns may lag. But unit holders may be less likely to leave.

These six reasons appeared to me neither quickly nor fully formed. They took their time to gel. What brought them into focus was my students.

I was teaching a masters-level course on value investing in stocks. It became popular enough to spark interest in a follow-on course. Bonds was the natural new topic. But smitten with the high returns from equities, I dragged my feet.

What kicked me into action was jobs. Many of my students were finding at least as many career opportunities in bonds as in stocks. And of course they were. The bond market is bigger.

But while writing the syllabus I hit a snag. My textbook choices were disappointing. There were plenty of bond books. But they were wordy. And bulky. Wordy, bulky, and narcoleptic. One dwarfed my toaster. I owe some of my finest naps to surveying the competition.

Those naps, and subsequent fits of typing, sired the work you now hold. To readers of my first book, it will seem familiar. It shares many characteristics.

For one, it's written with principals in mind. It's more for people investing their own money than for those acting as agents for others. It's useless on topics like how to round up capital to start a fund, for example, or how to work with regulators.

That said, the best fund managers think like principals. They run others' money as if it was their own. This book should serve them as well.

Second, it's written plainly. I choose simple over exhaustive. Just glance at the glossary. It's succinct. Take the word *derivative*. My definition of it is eight words long. The toaster-dwarfer's is 57.

Of course we will get pretty detailed. We have to. We can't gloss over topics like the *day count convention* or *bond-equivalent yield*. But expect a book more blunt than its plump peers.

Third, this book is international. Our examples come from Europe and Asia as much as they do from the Americas. But expect a U.S. tilt. That's because of my citizenship, and because of my experience. It's also because of my country's outsized role in global financial markets. So it's practical that we emphasize the U.S.

In fact my hope is that the whole book is practical. While born in a university, it's not academic. It doesn't treat bond investing as some ethereal field you're privileged to be given a glimpse of. Instead it treats it as a straightforward matter comprehensible by anyone. Because it is.

This practicality leads to objectivity. Whenever possible, we'll stick to facts. Often that's natural. There's only one way to figure *Macauley duration*, for example, or *yield to worst*.

Nevertheless, this book very much reflects my opinions. From my take on *credit ratings* to the way I frame the *cost of capital*, my personal views can't help but seep into these pages. So you'd do well to read each sentence as if it began with *I think that*.

When *Good Stocks Cheap* came out in 2017, interest rates were relatively low. The prime rate was 4 percent.[3] That made bonds look boring, and equities look promising.

But today interest rates are higher. As I write this in 2024 the prime rate is over 8 percent.[4] So bonds look more attractive. This has caused some colleagues to playfully accuse me of publishing arbitrage.

But I'm not that quick. If this book seems timely, that's by chance. If it seems out of season, that's also by chance. It's no more or less relevant today than it will be tomorrow, or in many tomorrows. It's about basics, not fads.

I'm also not quick enough to have come up with all of the case studies on my own. Most of them are trades done by investors that I respect, investors that figured out complicated situations faster than I did. Only in retrospect can I see their moves as clever.

These case studies require me to name specific companies. I also name some financial institutions to provide examples of investment products. But please know that I haven't been paid or otherwise encouraged to promote any of them. In the rare case that I own securities in one of them, I'll disclose that.

A final confession: this book contains errors. If I knew what they were, they wouldn't be here. But as with any first edition, a mistake or two is guaranteed. I'll post corrections promptly, at www.gooddebtcheap.com. Once there's enough of them I'll wipe the slate clean by publishing a second edition.

Many that read this book will become better active managers. They'll like picking bonds. But others won't. They'll conclude that the work is tedious relative to the upside, and opt for bond index funds. Others will eliminate their bond allocation entirely, and stick to just stocks and cash.

That's fine. Those are satisfactory outcomes. They're satisfactory outcomes because they're arrived at consciously, after a thorough look at the fixed income world.

This book aims to deliver that look. It serves you, not a class of securities. Its utility doesn't depend on your buying more bonds any more than the can opener manual's utility depends on your opening more cans.

ACKNOWLEDGMENTS

My core talent remains finding rooms in which I am the dumbest person, that is, putting myself in the company of those smarter than me. I'm made better by the good examples they set. Among them:

At the Stockholm School of Economics, professor Bo Becker for greenlighting my course on value investing in bonds;

Friends who heaved inspiration and expertise my way, chiefly Michael Cunningham, Niklas Edman, Allison Frankel, Pasquale Giannuzzi, Daniel Gustafsson, Ozgur Kaya, David Mindus, Darko Ristevski, and Julio Cesar Restrepo Ruiz;

Thousands of students I've taught at Berkeley, Stanford, and the Stockholm School of Economics, whose attention and questions motivated me to reach for clearer understanding;

And dear mother, editor of editors, who without which sentences made by me would read this one like.

These heroes get credit for anything in this book that works. But it is *moi*, imperfect author, who must accept responsibility for any mistakes, mistakes that this first edition is bound to have. May they be dinky.

INTRODUCTION

Entities borrow money. Often, they borrow from a bank. But other times they borrow from investors. And when they do, they issue *fixed income securities*.

If all goes well, fixed income securities pay a set amount. They may pay less if the entity runs into trouble. But unlike dividend-paying equities, they won't pay more. That's what's meant by *fixed*.

So fixed doesn't mean *guaranteed*, as much as some entities might like you to think that. It means *limited*. It's about a ceiling, not a floor.

Fixed income securities go by many names. One is *debt*. Others are *debentures, commercial paper, bonds, notes, covered bonds, munis,* and *Treasurys*. Each of those names says something. They say something about *seniority, security, maturity,* or something else. We'll cover all those. But in the broad scheme of things they're all still debt.

This book lays out a model for analyzing fixed income securities from a value investing perspective. The model is straightforward. It teases out the facts that matter, and ignores the far more voluminous fluff that doesn't.

The model has three core steps. Each is a question about the security. One, do I understand it? Two, is it good? And three, is it inexpensive?

The three steps are to be answered in order. They're sequential. And each must be answered *yes* before continuing. If an investment isn't understood, then one can't know if it's good. If it isn't good, then one can't know if it's inexpensive. If any question gets a *no*, there's no intelligent investment to be made at that moment.

The model is strict. Too strict, probably. It undoubtedly rejects some ideas that would have worked out well. That's a flaw. But it's unlikely to approve of ideas that would play out poorly. That's its virtue. One can miss many gems and still have a successful investing career. But one can't succeed by routinely betting on duds.

Investors in a fixed income security face two kinds of risk. First is *credit risk*. That's the risk of default. It's the chance that the issuer won't honor the debt.

Second is *interest rate risk*. That's the chance that interest rates will rise.

When interest rates rise unexpectedly, the prices of outstanding securities that pay fixed rates of interest fall. It's easy to see why. Consider an outstanding bond with fixed *coupon* and a *current yield* of 10 percent. That is, its annual interest payments divided by its price equals 10 percent.

Say that interest rates spike. Some entity then issues a new bond, comparable in all respects to the old bond except that— reflecting the spike—its current yield is 12 percent. For the old bond to remain competitive as an investment, its price has to drop such that its current yield is also 12 percent.

That's one reason why fixed income securities are grouped together as an asset class: their prices respond similarly to interest rate shocks. They act alike.

Admittedly, *value investing* means much less in the context of fixed income than it does in equities. With equities, value investing defines an approach that's really different from some widely-practiced alternatives.

Growth investing, for example. That's buying stocks in the hope that they'll increase in worth, often to the point of paying significant premiums for that hope. That's very different from the value approach of paying less than worth.

But what would growth investing mean in the context of debt? Bond payouts are limited, after all. So expecting debt values to soar seems silly.

There are exceptions. For example, there are junk bonds that jump in value once the creditworthiness of the issuer improves. And there are situations where a bond issued in one currency rises in value to an investor based in a country with a different, depreciating currency. There have even been cases where these two factors combine. But on balance the notion of growth investing in debt is odd.

Same with *momentum investing*. That's the application of the physics principle of inertia to stock prices. Some equity investors swear by it. But could a bond price that's just ticked up be reasonably expected to keep doing so? Again, odd.

So with bonds, value investing just means *not stupid*. It means thinking soberly when committing capital to an asset class, an asset class that's both older and bigger than equities.

An investor in fixed income securities has one of two priorities. The first is *capital preservation*. That's not losing money.

The second is *return*. That's making money.

Understandably, most investors want both. Those focused on capital preservation don't mind earning a return. And those focused on return don't want to sacrifice capital preservation. But the distinction is nonetheless useful because it helps to explain why one investor can see merit in a security that another finds revolting.

This book focuses more on the priority of return. Of course we'll touch on issues related to capital preservation. *Laddering*, for example. But those prioritizing return will get the most out of these pages.

Relatedly, this book deals more with bonds issued by companies than bonds issued by governments. Government bonds have their charm. They can have tax advantages, and can even pack some patriotic zing. But corporates are likely to deliver greater returns.

Debt is basic. Someone is borrowing money, and someone is lending money. That's it. Sure, there are wrinkles. For example, some bonds pay interest at rates that change. Others do so at intervals that change. Still others are backed by collateral that's difficult to value. Or even find, sometimes.

But debt isn't hard like science is hard. Physics—the principle of inertia by itself, even—is much harder.

And yet debt is often made to seem complex. It's wrapped up in unnecessarily incomprehensible phrases, like *option adjusted convexity*. It's complexified by nefarious financial professionals that owe their livelihood to a flummoxed laity.

A flummoxed laity that does not, starting now, include you.

PART I

FOUNDATIONS

CHAPTER 1

CAPITAL

Borrowing isn't the only way entities raise capital. There are alternatives. Those alternatives are worth understanding because they help to explain the behavior of entities towards their debtholders.

The alternatives vary by entity type. Governments have one set of alternatives, and companies have another.

Governments have four alternatives to borrowing.

One is taxes. There are different sorts, ranging from income tax to sales tax to property tax. Which sorts are available depend on whether a government is local, national, or somewhere in between. For example in the U.S., property tax is levied by county and municipal governments. Gift tax, meanwhile, is levied by the federal government (and by grabby Connecticut, but it's an exception).[1]

A second is fees. Those include everything from the price of renewing a drivers license to royalties on natural resource leases.

Third is grants from other governments. Such grants are often called *foreign aid*.

Fourth is printing money. That's an option available to governments that have the *power to coin*, or the right to create currency out of paper and ink. Printing money invites trouble, most notably inflation. But technically, it's an alternative to borrowing.

Corporations have different options. The main one is issuing stock. Stock is an ownership interest in a company. It's also called *equity* or *shares*.

Governments, of course, can't raise equity. They have no stock to sell.

When a corporation issues stock, it's selling part of itself. It's giving up claims on its future success in exchange for an inflow of capital now. There's no set ceiling on that success. There's no cap on the allowed amount of a company's sales, profits, or assets. So the cost of giving up those claims can be high.

When a company issues debt, by contrast, it doesn't give up any such claims. There are exceptions. But generally, it doesn't part with ownership. Instead it promises to pay a set amount in the form of interest. No matter how successful the business gets, the cost of that promise does not go up. To a company, that can make issuing bonds look more attractive than issuing stock. There are other considerations, obviously. But when borrowing looks better, that's why. It has a lower *cost of capital*.

Cost of capital is a big concept in corporate finance. It's the annual expense a business incurs by raising money. It's expressed as a percentage. Sometimes it's exact, and sometimes it's approximate.

With straight debt, it's exact. It's the interest rate. That's easy.

With equity, however, it's approximate. Financial academics spend entire careers tweaking formulas designed to nail it down. But they often rely on plucky assumptions. So the best thing such formulas can spit out are estimates. After all, how could one accurately figure the cost of giving up a permanent stake in a business of unknown future profitability?

Debt is *senior* to equity. That means that if a business fails, its lenders—bondholders, banks—get paid first. Any cash still around goes to them. Equity holders get paid second, or more commonly, never.

So what an investor in a company wants to own depends on how the business does. If the business succeeds, the investor wants to own stock. If the business fails, the investor wants—short of never having met the business in the first place—to own debt.

Capital structure is the mix of debt and equity used to finance a company. If there's a lot more equity than debt, a capital structure is often described as *conservative* or *solid*. If there's a lot more debt than equity, it's often described as *levered, leveraged, overleveraged,* or *geared.*

These terms are relative. They imply different ratios in different contexts. It depends on the issuer's industry, and on the investor's tolerance for thrills. But how equity-heavy or debt-heavy a capital structure is defines a company's *solvency*. That's the degree to which a company is able to meet its financial obligations. More on that in chapter 5.

Company managements have a *fiduciary duty* towards their owners. That means that they're obligated to put the interests of shareholders above their own. Sometimes they do, and sometimes they don't. But on paper, they have that obligation.

But managements don't have a fiduciary duty towards their debtholders. They must do certain things, of course. They have to do what's stipulated in the *indenture*, the contract between issuer and debtholder. They must pay *coupons* on time, for example. But they don't have to put the broad interests of debtholders above their own.

This strains relationships. It causes issuers to *call* bonds at the precise moment that debtholders wish they wouldn't. And it causes *convertible bond* owners to turn their debt into stock at the precise moment that it disadvantages issuers.

Of course there are tensions between issuers and shareholders too. Issuers might pay management higher salaries than shareholders would like. And shareholders might want higher dividends than an issuer wants to cough up.

But there's something more routine about the tensions with debtholders. It's ongoing. Management is forever optimizing the capital structure, forever pursuing a lower cost of capital. So notes get issued, and called. Lines of credit get drawn, and repaid. Preferred stock gets issued, and repurchased. Some investors wind up on the losing end of these changes.

But others don't. They profit. They profit because they understand how capital structure and the cost of capital drives issuer behavior. They can't predict the future exactly. But they know what's likely to happen. And their ranks are about to grow by one.

SUMMARY
  1. Entities can raise capital in ways besides borrowing.
  2. Governments can tax, charge fees, receive grants, and print money.
  3. Corporations can sell stock.
  4. The cost of debt capital is easier to measure than the cost of equity capital.
  5. Debt is senior to equity.
  6. Capital structure helps to define solvency.
  7. Companies don't have a fiduciary duty toward debtholders.

CHAPTER 2

ACCOUNTING

If you already know accounting, skip this chapter. But if you don't, you're in luck. That's because we'll tackle it here in just a few pages.

Accounting is a language. It's the language used to write *financial statements*. Trying to read financial statements without a grasp of accounting is like trying to play piano in boxing gloves.

Financial statements tell the history of an issuer in numbers. What form they take depends on whether the issuer is a business, a government, or something else.

If the entity is a business, it's probably a *corporation*. That's the type of entity most likely to issue fixed income securities of interest to value investors. So it's corporate accounting on which we'll focus.

A corporation's three key financial statements are the *income statement*, the *cash flow statement*, and the *balance sheet*.

The income statement covers a period of time, like a year. It's sometimes called a *profit and loss statement*, a *P&L*, or a *consolidated statement of operations*.

The income statement has several key lines. *Revenue*, for example. That's the top line. It's the sum of all sales during a period. It's sometimes called *turnover*.

The next key line is *cost of goods sold*. It's expenses that the issuer incurred to produce the revenue.

Next is *operating expenses*. It's costs recognized by the business regardless of what was sold. It's often called *selling, general and administrative expenses*, or *SG&A*.

Operating expenses differ from *cost of goods sold* in that they're not triggered by revenue. They happen no matter what sales were.

Picture a wholesale distributor of basketballs. Say that one month it bought basketballs from a manufacturer for $500 and sold them to retailers for $900, all from a warehouse that it rented for $300. The $500 is a cost of goods sold. The $300 is an operating expense.

Revenue minus *cost of goods* sold minus *operating expenses* equals the next key line: *operating income*. In the basketball example it's $100. That's just revenue of $900 minus cost of goods sold of $500 minus operating expenses of $300.

Operating income is one of several measures of income.

Next is *non-operating income*. It's income unrelated to the core business of the issuer. It can be positive, or it can be negative.

If the basketball wholesaler made $20 converting Thai baht into US dollars, that $20 would be non-operating income. That's because the wholesaler is in the basketball business, not the baht business.

Operating income plus *non-operating income* equals *earnings before interest and taxes*. That's another measure of income. It's commonly shortened to *EBIT*. In the basketball example it's $120.

Next comes *interest expense*. That's the entity's cost of borrowing money.

Earnings before interest and taxes minus *interest expense* equals *earnings before taxes*. And that minus *taxes* equals *net income*.

Revenue
– Cost of goods sold
– Operating expenses
= Operating income

+ Non-operating income
= *Earnings before interest and taxes*

– *Interest expense*
= Earnings before taxes

– Taxes
= *Net income*

The income statement, with important lines to a
  fixed income security investor shown in italics

Another financial statement is the *cash flow statement*. Like the income statement, it describes an entity over a period of time. It measures the cash that flowed into the entity, the cash that flowed out of the entity, and the difference between the two. So it measures cash *inflow,* cash *outflow*, and *net cash flow*.

The statement sorts cash flows into three groups. Each group has its own inflows, outflows, and net cash flow.

The first group is *cash flow from operations*. It's the cash flow that comes from the business doing its thing, like distributing basketballs.

Cash flow from operations is sometimes called *cash flow from operating activities* or *operating cash flow*.

The basketball wholesaler's cash flow from operations would include cash going out to pay bills from manufacturers, cash coming in from retailers paying their invoices, and cash going out to pay the warehouse landlord.

The second group on the cash flow statement is *cash flow from investments*. It includes payments for equipment that will last for multiple years, and money received from the sale of such equipment. The payments are called *capital expenditures*. They're often labeled *purchase of property, plant, and equipment*.

Cash flow from investments is also called *cash flow from investing activities*.

If the basketball wholesaler paid $3,000 for a forklift, then net cash flow from investments would go down by $3,000. If it sold an older forklift for $1,000, net cash flow from investments would go up by $1,000.

But if it paid $30 for a printer cartridge, net cash flow from investments wouldn't change, even if the printer cartridge lasts for several years. That's because $30 isn't *material*. It's too small. Instead what would go down by $30 is net cash flow from *operations*.

Issuers pick a threshold for determining whether a payment for a long-lasting thing is a cash outflow from operations or a cash outflow from investments. In the U.S. that threshold is often somewhere between $1,000 and $5,000.

The third group is *cash flow from financing*. When a company gets cash by issuing a bond or other security, that's a cash inflow from financing. If it pays cash to repurchase its own preferred stock or other security, that's a cash outflow from financing.

Cash flow from financing is sometimes called *cash flow from financing activities*.

> Cash flow from operating activities
> + Cash flow from investing activities
> + Cash flow from financing activities
> = Net cash flow

The basic organization of the cash flow statement

Usually it's obvious which group a cash flow belongs to. But not always.

Take interest payments. When an entity receives cash by issuing a bond, that inflow is a *cash flow from financing*. When it pays interest on that bond, that's an outflow. But which group should it belong to? *Cash flows from financing*, like the related inflow?

Or consider vendors. Normally, payments to a vendor are in *cash flows from operations*. But what if an entity is late paying a vendor's bill, and gets hit with an interest charge? When the entity pays that interest, is that also in *cash flow from operations*?

Logic turns out not to matter here. What matters instead is where the entity is located.

If it's in the U.S., interest payments are in *cash flows from operations*. It doesn't matter if they're to bondholders, vendors, or polar bears. What matters is that American entities prepare financial statements in accordance with *U.S. GAAP*. That's an accounting standard. It stands for *United States Generally Accepted Accounting Principles*. And it stipulates that interest payments are in *cash flow from operations*.

But if the entity isn't in the U.S., interest payments could be in either *cash flows from operations* or *cash flows from financing*. The entity can pick. That's because it's probably subject to *IFRS*. That's a different accounting standard. It's short for *International Financial Reporting Standards*. Most of the world uses it. And it gives entities that choice.

Even countries that don't use IFRS may offer that choice. Switzerland, for example. It uses *Swiss GAAP FER*. That standard also lets entities put interest payments in either *cash flows from operations* or *cash flows from financing*.[1]

Cash flow statements can be prepared by either the *direct method* or the *indirect method*. The difference shows up only in the first group, *cash flow from operations*.

The direct method organizes the first group in the way that we laid out earlier: cash inflows, followed by cash outflows, followed by net cash flow. It's simple.

The indirect method is messier. It starts with *net income*, the last line of the income statement. It then adds and subtracts various adjustments to get to *net cash flow from operations*.

Most listed companies use the indirect method. That's understandable, since it reveals less to competitors. It discloses neither total *cash inflows from operations*, nor total *cash outflows from operations*.

Say that an income statement reports an interest expense for a period. Will the corresponding cash flow statement for that period show an interest *payment* of the same amount?

Often, yes. But not always. That's because the income statement and the cash flow statement do different things.

The income statement judges. It determines what counts as revenue, and what counts as expenses, for a given period.

But the cash flow statement just sorts. It watches money slosh in and out of an entity, and sorts those flows into operations, investing, or financing.

For example say that on January 1, 2024 an entity issues 200 bonds. Each bond matures in one year, on December 31, 2024; has a *coupon rate* of 10 percent; and has a *par value*—the amount meant to be paid back at maturity—of $1,000. Assume further that this bond is the only interest-bearing liability that the entity has ever had. The interest expense the entity would recognize on its 2024 income statement would be $20,000. That's just 200 bonds times the $1,000 par value, times 10 percent.

But say that the entity didn't get around to paying that $20,000 until January 1 of the following year, 2025. What would the 2024 cash flow statement show as interest payments?

Zero. That's because the cash flow statement doesn't care about what the entity was *supposed* to pay. It just cares about what it *did* pay. It doesn't judge. It just reports money movements.

What about the 2025 statements? What would they show?

The 2025 income statement would show an interest expense of zero. The 2025 cash flow statement would show an interest payment—which since the company is American is a cash outflow from *operations*—of $20,000.

The income statement is prepared on an *accrual basis*. That's an accounting standard. The accrual basis gives the income statement the mandate to judge.

But the cash flow statement is prepared on a *cash basis*. That's a different accounting standard. The cash basis gives the cash flow statement a mandate to sort.

Incidentally, note that the term *accounting standard* can describe two different sets of things. It's used to describe the set that includes accrual basis and cash basis. But it's also used to describe the set that includes U.S. GAAP and IFRS.

Both the income statement and the cash flow statement measure an entity over time. They're like videos. They have a starting moment and an ending moment.

But the *balance sheet* doesn't. That's our last financial statement. It measures an entity at a single moment. It's not like a video. It's like a snapshot.

The balance sheet shows what an entity owns, what it owes, and the difference between the two.

What the entity owns is called *assets*. What it owes is called *liabilities*. And the difference between the two is called *equity*.

An *asset* is something that an entity got, has, and finds valuable. The word asset can mean other things too, like *holding* or *investment*. But in accounting it means something that an entity got, has, and finds valuable.

An asset is either *current* or *noncurrent*. If it could be used within a year, it's current. Cash, for example, is a current asset. So is *inventory*. Inventory is sometimes called *stock-in-trade*. It's stuff that, once sold, will flow through the income statement as a *cost of goods sold*.

Recall the wholesaler. Basketballs it received from the manufacturer but hasn't yet sold are inventory.

Noncurrent assets are different. They take more than a year to use. That new forklift, for example, is a noncurrent asset.

Consider the moment when the wholesaler pays $3,000 in cash for the forklift. On the cash flow statement, net cash flow from investments decreases by $3,000 and net cash flow decreases by $3,000. On the balance sheet, current assets decrease by $3,000 and noncurrent assets increase by $3,000. Cash becomes forklift.

Say that the forklift will last for three years. After that period, it will be worth zero. In other words, the wholesaler will *use* a third of the forklift's original cost each year. How is this accounted for?

For each of the next three years, the wholesaler will decrease the *book value* of the forklift on the balance sheet by $1,000. It will do this by recognizing an annual $1,000 operating expense on the income statement. That's called *depreciation*. It's the process of decreasing the book value of a noncurrent asset through periodic expenses on the income statement. Forklift becomes expense.

The forklift is a *tangible* asset. You can touch it. But some noncurrent assets are *intangible*. Patents, for example. Depreciation of an intangible asset is called *amortization*.

If an entity paid $10,000 for a patent that expires in a decade, the entity would recognize an amortization expense on its income statement of $1,000 for each of the next 10 years.

Amortization has another meaning, too. It's the process of reducing the principal on a loan. But here it refers to the periodic expensing of an intangible noncurrent asset.

Note that our depreciation and amortization examples are both *straight-line*. They're even. They expense the same amount for each year of the life of the noncurrent asset.

There are other methods. *Accelerated*, for example. That's where more gets expensed in the early years than in the later years. But straight-line is very common.

Not all noncurrent assets depreciate or amortize. Land, for example. It's a tangible asset that generally stays on the balance sheet at cost.

Same with *goodwill*. It's an intangible noncurrent asset. And it doesn't amortize.

Goodwill is simple to understand. It can appear on the balance sheets of companies that made acquisitions.

Say that the equity of company B is $5,000,000. And say that $5,000,000 is in fact the *fair value* of the equity. That's what it's really worth. Company A buys company B for $6,000,000. Right after it does, company A increases the goodwill on its balance sheet by $1,000,000. That is, goodwill equals acquisition price in excess of the fair value of the equity.

There are exceptions. Sometimes a portion of the acquisition price in excess of the fair value of the equity appears on the acquirer's balance sheet not as goodwill, but rather as an *identified intangible asset*. Usually that identified intangible asset amortizes, like the patent. But sometimes it doesn't.

The second section of the balance sheet is *liabilities*. Money raised through a bond issue is a liability. It's a liability because it must be paid back. It has a corresponding asset, of course. That corresponding asset is the cash that the issuer got by issuing the bond.

The bond issue is a kind of liability called a debt. If the maturity date is more than a year away, the debt is a *noncurrent* liability. Once the maturity date falls within a year, it becomes a *current* liability.

When the wholesaler receives basketballs from the manufacturer along with an invoice, the invoiced amount is a liability until it's paid. Since the invoice is probably due in less than a year, it's a *current* liability. Specifically, it's a kind of current liability called an *account payable*. Sometimes it's called a *trade payable*.

Note the difference between debt and liabilities. Debt is money owed to lenders, like bondholders and banks. It usually bears interest. Liabilities is a larger category. It adds in things like accounts payable. So debt is a subset of liabilities.

The third section on the balance sheet is *equity*. As noted, it equals assets minus liabilities. Sometimes it's called *shareholders' equity*, *net assets*, or *book value*.

An entity is *profitable* if it shows positive net income on its income statement. If it keeps that net income instead of—for example—paying it out as dividends, then balance sheet equity increases by that amount. Net income kept in the entity like that is called *retained earnings*.

At the moment a company issues a bond, both assets and liabilities go up. Equity, however, doesn't change.

That's assuming no related costs, like a fee paid to an investment bank for managing the bond issue. If there was such a fee, equity could tick down by that amount, having flowed through the income statement as an expense. Or that fee could be capitalized and amortized over the term of the bond, ticking equity down more gradually. But if there were no such costs, equity doesn't change.

The order of the three sections of the balance sheet varies. In the U.S., liabilities come before equity. Outside the U.S., the reverse is often true.

Assets = Liabilities   Assets = Equity
  + Equity   + Liabilities

Two possible organizations of the balance sheet

Such variety is normal. Financial statements often lay out unexpectedly. Take income statements. Some don't have an *interest expense* line. Others break *operating expenses* into separate lines, like *selling expenses* and *administrative expenses*.

Quirks aren't problems. They're simple to sort out on the fly. All that's necessary is a basic understanding of the financial statements and a readiness to see the unexpected.

Not all businesses are corporations. Some are *partnerships*. That's a different kind of legal entity. Their financial statements look like those of corporations. In America, they're also prepared in accordance with U.S. GAAP. But there are some differences.

For example, there's generally no income tax expense line on the income statement. That's because partnerships aren't taxed themselves. Instead, they pass through any tax obligations to their owners, the partners.

Relatedly, there's generally no income tax payments reflected on the cash flow statement.

Finally, the difference between assets and liabilities on the balance sheet isn't called equity. It's called *partners' capital*.

Some bond issuers are *agencies*. Agencies often have origins in government. The Tennessee Valley Authority, for example. It's a power utility owned by the U.S. government. And it issues bonds.[2]

Like partnerships, agencies have financial statements that look like those of corporations. In America they're also prepared in accordance with U.S. GAAP. But again, there are some differences.

One is on the balance sheet. Assets minus liabilities is called *proprietary capital*. It's analogous to a corporation's *equity* or a partnership's *partners' capital*.

State and federal governments also have financial statements that look like those of corporations. But again, there are differences. What those differences are is a big topic. Governments rarely issue bonds that deliver high returns, so it's a topic beyond the scope of this book.

What's within the scope of this book, however, is encouraging you to stay aware of changes in accounting rules. They can be big. In my lifetime the treatment of leases, goodwill, and unrealized gains in listed securities have all shifted significantly.

So if a financial statement looks different, check the accompanying section titled something like *notes to consolidated financial statements*. See if there's been a rule change. That's what I did when I first saw a balance sheet with the term *right-of-use assets*. I checked the notes. And indeed, there was something new for me to learn.

SUMMARY
1. Accounting is the language of financial statements.
2. Financial statements tell the history of an issuer in numbers.
3. The form financial statements take varies by issuer type.
4. Three key corporate financial statements are the income statement, cash flow statement, and balance sheet.

CHAPTER 3

ACCESS

If you want to buy stock in a company, you probably can. That's because most big company stocks are *listed*. They trade on exchanges like NASDAQ, the London Stock Exchange, or the Tokyo Stock Exchange. Your brokerage account is your ticket to the whole world of shares.

There are exceptions. IKEA[1] and Huawei,[2] for example. They're *privately held*. Their stocks aren't listed. But with most equities you can buy whatever you want.

Not so with fixed income securities. They're different. How they're different impacts how we both discover and access the opportunities they present.

The purchase of debt at issuance happens on the *primary market*. Some debt never trades after it's issued, making the primary market the only market it ever sees. Other debt does subsequently trade. It does so on the *secondary market*.

Stated differently, the primary market is where investors lend money to issuers. The secondary market is where investors buy outstanding debt from other investors.

These markets—the primary and the secondary—aren't physical, of course. They're not places. They're just figurative.

Fixed income securities that trade do so mostly *over-the-counter*. They're not listed on an exchange like NASDAQ. This means that at a single moment prices quoted by two different dealers for the same bond may be different. And it means that a bond offered by one dealer might not be offered by another.

All of this highlights the importance of *deal flow*. That's the amount and character of opportunities that an investor is able to access.

If you want to buy a bond on the primary market, the issuer or the investment bank managing the offering has to invite you into the deal. And if you want to buy a bond on the secondary market, you have to find a dealer that has it in inventory, and that offers it at a low price. Initiatives to make this process more open have been limited.[3]

Accessing preferred stocks can also be tricky. Many of them are convertible into common stock that's listed. And some are listed themselves, such as the one we'll see in chapter 15. But most aren't. So to commit capital to many of them you have to find them in the primary market.

This chapter isn't a guide as much as it is an alert. It's an alert that investing in fixed income securities requires legwork that investing in common stocks does not. What form that legwork takes depends on when you're doing it, and what country you're in. The goal, however, remains the same: to access the inventory you want.

This can be particularly hard with fixed income securities that interest value investors. That's because many of them are *fallen angels*. They're bonds that just had their credit rating downgraded from *investment grade* to *non-investment grade*. The problem with this is that some brokerages stop offering bonds that drop below investment grade. So the broker you rely on for stocks might not be able to get you the bonds that you want.

More on credit ratings later.

Discovering bond opportunities is inseparable from accessing them. That's because a broker that offers you the chance to buy debt on the primary market might be making you aware of that debt's existence. Bonds are often unpublicized like that.

The same is true with unlisted bonds on the secondary market. In offering you a security, a broker might quote a price that's otherwise unknowable. You couldn't have just looked it up.

So connecting with the right brokers isn't just about gaining access. It's about knowing what's out there. In the next chapter we'll start developing the model that lets you see if what you find out there is worth anything.

SUMMARY
1. A lot of debt never trades on the secondary market.
2. Debt that does trade on the secondary market does so mostly over-the-counter.
3. Deal flow matters with fixed income securities in a way that it doesn't with stocks.
4. Accessing fixed income security opportunities is inseparable from discovering them.

PART II

MODEL

CHAPTER 4

UNDERSTANDING

```
┌─────────────────────┐
│ Do I understand it? │
│                     │
└─────────────────────┘
    Issuer
    Currency
    Par value
    Issue date
    Maturity
    Payments
    Security
    Seniority
    Provisions
    Covenants
    Liquidity
```

The Value Investing Model for Fixed Income Securities begins with a simple question: *do I understand it?* It's simple to answer *yes*. Just be able to define the security along 11 parameters.

The first parameter is *issuer*. Who's borrowing the money? It could be a corporation, a country, a city, or some other entity.

The name of a security can reveal its issuer. *Munis*, for example. They're issued by cities and states. *Commercial paper* is issued by big corporations. *Treasurys* are issued by the U.S. government. And *gilts* are issued by the UK government.

Sometimes the issuer is a subsidiary of a corporation set up for the specific purpose of borrowing money. For example, Dooba Holdings Limited is a business based in Malta. In 2020 it borrowed money by issuing a bond. But the issuer of the bond wasn't Dooba Holdings Limited. Instead it was Dooba Finance AB, a Swedish subsidiary of Dooba Holdings Limited.[1] Such arrangements can have implications for the bondholder.

Second is *currency*. It's what the borrower is borrowing. It could be U.S. dollars, Japanese yen, or any other legal tender.

A fixed income security denominated in the currency of the issuer's home country that trades in that country is called a *domestic bond*. It's normal.

But a security's currency needn't match the issuer's local currency. Consider a *eurobond*. It's debt issued in a currency other than that of the issuer's home country. It doesn't have to be in euros, nor does the issuer need to be in Europe. In that way the word *eurobond* is a misnomer.

Somewhat confusingly, eurobond can also refer to a fixed income security issued by a European government.

Usually the currency the issuer borrows matches the currency in which it pays interest and principal. But not always. Sometimes it borrows in one currency, and makes payments in another. Other times it makes interest payments in one currency, and principal payments in another. Such securities are called *dual currency bonds*.

Some securities let holders choose the currency in which they receive those payments. They're called *currency option bonds*.

Dual currency bonds and currency option bonds aren't common. But like eurobonds, they happen. So the currency of an issue shouldn't be assumed from the location of the issuer.

The third parameter is *par value*. We've seen how that's the amount meant to be paid back at maturity. Sometimes it's called *face value* or—as in our description of currency option bonds—*principal*. It's usually the same as something called the *integral multiple*. It often matches the amount of the original borrowing. But not always, as we'll see.

Par values are commonly standardized. For example, U.S. corporate bonds generally have par values of $1,000.

Fourth is the *issue date*. That's when the money was originally borrowed.

The issue date is usually the same as the *dated date*. That's the date a fixed income security starts accruing interest. But sometimes it's different.

Fifth is *maturity*. We just used that word to help define par value. Maturity is the date when the par value is meant to be repaid. It's the intended end of the issuer's obligation.

The time between issuance and maturity is called the *term*. The time left until maturity is called the *tenor*. At issuance, term and tenor are the same.

The name of a security can imply its term. For example, *commercial paper* often has a term of 270 days. *Treasury bills* have a term of up to 52 weeks. And *notes* generally have shorter terms than *bonds*.

That said, the word *bonds* is often used to mean fixed income securities in general. It may say nothing about time. For example the phrases *zero-coupon bonds* and *coupon bonds* both use the word *bonds* without implying any particular term.

A fixed income security is *short-term* if the time between issuance and maturity is one year or less. It's *long-term* if it's more.

Term says something about the market of which a security is a part. A *short-term* fixed income security with particularly low *credit risk* is part of the *money market*. Such securities include Treasury bills, *certificates of deposit*, and *commercial paper*.

By contrast, a *long-term* fixed income security is part of the *capital market*. The capital market also includes *common stock* and *preferred stock*.

The sixth parameter is *payments*. With debt that means *coupon*. A *coupon bond* makes periodic interest payments. The frequency of those payments is commonly standardized. In the U.S. it's often *semi-annual*, meaning twice a year. But it could be anything. It could be annual, quarterly, monthly, or something else.

The *coupon rate* equals annual interest divided by par value.

A coupon rate can be *fixed* or *floating*. If it's fixed, it stays the same for the entire term of the bond. It may always be 6 percent, for example.

If it's floating, it changes. It resets at predetermined time intervals, often to a set *spread* over a *reference rate*.

A reference rate is a benchmark like *SOFR*. SOFR stands for the *Secured Overnight Financing Rate*. It replaced *LIBOR*—the *London Interbank Offered Rate*—in 2023.

A floating-rate coupon bond is sometimes called a *floater*.

Picture a floater that resets every six months at a 200 *basis point* spread over SOFR. Say that at the last reset SOFR was 4 percent, and half a year later it's 5 percent. The coupon rate would reset from 6 percent to 7 percent.

A *zero-coupon bond*, fittingly, doesn't make periodic interest payments. It just pays its par value at maturity. It has no coupon rate.

With preferred stock, payments means dividends. More on that in chapter 15.

The seventh parameter is *security*. That's the degree to which a debt is backed.

Debt can be either *secured* or *unsecured*. If it's secured, it's *collateralized.* It's backed by specific assets such as land, buildings, or vehicles. *Covered bonds*—often called *Pfandbriefe* in Europe—are an example of secured debt. They're generally backed by real estate.

By contrast, *unsecured* debt isn't collateralized. Instead it's backed by the issuer's assets generally, except those that back any secured debt. *Debentures* issued in the U.S., for example, are generally unsecured. Debentures issued in the UK are more likely to be secured.

Collateral is an example of a *credit enhancement*. A credit enhancement is something that an issuer tacks on to a debt to lessen the credit risk borne by holders. The result is a lower coupon rate. That's the hope, anyway. Smart issuers add credit enhancements if the cost of doing so is less than the projected reduction in interest expense.

Collateral is but one form of credit enhancement. Another is *financial guarantee insurance*. That's a promise by a third party— often a specialized insurance company—to assume the obligations of the debt if the issuer defaults. Bermuda-based Assured Guaranty Ltd. is currently the largest such insurer.[2]

Financial guarantee insurance is an *external* credit enhancement. It relies on an external party.

By contrast, collateral is an *internal* credit enhancement. An issuer can offer it by shuffling things around in house, without a third party.

The eighth parameter of understanding is *seniority*. Debt can be either *senior* or *subordinated*.

Senior debt is more likely to *perform*—that is, pay interest and principal as scheduled—if the issuer becomes *distressed*. That's because it's first in line to be honored. It has priority. Subordinated debt, meanwhile, is the first to become *non-performing*.

Any debt that is not explicitly called out as senior is subordinated. That's a good assumption, anyway. Securities tend to trumpet their strengths and downplay their weaknesses. So debts announce seniority, but keep mum about subordination.

Senior debt is also called *unsubordinated*. Subordinated debt is also called *junior*.

Like collateral, seniority is an *internal* credit enhancement. The issuer can offer it without involving a third party.

Ninth is *provisions*. Provisions are special features.

Callability, for example. It's a *redemption provision*. Some debt is *callable*. That means that the issuer has the right to pay the debt back prior to maturity. It's not required to. But it can.

An issuer is more likely to call outstanding debt if interest rates drop. That's because the drop gives the issuer the chance to refinance at a lower interest rate.

This creates *reinvestment risk*. It's sometimes called *call risk*. It's the chance that the investor won't be able to reinvest the proceeds from the call at an attractive rate.

A common kind of call is a *make whole call provision*. It gives the issuer the right to redeem debt at the greater of par value or the *present value* of the security's remaining payments. It protects investors if interest rates plunge.

Not to belabor definitions, but *present value* is a stream of future cash flows discounted back at some rate. It's the worth of promised payments in current currency terms. We'll revisit present value in chapter 7.

Another provision is *puttability*. It's the inverse of callability. Puttable debt gives the holder the right, but not the obligation, to demand repayment from the issuer prior to maturity.

A holder is more likely to put outstanding debt if interest rates rise. That's because the rise gives the holder the chance to invest in a higher-returning security.

A very different provision is *convertibility*. Convertible debt can be exchanged for a predetermined amount of another asset. Common stock in the issuer, for example. The right to convert usually belongs to the holder. But sometimes it belongs to the issuer.

The *conversion ratio* is the predetermined amount of the new asset that the holder gets for the old one.

Conversion can happen without a conversion provision. Take a bond without a conversion provision that's issued by a corporation that files for bankruptcy. A judge may turn all of the bondholders into shareholders. But how many shares will each bond become? And when the dust settles, how many shares will be outstanding? That is, how much of the issuer will a bondholder wind up owning?

These are hard questions. Distressed debt experts can come up with meaningful estimates. But novices can't. That's why distressed debt is best regarded as a prickly field into which the inexperienced do not stroll.

Provisions are *embedded options*. They're *embedded* in that they're features of securities instead of being securities themselves. And they're *options* in that they give someone the right to do something.

The tenth parameter is *covenants*. They're pledges made by issuers. They can be *affirmative*, requiring the issuer to do something like publish audited financial statements or limit its *debt-to-equity ratio*. Or they can be *negative*, prohibiting the issuer from doing something like selling assets or paying dividends.

Affirmative covenants are also called *positive covenants*. Negative covenants are also called *restrictive covenants*.

Sometimes a bond issue has no covenants. The issuer may be creditworthy enough to render them unnecessary.

Other times the covenants are extensive. Combing through them may be impractical. But a basic grasp of them makes it less likely that an investment will disappoint.

Eleventh is *liquidity*. That's how readily an asset can be sold for cash.

Some bonds are *listed* on *stock exchanges*. And some of them trade in high *volumes*, meaning that many change hands each day. Such bonds are liquid.

Take American chocolate manufacturer Hershey. As of this writing it has a fixed income security listed on the New York Stock Exchange. It has a coupon rate of 2.05 percent and maturity date of November 15, 2024.[3] And it trades plenty. It's liquid.

But most fixed income securities aren't listed. If they trade, they do so *over-the-counter*. That means privately, through brokers.

Of course that doesn't make them *illiquid*. Unlisted debt can still trade a lot. Take Treasurys. They trade over-the-counter in massive volumes. They're among the most liquid securities in the world.

But other unlisted securities don't trade. There's no volume. They're illiquid.

That doesn't make them bad, of course. Liquidity might matter, or it might not. It depends on the investor.

Liquidity matters if the security is *held-for-trading*. That means that the investor intends to sell the security within a year.

It also matters if the security is *available-for-sale*. That means that the investor intends to sell the security, but only after a year.

But liquidity might be irrelevant if the security is *held-to-maturity*. That means that the investor doesn't want to sell it.

Of course intent and reality can diverge. A security may be originally classed as held-to-maturity. But if the investor comes to need cash, the security may get sold. So liquidity can wind up mattering unexpectedly.

Incidentally, *held-for-trading*, *available-for-sale*, and *held-to-maturity* are accounting terms. They're used by institutional investors, like banks. They're categories in the assets section of a *balance sheet*. Among other things, they indicate whether unrealized gains or losses on a security flow through the institution's income statement. But they also nicely describe an investor's plan. That plan says how much liquidity matters.

Nailing down the 11 parameters of understanding requires research. How hard that research is depends in part on liquidity. If a debt is listed, the research is simple. Just go to the *investor relations* section of the issuer's website. A *prospectus* detailing the debt's features should be there. A contact email address should also appear. If the prospectus doesn't address a parameter, send a message requesting the missing information.

A backup source of information is brokerages. They summarize many of the 11 parameters. They're particularly useful for *issue date*. That's because prospectuses are written in advance, before the exact issue date is known.

To get data from a brokerage, first find the *CUSIP* or *ISIN* number in the prospectus. That's a nine or 12 character code that represents the security. Different brokerages organize their websites differently. But normally, entering that code into a search box leads to a page detailing the bond.

Brokerages usually provide accurate information. But not always. They're more likely than the issuer to mispublish data. So the prospectus is the preferred source.

If a debt isn't listed but the issue is large, a prospectus-like *offering memorandum* may be available. If it isn't, see if the issuer's stock is listed. If it is, an annual report can be downloaded from the investor relations webpage. Annual reports often contain information on unlisted fixed income securities.

American companies offer a particularly informative version of an annual report called a *10-K*. A quarterly equivalent, the *10-Q*, is also useful.

Research can be more difficult if the issuer is entirely private. Of course in that case one may never know that a bond existed at all.

Most investors don't take the time to fully understand the fixed income securities that they buy. They may have missed that a bond is subordinated, or fail to appreciate the implications of a redemption provision.

This means that investors who do take the time to understand their securities enjoy a great advantage. They have the confidence to manage portfolios ably during periods of market turmoil. After all, they know what they own.

SUMMARY

To understand a fixed income security is to define it along 11 parameters:
1. Issuer
2. Currency
3. Par value
4. Issue date
5. Maturity
6. Payments
7. Security
8. Seniority
9. Provisions
10. Covenants
11. Liquidity

CASE STUDY
Berkshire Hathaway Inc.
0.955% Senior Notes due 2026

Berkshire Hathaway (in which I am a shareholder) is a company based in Nebraska. In 2023 it issued five notes. One was a 0.955 percent senior note due in 2026. It's the first one listed in the prospectus, a prospectus that lets us nail down the 11 parameters of *understanding:*

http://www.gooddebtcheap.com/lp.htm

The first parameter is *issuer*. It's *Berkshire Hathaway Inc*. That's clear because that's the name emblazoned across the cover of the prospectus.

Second is *currency*. It's Japanese yen, per the ¥ sign. Plus page S-10 says "all payments of interest and principal, including payments made upon any redemption of the notes, will be made in yen."

Berkshire is an American company. That's clear because page S-v shows a headquarters address in Omaha, and page S-1 states "we are incorporated in Delaware." So the note is a eurobond, since the currency of the issuer's home country doesn't match that of the note. Because it's denominated in yen, it's a type of eurobond called a *euroyen bond*.

Incidentally, those page numbers aren't typos. It's odd that *SEC* filings use S-v, S-1, and S-10 instead of—oh, I don't know— one, two, and three. But they do. Finance is filled with pointless stunts like that. The *euroyen eurobond* thing, for example. Get used to it.

Third is *par value*. It's ¥10,000,000. That's not obvious, since the terms *par value* and *face value* aren't in the prospectus. But *integral multiple* is, right on the cover: "the notes will be issued only in minimum denominations of ¥100,000,000 and integral multiples of ¥10,000,000 in excess thereof." That means that the least an investor can pay for the notes at issuance is ¥100,000,000, and that any amount above that must be a factor of ¥10,000,000.

Prospectuses used to blurt par value right out. But now they cloak it in this *integral multiple* gobbledygook. How this moves civilization forward is beyond me.

Fourth is the *issue date*. The cover of the prospectus—written before the offering, as usual—refers to "the date of original issuance, expected to be November 29, 2023." Did that prediction prove correct? Brokerages provide the answer.

The CUSIP for this note is 084670DW5. That's on page S-5.[4] Entering that CUSIP into a brokerage's website reveals that the issue date was actually November 17, 2023. It was earlier than expected. But the *dated date*—the date the notes started accruing interest—was in fact November 29, 2023. Both dates can be relevant.

Fifth is the *maturity date*. It's November 27, 2026. That's right on the cover of the prospectus.

Sixth is *payments*. The coupon rate is part of the name of the note, also right on the cover: 0.955 percent. And page S-3 says when the coupon will be paid: "semi-annually in arrears on May 29 and November 29 of each year."

In arrears means *after becoming due*. For example the interest payment made on November 29, 2025 will satisfy the issuer's obligation that has accrued since the last payment was made on May 29, 2025.

Seventh is *security*. There is none. That's also right on the cover: "the notes will be our senior unsecured indebtedness."

Eighth is *seniority*. That's also easy: the notes are senior, as the sentence just quoted makes clear. Page S-3 spills more ink on this without adding much. It just says that the notes rank ahead of any subordinated debt—duh—and are *pari passu* with any other unsubordinated, unsecured debt.

Pari passu is Latin for *ranking the same*.

Ninth is *provisions*. There don't seem to be any. The prospectus doesn't mention calls, puts, or conversions. Further, page S-4 has a section called *repayment* that says the issuer can't repay the notes prior to maturity. Repay means call. So, no provisions.

There is a section called *redemption for tax reasons*. It's also on page S-4. It describes how Berkshire can buy the notes back at par in the freak case that a change in U.S. law requires bond issuers to pay some big new tax. That's a call provision of sorts. But an issuer can't unilaterally decide to use it. It comes into play only if a highly unlikely thing happens. So this standard clause isn't the kind of provision that interests us.

Tenth is *covenants*. Again, there don't seem to be any. The word covenant is mentioned, but only as a topic that a prospectus could address.

Borrowing without covenants is the privilege of issuers with high *credit ratings*. It's less available to more marginal outfits, issuers that have to be reigned in with restrictions. More on credit ratings in the next chapter.

Eleventh is *liquidity*. The cover states "the notes will not be listed on any securities exchange."[5] So they're not publicly traded, and therefore not as liquid as they could be. If they trade at all, they do so over-the-counter.

These 11 parameters give us a nice sketch of this security. It doesn't pay much interest. It comes from an issuer creditworthy enough to borrow covenant-free. It can't be called, put, or converted. It's all in yen. And it's unlisted.

So this bond might make sense for investors focused on capital preservation, particularly institutional investors of the *held-to-maturity* sort who either have yen, or who think the yen will appreciate against their home currency. It wouldn't make sense for retail investors, since it was never listed; nor for anyone seeking exposure to a different currency; nor for anyone focused on return.

Do you feel something? You should. You should feel that you now have a command of this bond. You *know* it. The chance that you misunderstand it is *nada*. What you feel is the foundation of outperformance.

CHAPTER 5

ISSUER

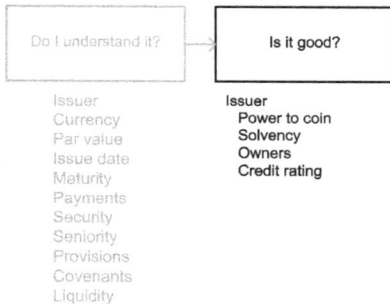

The second step in the model asks another basic question: *is it good?* In other words, is the fixed income security worth owning at *some* price? The answer depends on the investor's priority.

If the priority is capital preservation, good primarily means low credit risk.

If the priority is return, good has more to do with interest payments or *accretion*. It may also involve provisions like convertibility, particularly to a distressed debt investor. More on all of that later. But whether the priority is capital preservation or return, gauging goodness splits neatly into two parts: *issuer* and *issue*.

Gauging the goodness of an issuer means seeing if its promises are believable. Can it do what it says it will do in the indenture? That's answered in four points.

First is the *power to coin*. That's the ability to print money. An issuer either has it, or it doesn't.

If it has it, it's a country. In a pinch, it could print money to service its debt.

But just because an issuer is a country doesn't mean it has the power to coin. Take Latvia. It used to have the *lats*. That was its own currency. But in 2014 it joined the euro area.[1] It took on the euro as its sole legal tender. That brought the country some advantages. But it stripped it of its power to coin.

Of course Latvia today has a role in setting European monetary policy. Its central bank chief sits on the Governing Council of the European Central Bank.[2] But it can't just unilaterally power up some mint.

Or consider Ecuador. In 2000 it said *adios* to its *sucre* in favor of the U.S. dollar.[3] It didn't even join a currency union. It just embraced what it considered to be a more stable currency. Not only can't Ecuador print dollars, it has *no* say in monetary policy.

The power to coin is relevant to debt denominated in the issuer's currency. But a country can borrow other currencies. For example Indonesia's currency is the rupiah, but it issues bonds denominated in U.S. dollars.[4]

If such a country hits trouble, it can't just make the banknotes it needs. Theoretically, it could print its own currency and then exchange that for the currency required to make principal and interest payments. But that would put it at the mercy of a foreign exchange rate, a rate that the very act of printing could make unfavorable.

Even with borrowings denominated in its own currency, a country with the power to coin can't be cavalier. It can't just switch on the presses to make enough money to service its debt. That could spark inflation. But the power to coin does give a nation a stopgap way to make good on obligations denominated in its own currency.

The second point of issuer goodness is *solvency*. It's about how much money an issuer has relative to its obligations. It's assessed with ratios. Calculating these ratios is simple for someone with a grasp of accounting. You either had that grasp before getting this book, or you got it from chapter 2.

When the issuer of a fixed income security is a company, four solvency ratios are particularly useful. None is perfect. But they're all straightforward.

First is the *debt-to-equity ratio*. That's the issuer's total debt—current and noncurrent—divided by its book value. The lower the better.

The *liabilities-to-equity ratio* is another. The denominator is the same. But the numerator is bigger. It includes not only debt, but all other obligations as well. *Dividends payable*, for example. That's money that the company owes to stockholders. The lower the liabilities-to-equity ratio, the better.

Another solvency metric is the *quick ratio*. It assesses an issuer's ability to honor its debt in the near term. The numerator equals *current assets* minus *inventory*. The denominator equals *current liabilities*. The higher the quick ratio, the more solvent the issuer is thought to be.

Inventory is subtracted on the assumption that selling inventory for cash takes some time. Sometimes that's true, and sometimes it isn't. But subtracting inventory is a standard part of calculating the quick ratio.

The last is the *interest coverage ratio*. It measures an issuer's ability to service debt with *earnings before interest and taxes*. It equals EBIT divided by interest expense, both for the same period. Again, the higher the better.

Sometimes interest expense appears as a line on the income statement. But other times it doesn't. In that case it probably shows up elsewhere in the report.   Search for the term *interest expense*, *interest cost*, *interest incurred* or—as a last resort because it will return so many hits—simply *interest*.

Occasionally the only figure available is *financial expense*, *finance cost*, or some similar term. That number can work. But it's often too big. That's because it can include financial expenses besides interest, like foreign exchange fees.

Solvency metrics are most helpful when they're current. So they should be calculated from the most recent financial statements. Base the debt-to-equity, liabilities-to-equity, and quick ratio on the newest balance sheet. That could be in an annual report, a quarterly report, or an interim report. It doesn't matter. Just use whichever is most current.

Same with the interest coverage ratio. It should be based on the most recent income statement.

Often it's best to calculate the interest coverage ratio for a full year: 12 months of EBIT in the numerator, and 12 months of interest expense in the denominator. That's because of seasonality.

Take Toro. It's a Minnesota company that makes lawn mowers. For the full 12 months of 2023 its interest coverage ratio was eight. But for the second quarter alone it was 15. For the first quarter alone it was actually negative, because operating income was negative.[5] So throughout the year it was all over the place. And of course it was: Toro is a seasonal business. Who buys lawn mowers for winter?

Toro's interest coverage ratio for a single quarter could spark unnecessary panic, or unjustified comfort. That's why a full 12 month calculation makes sense. Bonus operating income from the summer helps fund the payment of interest in the winter.

If a company's most recent filing is an annual report, getting 12 months of figures is easy. Full year numbers are right there on the income statement. But if it's a quarterly or an interim report, some addition is required. One has to sum the most recent four quarters of EBIT for the numerator, and the most recent four quarters of interest expense for the denominator. That's the *trailing 12 months* method. It stitches together quarterly figures to create annual figures.

If a business isn't seasonal, calculating the interest coverage ratio for a shorter period—like the most recent quarter—works. It works especially well if the non-seasonal business recently changed its cost of debt capital. That keeps the pre-change interest expense from diluting the more relevant post-change interest expense. To judge an issuer's solvency by its interest coverage ratio right before it refinanced at a lower rate, for example, would be ridiculous.

As illuminating as the solvency metrics are, they're imperfect. Knowing how they're imperfect keeps them helpful.

The overarching imperfection is that they're historic. They say what happened, not what's happening. And they certainly don't say what *will* happen.

Take 10-Q's. They're usually published 40 days after the end of a period.[6] Toro's last one came out in 34 days. That's prompt. But even its numbers were already more than a month old. In the interim the company could have issued more debt, borrowed at a higher rate, or booked an expense that slashed equity.

That lag can distort. Consider again the interest coverage ratio. It can give a false read when interest rates change.

Say that a company is financed with floating-rate debt. Assume that it sells capital goods, like big boats, or heavy machinery. Assume that its customers borrow money to buy its products, as is common with capital goods. A spike in interest rates would increase the company's interest expenses. And it would increase its customers' borrowing costs, likely reducing the volume of products sold.

In other words, rising interest rates could turn a comfortably high interest coverage ratio into a frighteningly low one. The numerator would drop just as the denominator soared. Buying the company's bonds could be riskier than the interest coverage ratio would suggest.

Or consider the opposite. The company might show an alarmingly low interest coverage ratio. But plunging interest rates would decrease its floating-rate interest expenses. It would also reduce its customers' borrowing costs, likely increasing the volume of products sold. The numerator would rise just as the denominator soared. Buying the company's bonds could be safer than the interest coverage ratio would suggest.

The interest coverage ratio can mislead for other reasons, too. Take the numerator, EBIT. It can capture *revaluations*. Those are changes in the book value of assets made to reflect market prices. Sometimes revaluations have nothing to do with the income a company can use to service its debt.

Take Globe Trade Centre S.A. It's a commercial real estate landlord based in Poland. In 2022 Globe's EBIT was €69,218,000. Its interest expense was €28,914,000. So its interest coverage ratio was about 2.4. Some would consider that low.

But that figure might mislead. A closer look at the income statement reveals that Globe's 2022 EBIT captures revaluations of negative €29,422,000. That reflects the company's guess that had it sold its properties in 2022, it would have gotten €29,422,000 less than it might have in 2021.[7] IFRS—the company's accounting standard—requires that guess to look every bit as real as a payroll cost. So it's high up on the income statement. It's captured in operating income, even though it wasn't really an operation.

There's a workaround for calculating a more meaningful interest coverage ratio for Globe. It involves adding the revaluation back to EBIT. But that's not the point. The point is that for a ratio to be useful it must be examined, not just accepted.

The same is true with other solvency metrics. Consider *debt-to-equity* and *liabilities-to-equity*. Accounting rules can make their shared denominator deceptively dinky, and the resulting ratios needlessly terrifying.

Take *buybacks*. That's a company using cash to repurchase some of its stock. Picture a healthy company using $1,000,000 for that purpose. Think about how that would hit each financial statement.

On the income statement it doesn't do much, except maybe create a tiny expense in the form of a brokerage commission. So let's ignore that.

On the cash flow statement, $1,000,000 shows up as a *cash outflow from financing*.

On the balance sheet, the *current asset* of *cash* goes down by $1,000,000; and *equity* goes down by $1,000,000.

Remember, this is a healthy company. It had $1,000,000 available for buybacks probably because it had a positive *net cash flow from operations*. And yet the buyback increases both debt-to-equity and liabilities-to-equity. So it looks less solvent.

Same with dividends. Paying dividends hits the balance sheet by reducing both cash and equity. That also makes the company look less solvent.

To be clear, equity dropping because of buybacks or dividends isn't fiction. Both actions really do reduce the equity base of a company. But they can also create an illusion of weakness when in fact it was strength that made them possible.

Again, the point of highlighting these imperfections is not to discredit the solvency metrics. It's to encourage *thinking about what they're made of*. That renders any distortions harmless.

When we calculate the solvency metrics, we wind up with actual figures. How do we know what's okay, what isn't?

Speaking very generally, I like debt-to-equity to be no more than one, liabilities-to-equity to be no more than two, a quick ratio of at least one, and an interest coverage ratio of at least 10.

But these benchmarks are just starting points. They should flex with what an investor likes.

I like issuers that service their debts and are likely to continue doing so. But some investors don't. Distressed debt investors might hope that an issuer crumbles under the weight of its obligations so that bonds get converted into stock. It's the stock that they're after. So their debt-to-equity happy place might be 20 times higher than mine.

Benchmarks should also flex with the issuer's industry. Consider banking. As of this writing U.S. Bancorp's debt-to-equity ratio is about seven.[8] So is M&T Bank's.[9] And Truist Bank's is about eight.[10] Those seem perilously high compared to my benchmark of one.

But that's banking. Customer deposits—checking accounts and savings accounts—can be seen as debt. They can be added to outstanding fixed income securities and other borrowings to calculate the numerator. That leads to a top-heavy debt-to-equity ratio. But banks are heavily regulated. They have to meet strict capital guidelines. So their bonds may be safer to own than the ratio suggests. Banking rules provide protection that a generalized debt-to-equity benchmark obscures.

Or consider retailing. In the summer of 2023 Walmart had a quick ratio of 0.3.[11] Carrefour, a similar business based in France, had one of 0.6.[12] And BIM, a comparable retailer in Turkey, had one of 0.5.[13] Those seem unsettlingly lower than my benchmark of one.

But that's retailing. Much cash is tied up in inventory. And the numerator of the quick ratio is current assets minus inventory. So a big part of the top gets lopped off. That makes it microscopic compared to the chunky bottom.

Plus that bottom may be chunky in part due to extended payment terms that a retailer negotiated with its inventory vendors.

All those unpaid invoices are current liabilities. From that angle a small quick ratio signals strength.

Industry norms change, interest rates move, and capital structures shift. So it would be silly to present here a list of solvency benchmarks by industry. It would rapidly become outdated. What will not become outdated, however, is thinking about how quantitative standards should flex to best frame the health of an issuer.

The third point of issuer goodness is *owners*. Who owns the entity's outstanding equity? That's relevant because an owner may have both the ability and the motivation to pour additional resources into the issuer to improve its solvency. An owner flush with cash and keen to keep their holding alive may constitute an off-balance sheet resource.

Sometimes the name of the issuer alone suggests who the owners are.

Take Amtrak. It runs U.S. passenger trains. Many Americans know that it's owned by the federal government.[14] So someone analyzing its 3.6 percent senior secured notes due in 2033 might like that it's owned by a creditworthy country with the power to coin. In a bind, Uncle Sam could pitch in to keep the trains moving and the interest flowing.[15]

Other times the name of the issuer says nothing about owners. But some digging around does.

Take Axactor. It's a Norwegian debt collector. As of this writing its quick ratio looks fine, at 1.4. But the other solvency metrics don't. Debt-to-equity is 2.2, liabilities-to-equity is 2.4, and interest coverage is 1.4.[16]

But Axactor might be stronger than those numbers suggest. Almost half of its shares belong to Geveran Trading.[17] That's the investment vehicle of a European widely known to be a billionaire.[18] There's no guarantee that that person would provide capital in a pinch. But someone assessing Axactor's floating rate bond due in 2026[19] should know that a billionaire probably wants to keep the company alive.

Power to coin, *solvency*, and *owners* are points that investors gauge themselves. But *credit rating* isn't. It's an outside opinion. And it's the fourth point of issuer goodness.

A credit rating is a professional gauge of creditworthiness. It's expressed as a short combination of letters, sometimes ending with a number or a sign. It's assigned by a *credit rating agency*. Agencies aren't flawless. But more often than not, the higher the credit rating the healthier the issuer.

A credit rating is either *investment grade* or *non-investment grade*. If it's higher, it's investment grade. If it's lower, it's non-investment grade.

As of this writing, 10 credit rating agencies are deemed by the U.S. Securities and Exchange Commission to be *Nationally Recognized Statistical Rating Organizations*, or *NRSROs*. Those 10 are generally regarded as authorities outside of America as well.

Today the three largest NRSROs are Moody's, S&P, and Fitch. The others are A.M. Best, DBRS, Demotech, Egan-Jones, HR Ratings, Japan Credit Rating Agency, and KBRA.[20] The SEC publishes a current list of NRSROs:

http://www.gooddebtcheap.com/vb.htm

The SEC isn't the only arbiter of credit rating agencies. There's also the *European Securities and Markets Authority, or ESMA*. Today it recognizes 28 agencies, some of which are also NRSROs.[21] It also publishes its current list:

http://www.gooddebtcheap.com/uj.htm

	Fitch	Moody's	S&P
	AAA	Aaa	AAA
	AA+	Aa1	AA+
	AA	Aa2	AA
	AA-	Aa3	AA-
Investment grade	A+	A1	A+
	A	A2	A
	A-	A3	A-
	BBB+	Baa1	BBB+
	BBB	Baa2	BBB
	BBB-	Baa3	BBB-
	BB+	Ba1	BB+
	BB	Ba2	BB
	BB-	Ba3	BB-
	B+	B1	B+
	B	B2	B
Non-investment grade	B-	B3	B-
	CCC+	Caa1	CCC+
	CCC	Caa2	CCC
	CCC-	Caa3	CCC-
	CC	Ca	CC
	C	C	C
	D		D

Comparable ratings from the three major NRSROs[22]

Agencies publish guides that define what each credit rating means. I'm not sure why. They seem unnecessary, like an Olympic guide defining gold, silver and bronze.

Plus the language gets flowery. The *capacity to meet financial commitments* is described variously as *adequate, exceptional, vulnerable*, or *unsurpassed*. *Resilience to economic shocks* is described as *impaired*, *elevated*, *stressed*, or *limited*.

One is reminded of wine reviews: *hints of solvency with a leveraged bouquet*.

An issuer's credit rating may come with an *outlook*. That's a suggestion of any change that may take place over the *medium-term*. Medium-term means between six months and two years.

There are four outlooks: *positive*, meaning that the rating may notch up; *negative*, meaning the opposite; *stable*, meaning no likely change; and *developing*, meaning that the agency has—how can I put this—no idea.

When an unexpected event impacts an issuer, agencies may put a rating on *credit watch*. That means that they're reviewing it for a possible near-term change.

Incidentally, the term *agencies* here is just shorthand for *credit rating agencies*. They're different from government agencies like the Tennessee Valley Authority mentioned in chapter 2.

Issuers with low credit ratings are often distressed. They're challenged to meet their obligations. But just because an issuer is distressed doesn't mean it isn't paying interest on its outstanding bonds. Plenty of stretched entities find ways to service their debts.

Sometimes a low credit rating isn't even due to distress. It's due to some outside factor.

Consider Banco GNB Sudameris. It's a bank based in Colombia. Fitch rates it BB, and Moody's rates it Ba2.[23] Both put GNB squarely in the non-investment grade box.

But that's partly a result of the bank's location. Colombia has a low credit rating. Fitch gives Colombia a BB+,[24] and Moody's gives it a Baa2.[25] Generally speaking, a company's credit rating can't be higher than that of the country it's in. That's called the *country ceiling*.

To be sure, GNB has issues. And the macroeconomic problems of its home country are a challenge. But GNB isn't distressed. It's just subject to the country ceiling, an outside factor that results in a credit rating that may be lower than justified.

To the four points—*power to coin*, *solvency*, *owners*, and *credit rating*—one could add others. There can be deeper dives into issuer goodness.

Consider the solvency metric input of EBIT. It changes over time. So one could gauge the competitive dynamics behind it, like how market growth shapes revenue, or how the bargaining power of suppliers impacts operating expenses.

Or take distressed debt investors that expect a court to convert debt into equity. They bought bonds, but hope for stocks. To them the issuer's fundamentals—the breadth of the customer base, the threat posed by startups—matter greatly.

Both of these considerations might justify a full-blown workup of the sort described in *Good Stocks Cheap*. Adopting a long-term shareholder's view would tease out more insights.

But for most bond investors that would be overkill. It would take time and effort, and wouldn't lead to better decisions. So that energy might be better directed towards the next subject of goodness: *issue*.

SUMMARY
1. An issuer's goodness is based on its power to coin, solvency, owners, and credit rating.
2. Assessing solvency requires an understanding of accounting.
3. The debt-to-equity, liabilities-to-equity, quick, and interest coverage ratios are key solvency metrics.

CASE STUDY
Constellation Software Inc.

Constellation is a business software publisher based in Canada. It issued multiple tranches of debentures due in 2040. So an investor might want to assess its goodness.

Tranches are different editions of a security that vary by seniority, term, or other characteristics.

Constellation's interim report provides the information needed to assess its health as an issuer:

http://www.gooddebtcheap.com/gt.htm

First is the *power to coin*. Constellation doesn't have it. Its name ends in Inc. It's a company, not a country.

Second is *solvency*, starting with the debt-to-equity ratio. For that we need the balance sheet, which is on page 24 of the report. The numerator, of course, would include one or more *liabilities*.

The first line of the *current liabilities* section is *debt with recourse to Constellation Software Inc.* We can tell that it's debt by its name. It's $907,000,000.

Same with the next line: *debt without recourse to Constellation Software Inc.* It's $235,000,000.

Recourse, by the way, is a lender's right to seize extra assets in the event of default. It matters in distressed debt investing. But it doesn't matter in calculating the debt-to-equity ratio.

Another aside: even though Constellation is Canadian, it presents its financial statements in U.S. dollars. That's stated at the top of the balance sheet. This is not unusual.

The next line in the *current liabilities* section is *redeemable preferred securities*. Is that debt? Well, the words *redeemable* and *preferred* often describe a security that's more like debt than equity. But some clarity would help.

Fortunately the line refers to *note 9*. Note 9 starts on page 46, and runs for two and a half pages. Thrilling it is not. But it does help. For example, it says the securities pay "a fixed annual cumulative dividend of 5 percent per annum."

Dividend, coupon, spatula—whatever it's called, a 5 percent yearly obligation suggests debt to me. So does the paragraph titled "redemption at the option of the holder." It describes what sounds like a fixed income security put option. So in my view *redeemable preferred securities* is debt. It's $536,000,000.

Two more debts come from the *non-current liabilities* section. They're like what we saw in the *current liabilities* section, but they're due later. One is *debt with recourse to Constellation Software Inc.* It's $617,000,000. The other is *debt without recourse to Constellation Software Inc.* It's $1,275,000,000.

So we have five debts. Adding them up gives us a numerator of $3,570,000,000. That's the top of our ratio.

The bottom—equity—appears plainly on the balance sheet. It's $1,957,000,000. So the debt-to-equity ratio is almost two. That's just $3,570,000,000 divided by $1,957,000,000. That strikes me as a little too high.

The next solvency metric, the liabilities-to-equity ratio, has the same denominator. And the numerator is right on the balance sheet: $8,047,000,000. So the liabilities-to-equity ratio is about four. That also seems high.

Debt-to-equity and liabilities-to-equity aren't high because equity shrunk due to share buybacks. Take a look at the cash flow statement on page 29. See the section called *cash flows from (used in) financing activities*. If there had been buybacks, there would be a line in there called something like *purchase of treasury shares* or *common stock repurchases*. But there isn't.

The company did pay dividends, however. And that does shrink equity. Look back at that same section of the cash flow statement. There's a line in there called *dividends paid to common shareholders of the company*. During the quarter it was $21,000,000. That's $21,000,000 that got flushed out of the bottom of the debt-to-equity and liabilities-to-equity ratios.

Next is the quick ratio. For the numerator, the balance sheet shows *current assets* of $2,951,000,000. But $56,000,000 of that is *inventories*. So the numerator is $2,895,000,000. That's just *current assets* less *inventories*.

The denominator, *current liabilities*, is given as $5,098,000,000. So the quick ratio is 0.6. Against my benchmark of one, that too seems a little weak.

The interest coverage ratio is next. Should we calculate it for the trailing 12 months, or would the most recent quarter be sufficient?

Well, we know that Constellation is in the business software industry. That doesn't sound seasonal. It sounds year-round. Database licenses don't become popular for Halloween, for example.

A search for the term *seasonal* confirms this. The bottom of page 11 says that operating cash inflows ticked up in the first quarter due to "the timing of annual maintenance contract renewals." But that's *cash flow* seasonality. Our operating metrics aren't based on the cash flow statement. So calculating the interest coverage ratio for just the last quarter seems fine.

Figuring the numerator starts with some unexpected math. The income statement is on page 25. But something's missing. There's no line called *earnings before interest and taxes*, nor is there *operating income, operating profit, operating result*, or some other synonym. So we have to calculate it ourselves.

Revenue appears as $2,126,000,000. Subtracting from that *cost of goods sold* and *operating expenses* should give us operating income. But the lines *cost of goods sold* and *operating expenses* are missing too.

Instead what appears is a big fat *expenses* section totalling $1,799,000,000. It seems to be made up of things that are either a *cost of goods sold* or an *operating expense. Staff, hardware,* and *occupancy,* for example.

Right below that are seven lines that sum to $91,000,000. They seem to be of the *non-operating income* variety. *Foreign exchange loss,* for example. The outlier is *finance costs* of $50,000,000. Note 13 on page 51 tells us that that includes *interest expense on debt and debentures* of $38,000,000.

So EBIT equals revenue of $2,126,000,000, minus expenses of $1,799,000,000, plus non-operating income of $91,000,000, plus interest expense of $38,000,000. That's $456,000,000. It's our numerator.

Note that we plucked all of these numbers from the left-most column of the income statement. That's because we decided that the ratio should be for the most recent three months only.

Our denominator is simply the interest expense of $38,000,000.

But wait a minute: didn't we decide that *redeemable preferred securities* was debt? And doesn't it pay a dividend? Yes we did, and yes it does. Then for consistency, we should probably add that dividend to *interest expenses* to figure the bottom of the ratio. So: what was the redeemable preferred securities dividend during the quarter?

Well, the income statement has a line called *redeemable preferred securities expense.* It's $37,000,000. Is that the dividend? The line references note 9, the same note that we saw earlier. In a convoluted paragraph at the bottom of page 46 it says "the change in fair value" is "recorded as a redeemable preferred securities expense."[26] So the $37,000,000 sounds like a revaluation, not a dividend. Hmm.

This confused me. I was stuck. So I emailed the chief financial officer.

Messaging the CFO of a public company might seem bold. Rude, even. But it isn't. There was no investor relations contact person named on Constellation's website, and I needed an answer. So I found the CFO's name, got the company email addresses format from the online biography of one of its salespeople, and sent a succinct question: where in the financial statements could I see the Q3 2023 redeemable preferred security dividend?

The CFO replied that day, referring me to a Canadian statutory filing called *management's discussion and analysis*, or *MD&A*:

http://www.gooddebtcheap.com/zp.htm

The CFO pointed out that page nine showed an annual version of the number I was looking for: a "dividend of $11 million." It covered all of 2023.[27] So I divided $11,000,000 by four to estimate a quarterly figure of $2,750,000.

Adding $2,750,000 to the interest expense of $38,000,000 produces a denominator of $40,750,000. And dividing EBIT of $456,000,000 by $40,750,000 gives an interest coverage ratio of 11. That's satisfactory.

Note that I took some liberties calculating the interest coverage ratio, liberties that could be reasonably challenged. For one, I assumed that the annual preferred dividend amount applied evenly throughout the year. If the balance of the redeemable preferred security fluctuated during the year—as it seems to have—then that's imprecise.

But it's probably not dangerously imprecise. Remember, we're using that estimate to increase a denominator that already has an interest expense of $38,000,000 in it. Adding $2,750,000—or anything close—wouldn't change the denominator enough to produce a wildly different interest coverage ratio.

Another liberty I took regards that revaluation of \$37,000,000. Remember Globe Trade Centre? Its published operating income figure was cut by a negative property revaluation. That revaluation had nothing to do with operations, we realized, so perhaps it should be added back. After all, it didn't really reduce the income available to cover interest expenses. But with Constellation, I ignored all that.

Again, however, we're not talking big numbers. Adding the \$37,000,000 revaluation back to the \$456,000,000 of operating income that's already in the numerator isn't going to take the interest coverage ratio from 11 to 20 or something. It barely takes it to 12, actually. So again we have an imperfection that's excusable because it has no serious consequences. It wouldn't change our assessment.

Calculating these solvency metrics was tricky. We had to figure EBIT. We had to hunt for interest expenses. And we had to sort out the whole redeemable preferred securities dividend thing. But even with those complications it was doable:

http://www.gooddebtcheap.com/iv.xlsx

Third is *owners*. If Constellation was American, major shareholders would be named in the *proxy statement*, also known by its adorable SEC nickname *DEF 14A*.

But Constellation is Canadian. So owner information appears in a filing called the *management information circular*:

http://www.gooddebtcheap.com/aw.htm

Page 22 reveals that a big owner is the president. Some internet sleuthing reveals that he's also the founder. He has 430,282 shares.[28]   As of this writing Constellation's share price is about

$2,700.[29] Multiplying that price by 430,282 suggests a holding that totals over $1,100,000,000.

From this fact alone we can't really conclude that the president is a billionaire. He could have personal debt, for example. And of course the stock price can drop. But someone considering the purchase of Constellation debentures should find it reassuring that the person running the company is very motivated to keep it healthy.

Fourth is *credit ratings*. Constellation is an investment-grade issuer. But not by much. S&P gives it a BBB,[30] and Fitch gives it a BBB+.[31]

The four points of issuer goodness let us see that Constellation is—shall we say—*fair*. While it obviously can't print money, it's able to service its debt, with an interest coverage ratio just above 10. But its other solvency metrics are weaker. That said, its big owner runs the company and is rich enough to potentially provide emergency funds. The credit ratings agencies seem to agree with all this, seeing Constellation as a skinny player on the investment grade team. So a smart investor could, with caution, proceed to assess the goodness of the company's debentures.

CHAPTER 6

ISSUE

Do I understand it?	→	Is it good?

Issuer
Currency
Par value
Issue date
Maturity
Payments
Security
Seniority
Provisions
Covenants
Liquidity

Issuer
  Power to coin
  Solvency
  Owners
  Credit rating
Issue
  Performance
  Credit rating
  Duration
  Convexity

We've assessed the issuer. That's the first part of gauging goodness. The second is assessing the *issue*. That's the fixed income security itself. Gauging its goodness involves four points.

The first is *performance*. As we know, a fixed income security that pays interest and principal as promised is said to be *performing*. One that doesn't is said to be *non-performing* or *in default*.

Most investors want a security that's performing. But not all. Non-performing securities can drop in price so precipitously that they become attractive to distressed debt investors. Some of these investors expect the security to start performing again. Others expect it to get converted into equity. There are actually funds chartered to pursue such thorny opportunities. So the relationship between performance and goodness depends on the investor.

Say that a fixed income security is performing. How can one know if it's likely to continue doing so? There are two routes: analyze it, or accept someone else's analysis.

Analyzing it starts with calculating the four issuer solvency ratios. It then weighs any characteristics of the issue that make it more or less likely to perform than issuer goodness would suggest. Credit enhancements or subordination, for example.

But most do the latter. They accept someone else's analysis. Specifically, they trust credit rating agencies.

This holds for *issuer* credit ratings, too. Most folks don't calculate solvency metrics, or check to see who the owners are. They just assume that someone over at the credit rating agency did all that, and encapsulated their findings in a tidy little *Baa3* or *AA-*. You shall not sink to such sloth.

Anyway, that's the second point of issue goodness: *credit rating*. Issuers pay credit rating agencies to score the creditworthiness of their debt.

Agencies use the same scales to rate *long-term* issues as they do to rate issuers. Fitch and S&P use their AAA to D scale, and Moody's uses its Aaa to C scale.

Long-term issues have an original time to maturity—a term— of at least one year.

Agencies do have separate scales for *short-term* issues. That's debt with a term of less than a year. We'll introduce those scales in chapter 14 when we look at a common form of short-term debt, *commercial paper*.

Like issuers, an issue is either investment grade or it isn't. If it's investment grade, an agency has judged it as likely to perform.

If it's not investment grade, one of two conditions holds. First, an agency may have judged it as less likely to perform. Such debt is commonly called *speculative*, *high-yield*, or—lovingly—*junk*. Second, no agency may have been asked to rate it. It may simply be *unrated*.

Many institutional investors are restricted from buying fixed income securities that aren't investment grade. That's why issuers are motivated to pay for ratings services.

As with performance, most investors require a security to be investment grade to consider it good. But not all. There are high-yield bond funds that buy junk with the view that the agencies judged them too harshly. Others buy unrated debt, confident in their own assessments. They have no use for agency opinions. So again, the relationship between credit rating and goodness depends on the investor.

With stocks, third-party ratings do nothing for me. But bonds are different. Their performance hinges on fewer variables. They're relatively simple for a paid analyst to gauge. So credit rating agencies usually get it right. Investment grade debt generally performs, and debt that doesn't often wasn't investment grade.

But sometimes they get it wrong. For example in the runup to the 2008 financial crisis NRSROs gave investment-grade ratings to *mortgage-backed securities* backed by subprime residential mortgage debt. They shouldn't have, but they did. That became clear when the mortgage-backed securities defaulted.

For this reason it's best not to rely too heavily on credit ratings. They're part of gauging goodness, sure. But just part.

Bonds often have the same credit rating as their issuers. But not always.

Consider a city in modest financial shape. It can issue a muni with a higher credit rating by tacking on financial guarantee insurance. We met that back in chapter 4. It's an external credit enhancement where an insurance company assumes the obligations of the bond if the city defaults.

Corporations can do this too. Take Heathrow Funding Ltd. It's a subsidiary of the company that runs the UK's biggest airport. In March 2023 its S&P rating was BBB+.[1] But it was able to sell two tranches of a bond—one due 2058 and one due 2059—with an

S&P rating of AA. It did this by buying financial guarantee insurance from Assured Guaranty.[2]

A bond rating can be lower than that of its issuer, too. Take Citicorp, the New York financial services giant. As of this writing Fitch rates it A. Many of its securities are also rated A, like its 4.65 percent senior notes due 2045. But not its 4.6 percent subordinated notes due 2026. Fitch rates that two notches below, at BBB+.[3] That's because it's subordinated. In distress, it would perform only if the seniors perform.

I'm not aware of an accepted counterpart to the term *credit enhancement*. But there should be one. I propose *credit debasement*. And I nominate subordination as its best example.

The third point of issue goodness is *duration*. It's a stab at quantifying interest rate risk. There are a few versions of it.

The foundational version is *Macaulay duration*, named after its inventor. It equals the *weighted average* time until cash inflows from a fixed income security, including the principal received at maturity. It's measured in years.

Macaulay duration can't be longer than tenor. With zero-coupon bonds, it equals tenor. That's because zeroes have just one big fat cash inflow at maturity. So a zero with a one-year tenor has a Macaulay duration of one.

A coupon bond with the same one-year tenor has a Macaulay duration that's shorter. That's because it throws off some cash prior to maturity. It pays interest.

Macaulay duration can be figured from five inputs: price, par value, tenor, coupon, and coupon frequency. Online calculators make it simple:

http://www.gooddebtcheap.com/pl.htm

Another version is *modified duration*. It turns Macauley duration into a prediction. It's a percentage. A 1 percent change in interest rates is estimated to cause a bond's price to change in the opposite direction by its modified duration.

Picture an outstanding bond with a modified duration of 2 percent. If interest rates fall 1 percent, the price of the bond should rise 2 percent.

Now picture that same bond when interest rates *rise* 1 percent. The price should *fall* 2 percent. That's why interest rate risk is sometimes called *duration risk* or *price risk*.

The online calculator that figures Macaulay duration also spits out modified duration. It can also be calculated by hand, as we'll see in the next chapter.

Another version is *dollar duration*. It's expressed in money. It's just modified duration times price. A 1 percent change in interest rates is estimated to change a bond's price in the opposite direction by its dollar duration.

A final version is *effective duration*. It's for bonds with provisions like calls or puts. Such securities need a different kind of duration because a change in interest rates can change their cash flows completely.

Take an outstanding bond with a fixed coupon and a redemption provision. Modified duration and dollar duration suggest that if interest rates fall, its price should rise. But if interest rates fall a lot, the bond could get called because the issuer could borrow at a lower rate. The cash flows would then change. Instead of a string of future coupons plus the principal at maturity, the holder would suddenly get the principal, plus any *call premium* stipulated in the indenture, plus maybe some accrued interest, and that's it. It's over.[4]

The term duration is often cast about sloppily, even by financial professionals. Often it means *modified duration*. Sometimes it means *Macauley duration*, *dollar duration*, or *effective duration.* Occasionally it's misused to mean *term* or *tenor*. A careful look at context can reveal what was meant.

Books can muddle things up further. One—a popular one— describes the formula for duration as "wickedly complex."[5] How encouraging.

Bonds with longer tenors tend to have higher durations. This is easy to see. Recall our zero-coupon bond with a tenor of one year. Its Macaulay duration is one.

Now picture a different zero-coupon bond, one with a tenor of two years. Its Macaulay duration is two. Therefore its modified duration is also higher. So its price is more sensitive to interest rates. And that makes sense. It makes sense because a change in interest rates has more time to act on the value of its sole cash flow.

If you leave rottweilers in the living room for a minute, there's only so much damage they can do. But if you leave them in there all day, they could shred the furniture. You could return to piles of splinters and shards under clouds of dust. That's because the dogs had more time to act on the value of the furniture.

Let's run with this rottweiler logic a bit. A zero has higher modified duration than a coupon bond with the same tenor.

Consider two bonds, each with a tenor of one year. One's a zero. The other makes semiannual coupon payments. Both pay principal at maturity, obviously. But only the coupon bond pays an additional amount. It pays interest. And it does so *before* maturity. It pays *sooner*. That drags its weighted average time until cash inflows *down*. So the coupon bond's duration has to be lower than that of the zero. The dogs have less average time to chomp the furniture to bits.

Now compare two coupon bonds. Assume that they both have a one-year term, and pay interest semiannually. One has a coupon rate that's fixed. The other has a coupon rate that floats, and the rate resets every time it pays interest. Which has lower duration?

Well, the fixed coupon bond is stuck making the same payments no matter what interest rates do. It's locked into a rate for the full term of one year.

But the floater is stuck for only *half* a year. That's because its rate resets whenever it makes a semiannual payment. So it has lower duration.

That's an appeal of floating rate bonds: low interest rate risk. Resets protect the bondholder from being chained to a low rate in a rising rate environment. In fact, floaters that reset frequently are often thought of as having durations of zero.

So to recap in broad terms: zeroes have high duration, floating rate coupon bonds have low duration, and fixed rate coupon bonds are somewhere in between.

Duration has its place. It's useful for managing portfolios of many different bonds with high credit ratings, like a pension fund with hundreds of different AAs. Investors focused on capital preservation like it.

So do some investors who regard their bonds as either *held-for-trading* or *available-for-sale*. Those that expect interest rates to rise prefer low duration. Those expecting the opposite prefer the opposite.

But duration is less useful to those intending to hold to maturity. They don't foresee selling, so duration tells them nothing. It's like a Mumbai weather report to someone who has nothing to do with India. What price does on the road to principal payment is noise.

Duration is also less useful to value investors hunting for gems in the junk bond dumpster. It's not as helpful if the focus is return. That's partly because performance and solvency matter more than interest rate changes. But it's also because of how the duration formula weights cash flows.

We're going to revisit duration in the next chapter, after we've defined something called *yield to maturity*. With yield to maturity we can calculate duration by hand. And that will reveal an important quirk that can mislead the uninformed. That same quirk advantages those who see it.

Some predictive measures are perfect. The area of a square, for example. It's length times width. Always. It doesn't matter if the square is a chessboard, a microchip, or a waffle. The area of a square is length times width. Always.

Duration is not like that. It's a guess. A messy guess. That's partly because a change in interest rates is never the sole event acting on the price of a bond. Something else is always happening. An economist is making a speech, two banks are merging, a kingdom is printing money—all kinds of things impact debt prices. But it's also because of how it's calculated, as we'll see.

The fourth point of issue goodness is *convexity*. While duration estimates the change in price given a change in interest rates, convexity estimates the change in *duration* given a change in interest rates. It's a stab at patching some of duration's inaccuracy.

In the language of calculus, duration is a first derivative, and convexity is a second derivative. The first is the rate of change, and the second is the rate of change of the rate of change. You don't need to know calculus to appreciate convexity. But if you do, that characterization should help.

Convexity has some things in common with duration. It can describe an individual security, or a portfolio of securities. It's most useful for managing portfolios of many different bonds with high credit ratings. And it's less useful to value investors hunting for unloved securities.

The same online calculator we used to spit out duration spits out convexity. No additional inputs are required. But grasping convexity's limitations is. Convexity is an attempt to improve duration's predictive ability. Though the result of admirable effort, it strikes many value investors as inessential.

SUMMARY
1. The goodness of a fixed income security is based on its performance, credit rating, duration, and convexity.
2. How investors interpret each of these parameters depends on their priorities.
3. Versions of duration include Macaulay duration, modified duration, dollar duration, and effective duration.

CASE STUDY
OneMain Holdings, Inc.
9% Senior Notes due 2029

OneMain Holdings is a financial services company based in Indiana. It borrows money at one rate, and lends it out at a higher rate. But it's not a bank. Instead of borrowing money by accepting deposits, it borrows money by issuing fixed income securities.

On June 22, 2023 its subsidiary OneMain Finance Corporation issued 9 percent fixed rate senior unsecured notes due January 15, 2029 with CUSIP 682695AA9.[6] The prospectus lays this all out:

http://www.gooddebtcheap.com/zw.htm

As with any issue, gauging goodness starts with *performance*. The notes are performing. As of this writing in March 2024, there's no mention of default in any news story about OneMain. The company's most recent SEC filing, a 10-K, supports this. A search for *2029* turns up several mentions of the note, all of which suggest that they are paying as promised:[7]

http://www.gooddebtcheap.com/yu.htm

Second is *credit rating*. It's junk. But good junk.

Entering the CUSIP number into a brokerage website reveals that Moody's gives the issue a Ba2, and S&P gives it a BB. So on both scales it's two notches below investment grade. But it's also at least nine notches away from the bottom.

Recall that these notes are senior unsecured. That means that they're not subordinated, nor are they backed by any special collateral. So it would be logical for their credit rating to match that of their issuer. And indeed, it does.[8]

Third is *duration*. Let's focus on modified duration, since that's often the most useful version. It's easy to gather the information an online calculator needs to figure this.

As of this writing the price is 106.[9] That's the *ask*—the price a potential seller is seeking—given by several brokerage websites. A price quote of 106 means 106 percent of par. The issue is an American corporate, so par should be $1,000. The prospectus confirms this, referring on page S-11 to "integral multiples of $1,000."[10] So the bid price is $1,060. That's 106 percent of $1,000.

The tenor is also simple to spot. It's 4.85 years. That's figured by entering today's date—March 9, 2024—and the maturity date into an online calculator:

http://www.gooddebtcheap.com/gg.htm

The coupon rate is in the name of the issue: 9 percent. The prospectus doesn't say that the rate is floating or variable, so we can safely assume that it's fixed. Interest is "payable semiannually in arrears," as page S-3 of the prospectus says.[11]

So our inputs for the online calculator are straightforward:

Price	$1,060
Par	$1,000
Years to maturity	4.85
Annual coupon rate	9%
Coupon payment frequency	Twice a year

The calculator tells us that modified duration is 3.669 percent. That's less than the tenor, since there are coupons. But it's not nothing.

Fourth is convexity. Our duration calculator spits that out as 18.432. Also not nothing.

So, are the notes good? Well, we're just using them for illustration in the narrow context of issue goodness. We've ignored the broader frame of understanding and issuer goodness. But at least we can see who they're *not* good for.

They're not good for anyone that needs their bonds to be investment grade. That rules out the majority of the bond buying crowd.

They're also probably not good for anyone that needs conventional assurance that price isn't sensitive to changes in interest rates. That's because the coupon rate doesn't float, and most of the cash flow comes at maturity. So duration and convexity aren't zilch.

That said, some studies suggest that duration and convexity are less reliable for non-investment grade bonds than for investment grade bonds. There's some weight behind those studies, as the next chapter will show. But in any case, someone needing *conventional* assurance of low sensitivity won't find it at OneMain.

CHAPTER 7

INEXPENSIVENESS

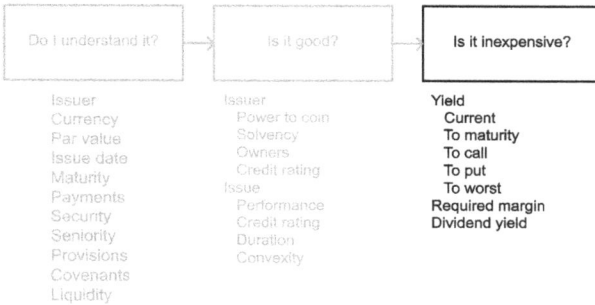

The third step in the model asks a final question: *is it inexpensive?* Answering that involves *yield*. Yield shows what a bond returns in a year relative to its price. It's a percentage. We'll cover it shortly. But first, a painless dash through some bond market mechanics.

We saw in chapter 3 how bonds are issued on the *primary market*, and that only some subsequently trade on the *secondary market*. And we saw that bonds that do trade do so mostly *over-the-counter*.

Brokers post a *bid*—the price proposed by potential buyers—and an *ask*—the price proposed by potential sellers. The bid is lower than the ask. The difference is called the *bid-ask spread*, commonly shortened to just *spread*. More liquid bonds tend to have tighter spreads. Less liquid bonds have wider spreads.

Spread has other meanings in finance as well. But it always refers to the distance between two numbers. For example, in chapter 4 we saw how it can refer to the space between the coupon rate and reference rate on a floater.

Bonds bought for less than par are said to be bought at a *discount*. Bonds bought for more than par are bought at a *premium*.

Bond prices are quoted as a percentage of par value. We saw this in the OneMain case study. If the ask on an American corporate is quoted as 101.125, it can be bought for $1,011.25. That's just 101.125 percent of the normal American corporate par value of $1,000.

There's also an old-timey method where bond prices are actually quoted as fractions of some weird denominator, like eight or 32. Ridiculous, I know. This dates from back when most New Yorkers washed their clothes in buckets.

The telltale sign of this anachronism is a hyphen or a colon. For example, an ask of 101-04, or 101:04, can mean 101 4/32. Four divided by 32 equals 0.125. So both 101-04 and 101:04 can mean 101.125. In other words, the ask is 101.125 percent of par value.

If a plus sign also appears, that means add 1/64. Yes, I'm serious. For example, an ask of 101-04+ can mean an ask equal to 101.140625 percent of face value. That's just 101 plus 4/32 plus 1/64. Some people just like buckets.

The day a fixed income security trade is executed is called the *trade date*. The day the transaction is finalized is the *settlement date*. That's when the buyer gets the securities and the seller gets the money.

The time between trade date and settlement date is standardized by market. As of this writing it's one business day in North America. That standard is called *T+1*, for "trade date plus one day." Before 2024 the standard was *T+2*.

The timing of the settlement date can create a pricing wrinkle. An example shows how. Picture a coupon bond with a par value of $1,000 that pays 10 percent interest semiannually, on June 30 and

December 31. Say that an investor buys it on June 30 at 100. The amount paid is therefore $1,000. Then on December 31 the investor gets a coupon payment of $50. That's just half of the 10 percent coupon rate times the $1,000 par value.

Now say that instead of June 30, the investor buys the bond on December 16. That's five and a half months later. And it's just a couple of weeks before a coupon payment. Assume that everything else is the same, including the quoted price of 100. On December 31 the investor gets $50 in interest. Did the investor pay $1,000 for the bond?

Probably not. The investor paid a little more. That's because the investor gets the full $50 despite having become a holder just two weeks before the coupon date. So the investor pays extra to compensate the seller for the interest that accrued on the bond between the last coupon date and the settlement date.

The quote of 100 is the *clean price*. It's the ask ignoring the extra added for the accrued interest. A quote that includes that extra is called the *dirty price*. On the date of a coupon payment the clean price and the dirty price are the same.

Quotes are usually clean. But sometimes they're dirty. Regardless, the dirty price is what the buyer winds up paying.

Calculating the amount of accrued interest is an automated affair. But knowing how it's done helps to explain some dirty prices that otherwise seem puzzling. They're puzzling because of the *day count convention*. That's the standard a particular market uses to calculate accrued interest.

Actual/actual, for example. That's one day count convention. It's based on the actual number of days in a month and the actual number of days in an accrual period.

To illustrate, consider again the coupon bond with a par value of $1,000 that pays 10 percent interest semiannually, on June 30 and December 31; bought at 100 on December 16. Recall that each semiannual coupon payment is $50. So accrued interest can never be more than that.

With the actual/actual day count convention, accrued interest equals $45.65. That's easy to figure.

Start by counting the *actual* number of days between the last coupon date and the settlement date. July has 31 days, August has 31, September has 30, October has 31, and November has 30. Then there's 15 for December (it's standard to always count the first date, July 1 in this case; but not the last, December 16). So the math is 31+31+30+31+30+15=168. The actual number of accrual days is 168.

Then count the *actual* number of days in the full accrual period. That's simple too. It's 31 for July, 31 for August, 30 for September, 31 for October, 30 for November, and 31 for December. So the math is 31+31+30+31+30+31=184. The actual number of days in the period is 184.

The coupon payment of $50 times 168 actual accrual days divided by 184 actual period days equals $45.65. So that's the accrued interest. And since $1,000 plus $45.65 equals $1,045.65, the dirty price is $1,045.65.

A different day count convention is *actual/360*. The numerator is the same. But the denominator assumes that there are 360 days in a year. To illustrate, consider again our 10 percent coupon bond.

The number of days between the last coupon date and the settlement date is the same *actual* figure: 168.

Next, the number of days in the full accrual period is 180. Of course it's not *actually* 180. It's actually 184. But now we're assuming that there are 360 days in a year. Half of 360 is 180.

The coupon payment of $50 times 168 actual accrual days divided by 180 assumed period days equals $46.67. So *actual/360* sees the accrued interest as $46.67, and the dirty price as $1,046.67.

A final day count convention is *30/360*. It assumes that there are 30 days in a month and 360 days in a year.

Sticking with our 10 percent bond example, we first count the number of days between the last coupon date and the settlement date. July, August, September, October, and November are each assumed to have 30 days. Then there's 15 for December, since this day count convention has us count actual days for partial months. So the math is 30+30+30+30+30+15=165.

As before, the number of days in the full accrual period is assumed to be 180.

The coupon payment of $50 times 165 accrual days divided by 180 period days equals $45.83. So *30/360* sees accrued interest as $45.83, and the dirty price as $1,045.83.

Different markets use different day count conventions. Treasury bonds and Treasury notes use actual/actual. Money market instruments like commercial paper use actual/360. And American corporates and munis use 30/360.

There are plenty of other day count conventions. There's *30E/360*, *actual/365*, and *actual/365L*, for example. They're all in the glossary. Knock yourself out. But the key point for the investor is this: if a given dirty price differs from your calculation, make sure that you're using the day count convention that's right for that market.

While bond prices are usually quoted in percentages, they're thought of in yield. As such, prices are often discussed in terms of yield. If one bond has a higher yield than another bond that's otherwise identical, it's cheaper.

There are five types of bond yield.

First is *current yield*. It's basic. It equals annual interest divided by price.

Current yield doesn't apply to zero-coupon bonds, obviously, since those don't pay interest. And even with coupon bonds, current yield rarely offers great insights. But sometimes it does, and it's easy to calculate. So we calculate it.

Second is *yield to maturity*. It's commonly shortened to *YTM*. It's the annualized return from a bond assuming that it's held until the end of its term. It's the discount rate that, when applied to all of the bond's future interest and principal payments, equals its price.

The inputs for calculating yield to maturity are price, par value, tenor, coupon, and coupon frequency. Those are the same inputs needed to figure duration and convexity. The same online calculator we used for those numbers spits out yield to maturity as well:

http://www.gooddebtcheap.com/pl.htm

Incidentally, yield to maturity says nothing about what happens to coupon payments once they're paid. It makes no reinvestment assumptions.[1] I mention this because there's a widely held misperception that it does.[2] It doesn't.

Of course what the coupon payments do once paid is certainly relevant to the investor. It's very relevant. That's because every coupon payment creates a reinvestment risk. It introduces the chance that the cash can't be redeployed at a satisfactory rate of return. But YTM couldn't care less about that.

Even though a zero-coupon bond pays no interest, an online calculator can still show its YTM. Just set the coupon payments to zero.

One could also calculate a zero's YTM by hand. That's easy, because there's just one cash inflow. The formula is:

$$(\text{par value} / \text{price}) \wedge (1 / \text{tenor}) - 1$$

Not to play math teacher, but the symbol $\wedge$ is called a *caret, circumflex*, or—in vernacular—*hat*. It means *raised to the power of*. It turns whatever follows into an exponent. For example $8\wedge2$ means eight squared, or 64.

The third type of yield is *yield to call*. It matters when a security has a redemption provision. It's basically *yield to maturity* with the maturity date set equal to the *call date*. The issuer usually has to pay a *call premium*, which when added to par value equals the *call price*. Call price is what the holder of a called security gets. So a different online calculator is useful:

http://www.gooddebtcheap.com/mo.htm

Sometimes a security can be called on multiple dates, often with different call premiums on each date. In that case it can be smart to calculate yield to call for each call date. One can do this with shortcuts, as we'll see.

Fourth is *yield to put*. Predictably, it's relevant with putable bonds. It's like *yield to maturity* with the maturity date set equal to the *put date*. The issuer buys the security back at a predetermined *put price*, which may differ from par value. So again, a different online calculator helps:

http://www.gooddebtcheap.com/mp.htm

If a security can be put on multiple dates at multiple put prices, calculate yield to put for those different dates. We'll see some shortcuts for this as well.

Fifth is *yield to worst*. It's the lowest of yield to maturity, yield to call, and yield to put. Assuming performance, it's the worst case scenario. Absent any special insight as to what will happen, it's a reasonable basis for comparing different fixed income investment opportunities.

Of course if one knows what's likely to happen, yield to worst can mislead. It can be too pessimistic. Take an outstanding fixed-rate bond with a redemption provision. Say that its credit rating goes up just as prevailing interest rates drop. For two reasons, then, the issuer could probably refinance at a lower rate. That makes a call likely. So the most accurate forecast may be yield to call, not yield to worst.

Note that current yield isn't one of the candidates for yield to worst. That's because it's an entirely different animal. It considers only interest payments. It forgets that principal will eventually be received as well. So it would understate yield to worst.

All of the yield measures are fiction if a bond doesn't perform. They're only illuminating if interest and principal are paid as promised. After all, a bond that defaults immediately has a yield of zippo, no matter how hefty its stated coupon is. So performance is the assumption that makes yield meaningful.

Often yield is the goal. It's what the investor wants. But sometimes it isn't. Instead, the investor wants a *capital gain*. That's money made by selling a bond after it increases in price.

Consider a performing bond. Say it has a price of $950, a par value of $1,000, a tenor of two years, a coupon of 8 percent paid once a year, and no put or call provisions. Its yield to maturity is 10.916 percent. That's given to us by the same online calculator we used before:

http://www.gooddebtcheap.com/pl.htm

So 10.916 percent is what an investor could get by buying and holding. Not bad.

But say that other bonds identical in tenor, coupon, credit rating—everything—sell for 30 dollars more. They're $980. And assume that the $950 bond soon joins its peers at that higher price level. Say it does so after a month, and that the investor sells it at that moment. The return would be around 3.16 percent. That's just the proceeds of $980 minus the investment of $950, all divided by the investment of $950. Thirty over 950 equals 0.0316.

But remember, the holding period was just a month. So the *annualized* return was more like 38 percent. That's just 3.16 percent times 12 months. It's the number to compare to yield to worst. And it's much better.

Of course this example is extreme. It would be unusual for a bond to be priced so much lower than other, virtually identical bonds. But it illustrates how capital gains can be the goal of a smart bondholder. Yield can reveal the opportunity, but it might not be what the investor is after. Better returns may come from seeing a bond as held-for-trading, not held-to-maturity.

Yield makes sense with fixed-rate coupon bonds. But it makes less sense with floaters. That's because floaters have coupon rates that change. So for them, metrics besides yield to maturity, yield to call, and yield to put are useful. *Required margin*, for example. That's the spread over the reference rate adjusted for any change in the price. More on that in chapter 13.

An additional type of yield is *dividend yield*. It's for preferred stock. We'll address it in chapter 15.

Recall that YTM is the discount rate that, when applied to all of a bond's future interest and principal payments, equals its price. With that understanding, let's revisit duration.

The foundational version—Macaulay duration—was invented in 1938 by Canadian economist Frederick Macaulay. His insight was that maturity is but one part of the *longness*, if you will, of a debt:

> *We must remember that the 'maturity' of a loan is the date of the last and final payment only. It tells us nothing about*

the sizes of any other payments or the dates on which they are to be made.[3]

To maturity can be added other things that paint a clearer picture of longness:

> *Whether one bond represents an essentially shorter or an essentially longer term loan than another bond depends not only upon the respective 'maturities' of the two bonds but also upon their respective 'coupon rates'—and, under certain circumstances, on their respective 'yields'.*[4]

Macaulay then establishes *weighted average* as the way to take all of these factors into account:

> *It would seem almost natural to assume that the 'duration' of any loan involving more than one future payment should be some sort of a weighted average of the maturities of the individual loans that correspond to each future payment.*[5]

He then notes that calculating the weighted average requires a discount rate, like the YTM of the debt:

> *We have, for purposes of computation, used as 'yield' the yield of the individual bond whose 'duration' we were discussing.*[6]

Macaulay allows that this can create complications:

> *The difficulties connected with the problem of arriving at a completely satisfactory concept of 'duration' are, indeed, extremely great. Any proposed solution almost necessarily involves some paradoxes.*[7]

Let's dive into those paradoxes.

Consider again our bond with a price of $950. Recall that it has a par value of $1,000, tenor of two years, and annual coupon of 8 percent. Our online calculator says Macaulay duration is 1.924. It also said that YTM was 10.916 percent. Here's that calculator again:

http://www.gooddebtcheap.com/pl.htm

Online calculators are great. But they hide what's going on behind the scenes. So to get a better feel for duration, let's use that YTM of 10.916 percent—or 0.10916—to calculate duration by hand.

Each annual coupon payment is $80. That's just 8 percent of $1,000. There are two coupon payments: one in year one, and one in year two. The second one also comes with the principal payment of $1,000. So the bond has two cash flows:

Years	Amount
1	80
2	1,080

Now let's use the YTM of 0.10916 to weight each amount by the time it takes to arrive. In other words, let's calculate each one's present value. We do that by dividing each amount by a factor. That factor equals the quantity one plus YTM, raised to the number of years it takes the amount to arrive. One plus YTM equals 1.10916. So:

Years	Amount		Present value
1	80 / 1.10916^1 =	72.12
2	1,080 / 1.10916^2 =	877.88

The two present values add up to 950. That's the price of the bond, as it should be:

Years	Amount		Present value
1	80	/ 1.10916^1 =	72.12
2	1,080	/ 1.10916^2 =	877.88

$$950.00$$

Dividing each amount's present value by 950 gives us another factor. That factor says how much each amount contributes to the bond's total present value. As percentages the factors should add up to 100 percent. So as decimals they add up to one:

Years	Amount		Present value			Total present value
1	80	/ 1.10916^1 =	72.12	/	950	= 0.076
2	1,080	/ 1.10916^2 =	877.88	/	950	= 0.924
			950.00			1.000

Finally we multiply that last factor by years:

Years	Amount		Present value			Total present value
1	80	/ 1.10916^1 =	72.12	/	950	= 0.076 x 1 = 0.076
2	1,080	/ 1.10916^2 =	877.88	/	950	= 0.924 x 2 = 1.848
			950.00			1.000

The sum of those products equals Macauley duration:

Years	Amount		Present value		Total present value			
1	80	/ 1.10916¹ =	72.12	/	950	= 0.076 x 1 =	**0.076**
2	1,080	/ 1.10916² =	877.88	/	950	= 0.924 x 2 =	**1.848**
			950.00			1.000	**1.924**

So the hand calculation gives us 1.924, just as the online calculator did.

Okay: go back to the online calculator. Let's change an input. Change tenor from two to three. You'll see that Macauley duration changes to 2.777. It increases.

That makes sense, right? That makes sense because the principal will now take an additional year to get to us. Longness has increased.

Okay, put the tenor back to two.

Now change the coupon rate, from 8 percent to 5 percent. That also increases Macauley duration, to 1.951. That also makes sense, since the cash flows that arrive first—the coupons—are now smaller. That gives more relative weight to the last cash flow, the principal paid at maturity. Again, longness has increased.

Okay, put the coupon rate back to eight.

Now change price. Change it from 950 to 980. Macauley duration increases, to 1.925. Should it?

Mechanically, yes. That's because YTM is an input in the Macauley duration formula. And price is an input in the YTM formula. That's easily seen by recalling the formula for the YTM of a zero:

$$(\text{par value} / \textbf{price}) \char94 (1 / \text{tenor}) - 1$$

So price is a hidden input in the formula for Macauley duration.

Does that distort things? If so, not harmfully. Macauley duration is just longness, after all. But what about modified duration?

Recall that modified duration turns Macauley duration into a prediction. A 1 percent change in interest rates is estimated to cause a bond's price to change in the opposite direction by its modified duration. Pension fund managers, bank treasurers, and chief investment officers count on that prediction to be basically sound.

The formula for modified duration is:

$$\frac{\text{Macaulay duration}}{1 + (\text{YTM} / \text{number of coupon payments per year})}$$

The same online calculator we've been using spits out modified duration as well. Consider how changes in the inputs change the output.

Take tenor. When we changed the tenor of the bond from two years to three, modified duration went from 1.735 percent to 2.525 percent. It increased. So tenor and modified duration are positively correlated.

That makes sense. It makes sense because a longer time to maturity gives a change in interest rates more time to impact the worth of the bond.

Remember the rottweilers? Letting them stay in the living room longer gives them more time to act on the value of the furniture.

Now consider the coupon rate. When we decreased the coupon rate from 8 percent to 5 percent, modified duration went from

1.735 percent to 1.810 percent. It increased. So coupon rate and modified duration are negatively correlated. That's because a lower coupon rate means lower coupon payments, giving a change in interest rates relatively smaller amounts to impact early in a bond's term. That makes sense too.

Now price. When we changed the price of the bond from 950 to 980, modified duration went from 1.735 percent to 1.764 percent. It increased. The implication is that a rise in a bond's price increases the impact that a change in interest rates has on the bond's price. Is that correct?

No, in my view. It's wrong. It's wrong for three reasons.

First, there's less logic to price impacting sensitivity than there is to maturity and coupon impacting sensitivity. Changes in maturity or coupon really do give interest rate changes more of a chance to impact price. But price doesn't have as clear a chance to do that. Yes, price impacts the conventional calculation of longness. But it doesn't impact longness itself.

Second, prices flit around. Unemployment rates, housing starts, and other economic factors bat price around like a toddler bats a balloon around. So the formula lets price bat sensitivity around.

Contrast this with maturity and coupon. When maturity changes, that's a real change. When it's raised from two years to three, it stays at three unless changed again. Same with coupon. When the coupon rate drops from 8 percent to 5 percent, it stays at 5 percent unless changed again. But prices of listed securities change more—shall we say—capriciously. Does duration acknowledge this capriciousness?

No. Lurking deep within the formula for duration is a view that price changes aren't capricious at all. That view is the *efficient market hypothesis*. It's the idea that the price of something equals its worth. It's premised on rationality. It sees people soberly weighing facts before acting in a market that, as a result, generates accurate prices.

Value investors generally reject this. We chuckle at the efficient market hypothesis because if it were true, the outperformance that characterizes so many value investing careers wouldn't happen. And yet it's baked into duration as if it were as reliable a driver of sensitivity as maturity and coupon. It's baked in there as if it were the efficient market *theory*.

A theory is proven. But a hypothesis is just a proposal.

Third, bond investing opportunities that interest value investors have, by definition, prices that are *wrong*. After all, what's value investing? It's buying assets for less than worth. It thrives in situations where the ask is too low. So why would we let a wack variable guide our view on sensitivity?

For these three reasons duration tends to be less relevant to value investors than to managers of diversified portfolios of investment-grade bonds. Yes, we include it in the model. But that's mostly to help explain the behavior of other market participants. It's not a metric on which we hang our hat.

One last note on the model. *Inexpensiveness*, obviously, appears towards the end. It pops up only after we've understood the security, assessed the issuer, and weighed the issue.

In practice, yield is often the first thing an investor looks at. That's the natural result of *screening*, the hunt for securities meeting quantitative criteria.

By pushing a deeper look at inexpensiveness out until later, we create a safeguard. We reduce the chance that we'll fixate on some premature illusion of high returns. We don't want to let a delectable YTM blind us to a foreign exchange exposure embedded in a dual currency bond, or a reinvestment risk posed by a call provision, or a solvency problem revealed by a low quick ratio. We want to check those things first. By starting with a thorough look at the security, we make it less likely that we'll be seduced by illusory yields, bettering our shot at long-term outperformance.

SUMMARY

1. Different markets calculate accrued interest with different day count conventions.
2. Yield is the basic inexpensiveness metric for fixed income securities.
3. Performance is the assumption that makes yield meaningful.
4. The five main versions of yield are current yield, yield to maturity, yield to call, yield to put, and yield to worst.
5. Yield to worst is often the best basis for comparing different fixed income investment opportunities.
6. While yield can reveal an opportunity, a capital gain may offer a higher return.
7. Yield is more useful with fixed coupon bonds than with floaters.
8. Because duration is influenced by price, it's less helpful to the value investor.

CASE STUDY
Santander Issuances, S.A. Unipersonal
5.179% Subordinated Notes due 2025

Santander Issuances, S.A. Unipersonal is a subsidiary of a big financial services company in Spain. On November 19, 2015 it issued a note. It matures on November 19, 2025, and has a fixed 5.179 percent coupon paid semiannually. Brevity was clearly not a goal of whoever wrote the prospectus. So give thanks for the summary that starts on page S-1:

http://www.gooddebtcheap.com/st.htm

As usual the prospectus doesn't blurt out the par value. Instead on page S-7 it says that the notes are issued in "denominations of $200,000 and integral multiples thereof." We saw in chapter 4 how the integral multiple means par value. But what's the number?

Since the note is a U.S dollar-denominated corporate, probably $1,000. In any case, we can safely assume that to calculate yield.

A search for the term "redemption" uncovers what at first seems to be a call provision. It's on page S-5, in the sections titled "tax redemption" and "regulatory redemption." Apparently Santander can call the notes at par—page S-5 uses the term "principal amount"—plus any accrued interest. But it can only do this if tax laws or regulations change in certain ways.

This is the same boilerplate clause that we saw in the Berkshire Hathaway case. It only takes effect under exceptional circumstances. It's not the kind of call provision that interests us. So we can ignore it.

Further, a search for the term "put" returns nothing.[8] So we won't calculate yield to put just as we won't calculate yield to call. We'll calculate current yield, since that's easy. But we'll focus on yield to maturity, which—since there are no other contenders—will equal yield to worst.

As of this writing on June 28, 2024 the ask on the note is 99.02.[9] That's the clean price.

The maturity date is 509 days away. That's in 1.39 years, since 509 divided by 365 equals 1.39.

So the current yield is 5.23 percent. That's just the 5.179 coupon divided by the 99.02 price. Today that's better than a good bank savings account. But not by much.

For yield-to-maturity, we turn again to the online calculator:

http://www.gooddebtcheap.com/pl.htm

Our inputs are:

Price	$ 990.20
Par	$1,000.00
Years to maturity	1.39
Annual coupon rate	5.179%
Coupon payment frequency	Twice a year

The calculator tells us that yield to maturity is 5.924 percent. Again, that's not much better than a bank savings account.

So is the note inexpensive? Not to this value investor. Of course we're looking at it narrowly, just to illustrate inexpensiveness. Maybe there's something in understanding, issuer, or issue that we should appreciate. But absent that, the note is more for managers of diversified investment-grade portfolios than for return hunters.

CHAPTER 8

IRRATIONALITY

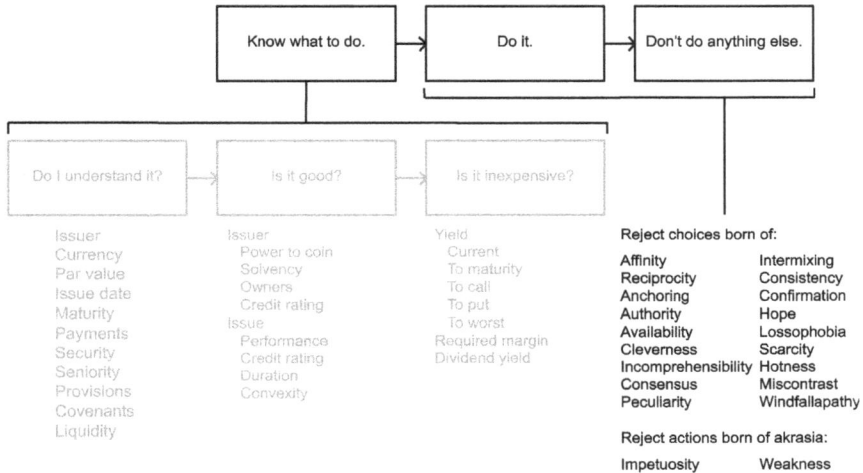

| Know what to do. | → | Do it. | → | Don't do anything else. |

| Do I understand it? | → | Is it good? | → | Is it inexpensive? |

Issuer	Issuer	Yield
Currency	Power to coin	Current
Par value	Solvency	To maturity
Issue date	Owners	To call
Maturity	Credit rating	To put
Payments	Issue	To worst
Security	Performance	Required margin
Seniority	Credit rating	Dividend yield
Provisions	Duration	
Covenants	Convexity	
Liquidity		

Reject choices born of:

Affinity	Intermixing
Reciprocity	Consistency
Anchoring	Confirmation
Authority	Hope
Availability	Lossophobia
Cleverness	Scarcity
Incomprehensibility	Hotness
Consensus	Miscontrast
Peculiarity	Windfallapathy

Reject actions born of akrasia:

| Impetuosity | Weakness |

My first book, *Good Stocks Cheap*, has a chapter called *misjudgment and misaction*. It's key. Many smart people make bad investments because they—well—misjudge or misact. They analyze well. But when it comes time to decide, they stumble. They fall prey to the irrationality to which we, as humans, are all subject. So they buy what they shouldn't, and don't buy what they should.

Managing this problem is simple. We identify our cognitive biases. We give them names, and learn to recognize their symptoms. Then when they pop up to botch our choices, we can spot them as the hellions they are and squash them.

Admittedly, irrationality is a bigger issue with stocks than with bonds. It's easy to get emotional about a stock. That's because it's an ownership stake in a business whose products we may love, or whose CEO we may admire, or whose advertisements we may like. But it's harder to get emotional about bonds. They're all rates, pars, and yields. They're colder.

It's like falling in love with a puppy versus falling in love with a lizard. One's just more conceivable.

But psychological traps litter the fixed income landscape as they do any sphere of human endeavor. We're not suddenly foolproof just because we pivot from stocks to bonds. So into the fixed income world we carry our map of mental shortcomings, reframed for that asset class.

The first three steps of the model—*do I understand it? is it good?* and *is it inexpensive?*—form a row. The lower of two rows, actually, because above it is a row of three supra-steps: *know what to do*, *do it*, and *don't do anything else*.

The first supra-step, *know what to do*, is the umbrella category for the lower row. We *know what to do* after we *understand* a security, know whether it's *good*, and know whether it's *inexpensive*.

The second supra-step, *do it*, means taking decisive action when that's appropriate. It means buying an understood, good bond when it's underpriced. That turns out to be tough. It's tough because the reason a bond becomes underpriced is because hordes are selling it. So we have to commit capital to an asset that everyone else is dumping. We get no social reinforcement.

The third supra-step, *don't do anything else*, is tougher still. It means that when we don't understand a bond, or understand a bond that comes from a questionable issuer, or understand a good bond that's expensive, we sit tight.

That's hard for people of ambition. We *itch* to take action. But acting just because of an itch can hurt us. To paraphrase the philosopher Pascal, investors' problems stem from their inability to keep still.

The great resource on this subject is Robert Cialdini, an American psychology professor. His book *Influence* remains helpful reading for any intelligent investor.

A second great resource is a Cialdini apostle, the late investor Charlie Munger. His 1995 Harvard talk is the north star on human misjudgment. It contains some indelicate language, and the recording quality is marginal. But if you haven't yet heard it, a remunerative hour awaits you:

http://www.gooddebtcheap.com/al.htm

Third is Amos Tversky and Daniel Kahneman, psychologists whose 1979 paper *Prospect Theory* ushered in the modern field of behavioral finance. Their research is nicely summarized in Kahneman's bestselling book *Thinking Fast and Slow*.

Anything I know about investor irrationality comes from these four thinkers. They get credit for the following list of 18 cognitive biases that bond investors would, in my view, do well to conquer.

First is *affinity*. That's liking something. The affinity bias urges us to buy a bond because we're fond of something associated with it. Stock from the same issuer, for example.

Affinity can also work in reverse. We may prematurely stop considering a bond because we find the issuer's industry humdrum. Or we may skip a solid muni because we don't like spending time in the city that is the issuer.

Second is *reciprocity*. Reciprocity is the tendency to treat others as they have treated us. It infects bond investing because so many fixed income securities are unlisted. We rely on over-the-counter brokers to bring us inventory. When they do, we can feel obligated to reciprocate by buying whatever they're offering.

Reciprocity can also work backwards. We may stop considering a security brought to us by a broker that we perceive to have done us a disservice. That's equally unproductive.

Reciprocity differs from affinity. Reciprocity requires a specific action by someone towards the investor. But affinity doesn't.

Third is *anchoring*. Anchoring is benchmarking against an insignificant standard. It pushes us to buy a bond just because its yield has increased from a low level. If it's still too low and there are no extenuating circumstances, we'd do better by waiting.

Anchoring works with capital gains, too. An investor may sell a bond just because the bid soars past the purchase price. But if the yield remains too high, the bid is likely to increase more.

Fourth is *authority*. The authority bias motivates us to copy trades made by investors we admire. There's nothing wrong with looking up to experts. But it's dangerous to let reverence eclipse objectivity.

On the flip side, the authority bias can encourage us to ignore ideas from junior people. It could cause a fund manager to reject an opportunity proposed by a just-hired analyst, for example. That's unproductive. Good ideas can come from anywhere.

Fifth is *availability*. The availability bias highlights information received recently or vividly. It blinds us to information that's older or duller, even if it's more relevant.[1] It can keep us from considering a solid, high yield-to-maturity bond just because the issuer is quiet. And it can attract us to a low-yield bond just because the issuer has a good publicist.

Sixth is what I call *cleverness*. The cleverness bias inclines us toward ideas that make us feel intelligent. It favors opportunities that call out our analytical best, opportunities that remind us of how brilliant we are.

Convertible bonds are nasty cleverness traps. They're convoluted. Often their convertibility is contingent on hard-to-predict events, their conversion ratios are variable, and the common stock we would get by converting is hard to value. Figuring them out takes more time than figuring out a *plain vanilla bond.* And yet that very challenge can fool us into thinking that we've uncovered something great.

Flipped over, the cleverness bias repels us from securities that seem too simple. It makes us wary of situations we can sort out easily. It pushes us away from that plain vanilla bond, even if it has a high yield-to-worst and a solvent issuer.

Seventh is what I call *incomprehensibility.* The incomprehensibility bias makes us want a security more if we understand it less. It makes us mistake unintelligibility for opportunity. It makes a broker who uses complicated language seem like a pro, endowed with insights we couldn't possibly have had ourselves.

Inverted, the incomprehensibility bias makes us reject opportunities described to us simply. We hate them because they're not obfuscated. They deny us the exercise of interpretation. And yet the best ideas are often plain, and the best brokers often communicate in a straightforward way.

Incomprehensibility is different from cleverness. The cleverness bias is about ideas that are truly complex. But the incomprehensibility bias is about ideas that are merely expressed in a complex fashion.

Eighth is *consensus.* Consensus is agreement among many. It moves us to buy the bonds that everyone else is buying. The problem is that these are often low yield, since popularity drives up price. It's when an investment becomes unpopular that its yield gets promising.

Of course just because a bond is unpopular doesn't make it a great investment. The unpopularity may be justified by deteriorating credit quality. The high yield may be fiction because a default is likely. So a consensus view that a security is bad isn't enough to make it attractive. Unpopularity is helpful, but it's not sufficient.

Ninth is what I call *peculiarity*. Peculiarity motivates us to want bonds that are unique. It's the opposite of consensus. It may make us seek debt from exotic countries just because they're from exotic countries, or century bonds just because they mature in 100 years. It's similar to the cleverness bias except that it showcases securities that are merely different, not necessarily complicated.

Acting inversely, the peculiarity bias repels us from ideas that aren't obscure enough. It keeps us from buying domestic, plain vanilla bonds that are excellent. It unnecessarily restricts our universe of opportunities.

Tenth is what I call *intermixing*. It biases us towards bonds that are different from others in our portfolio. To an investor in high-yield corporates it may make an investment-grade muni appealing, even if it yields less.

When the intermixing bias operates in reverse, it pushes us away from opportunities that don't stand out in our portfolio. This is like the peculiarity bias, but against the background of our own holdings as opposed to those of others.

Intermixing is not the same thing as diversification. Diversification is buying different bonds so that not all of them drop in price simultaneously, or mature simultaneously. If capital preservation is the priority, diversification can make sense. But intermixing doesn't. It's just variety for variety's sake.

Eleventh is *consistency*. Also called *commitment and consistency*, it makes us act in concert with our prior actions. It keeps us from productively changing our mind, especially when doing so would require us to reverse a stand that others know we took. It could cause us to hold on to a bond whose issuer just went on credit watch with a negative outlook, even if we could still sell profitably.

Consistency is different from perseverance. Perseverance is sticking with a security when any contrary indicators that have emerged don't matter. Perseverance is good. If a great preferred stock drops in price for no good reason, holding makes sense. Consistency, however, is holding that preferred merely because you already own it. If the fundamentals of the issuer have truly deteriorated, not selling in the name of consistency is absurd.

Twelfth is *confirmation*. The confirmation bias tilts us toward opportunities that support views we already hold. It's like consistency, but based on beliefs instead of prior actions.

Acting in reverse, the confirmation bias repels us from ideas that clash with our old convictions. It makes us dismiss good opportunities because they go against our preexisting views. It both shrinks our investment universe and keeps us from updating our beliefs to reflect new realities.

We may have once rejected bonds from an issuer that wasn't sufficiently solvent. But if that issuer has recapitalized to the point that its solvency ratios are now excellent, ignoring the bonds just because we used to is wrong.

Thirteenth is *hope*. The hope bias urges us to believe in an investment. It spotlights facts that make a security look good, and deemphasizes those that don't. It might have us focus on a high yield to call when there's little chance that the security will be called, or on yield to worst when there's little chance the security will perform.

Socially, hope is a virtue. It's optimism. We get along well with others by projecting a positive attitude. But with fixed income securities, there's no way for hope to usefully manifest itself. A bond doesn't care if we believe in it. It won't perform just because we're optimistic.

Fourteenth is what I call *lossophobia*. It's the fear of loss that urges us to sell a security just because its price has dropped. It's the panic that pushes us to realize a loss, even if the issuer's fundamentals remain solid.

Of course if the preferred dividend coverage ratio plunges below one, or the debt-to-equity ratio soars above one, or the fundamentals deteriorate in some other way, selling might make sense. But an issue's value doesn't drop just because its price flits around.

Fifteenth is *scarcity*. Like reciprocity, it pops up because many fixed income securities are unlisted. We want them merely because they're hard to get.

Correspondingly, the scarcity bias repels us from securities that seem abundant. It can make a listed bond look bad, as if availability itself indicated low quality.

Scarcity also works when selling. If we own preferred stock from a deteriorating issuer whose price has yet to fall, we may hold since the chance to sell at a good price seems lasting.

The sixteenth is what I call *hotness*. It's the belief that we're on a winning streak. More formally called the *hot hand fallacy*,[2] it pops up after a string of good investment outcomes. We make the next buy because it feels like it will go as well as the last one. It's a false sense of confidence that can leave us with an issue we never should have purchased.

Operating inversely, hotness keeps us from making a good investment after a string of bad results. We feel like we're on a losing streak, so we skip opportunities that are entirely solid.

The seventeenth is what I call *miscontrast*. It pushes us to make investments that aren't good in an absolute sense, but that are better than others we're seeing at the time. It's the illusion that an environment of low caliber deals will sustain. It creates the risk that we'll commit capital to weak opportunities, leaving us without the *dry powder* needed for the strong ones that eventually surface.

Miscontrast is most relevant to managers. Consider bond funds. Sometimes staying in cash is the right thing for managers to do. But their investors signed up to be in bonds, and the charter of the fund promises that they'll be in bonds. So dry powder can make managers look lazy instead of judicious.

The eighteenth is what I call *windfallapathy*. It's apathy caused by a windfall, a carelessness that emerges when people unexpectedly come into a large sum of money. It's being less selective about investments because it seems like such selectivity is no longer essential.

Relaxing our investment standards may remind us that money isn't as scarce as it once was. That's a pleasant feeling. But it leads to substandard returns and losses. The math on that is vicious, quickly destroying newfound wealth. So however understandable windfallapathy may be, it's to be stopped the moment it surfaces.

Just because an opportunity conjures cognitive biases doesn't mean it should be rejected. It should only be rejected if cognitive biases distort our judgment.

Take a convertible floater. It may be truly complex. It may be convertible only under esoteric circumstances, and its coupon may reset at irregular intervals according to some unfamiliar index. We need extra time to figure it out. But that doesn't mean that the cleverness bias is in action. It's only in action if the model doesn't recommend the convertible floater and we buy it anyway.

That's why the judgments to reject are those *caused* by cognitive biases. We reject them because they come *exclusively* from mental flaws.

Cognitive biases can team up. Several can act simultaneously. If after a string of good investment outcomes we're offered a block of preferred stock that stands out from the corporates we usually buy, both the hotness bias and the intermixing bias may be acting. This double threat heightens the chance that we'll misjudge.

Sometimes there is no misjudgment. We steer clear of all 18 biases. But we still misact. We buy the wrong thing, refrain from buying the right thing, or sell something we should hold. Why?

The ancient Greek philosopher Aristotle tackled this question centuries ago. He called misaction *akrasia*, meaning *lack of restraint*. In his *Nicomachean Ethics*, he defined two forms of akrasia.

First is *impetuosity*. It's acting on impulse. It's doing something without thinking it through. It's hard to combat because it feels like instinct, the kind of instinct that serves us so well in other aspects of life.

Managing impetuosity requires seeing it as fleeting. It passes. It's forceful when it first surfaces. But it disappears just as quickly. And yet bad investments made during its brief visit last. Don't make them.

The second form of akrasia is *weakness*. It's giving in to an urge after deliberation. It's doing something stupid knowing that it's stupid.[3]

Weakness can be hard to distinguish from a bias that it masks. Picture an investor buying a plain vanilla bond with a miserable yield to maturity through a highly respected broker. Was it the authority bias that forced the purchase? Or did the investor know that buying was wrong, and just succumb to weakness? It can be hard to tell. But this imperfection delivers a benefit of redundancy. It provides multiple chances to catch an error before it happens.

Akrasia is embarrassing. It's us at our worst. Why we're afflicted by it I don't know. But we are. People do all kinds of things—consciously and unconsciously—that do them harm. When akrasia sets upon investors, it causes real economic damage.

So do the 18 cognitive biases. But the solution is simple. Know about them. Recognize them. That's all the inoculation you need.

SUMMARY

Investor misjudgment comes from some combination of 18 biases:

1. Affinity
2. Reciprocity
3. Anchoring
4. Authority
5. Availability
6. Cleverness
7. Incomprehensibility
8. Consensus
9. Peculiarity
10. Intermixing
11. Consistency
12. Confirmation
13. Hope
14. Lossophobia
15. Scarcity
16. Hotness
17. Miscontrast
18. Windfallapathy

Investor misaction comes from one of two forms of akrasia:

1. Impetuosity
2. Weakness

Don't do anything else.

Do it.

Know what to do.

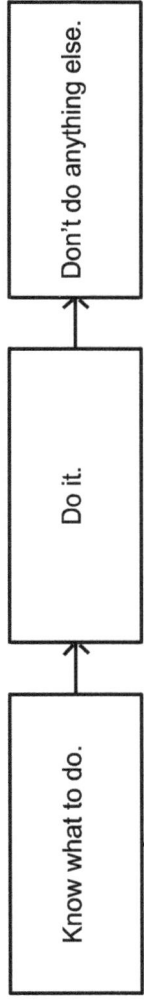

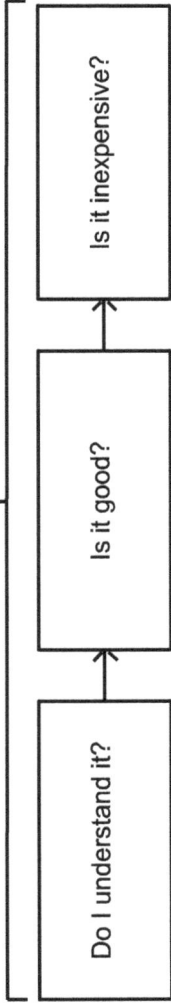

Do I understand it?

Is it good?

Is it inexpensive?

Do I understand it?

Issuer
Currency
Par value
Issue date
Maturity
Payments
Security
Seniority
Provisions
Covenants
Liquidity

Is it good?

Issuer
Power to coin
Solvency
Owners
Credit rating
Issue
Performance
Credit rating
Duration
Convexity

Is it inexpensive?

Yield
Current
To maturity
To call
To put
To worst
Required margin
Dividend yield

Reject choices born of:

Affinity	Intermixing
Reciprocity	Consistency
Anchoring	Confirmation
Authority	Hope
Availability	Lossophobia
Cleverness	Scarcity
Incomprehensibility	Hotness
Consensus	Miscontrast
Peculiarity	Windfallapathy

Reject actions born of akrasia:

Impetuosity	Weakness

PART III

TYPES

CHAPTER 9

ZEROS

Some fixed income securities share characteristics. They may share the same kind of issuer. They may share the same term. Or they may share the same coupon. Such securities are grouped into types.

These types aren't mutually exclusive. A single security can be of several types.

Ours will not be a comprehensive look at all of the types. It will be limited. We'll focus on those that are foundational, and those that offer the greatest opportunities to value investors.

One type is *zero-coupon bonds*. They're often called *zeros*. As we know, they don't pay interest. That's their common characteristic: the coupon. It's nil.

The return on a zero comes purely from the discount to par paid for the bond. That's why zeros are sometimes also called *pure discount bonds*. The discount can be offered at issuance, on the primary market. And it can be offered later, on the secondary market. The greater the discount, the greater the return.

Recall that yield to maturity is the discount rate that, when applied to all of the bond's future interest and principal payments, equals its price. We know that the formula for the YTM of a zero is:

$$(\text{par value} / \text{price}) \wedge (1 / \text{tenor}) - 1$$

A zero doesn't have a coupon rate, obviously. But it does have an *accretion rate*. That's the speed at which its worth marches from its discounted price at issuance towards par value at maturity. At issuance, the accretion rate equals YTM.

The *accreted value* of a zero is a measure of its worth at a particular moment during its term. At issuance, accreted value equals price. At maturity, accreted value equals par. In the interim, it's somewhere in between.

Consider a zero with a $1,000 par value and 10-year term issued at 87.020 on January 1, 2024. Its price at issuance is, obviously, $870.20. On December 31, 2028—midway through its term—its accreted value is $932.84. That's easy to calculate:

http://www.gooddebtcheap.com/av.xlsx

It's also easy to visualize:

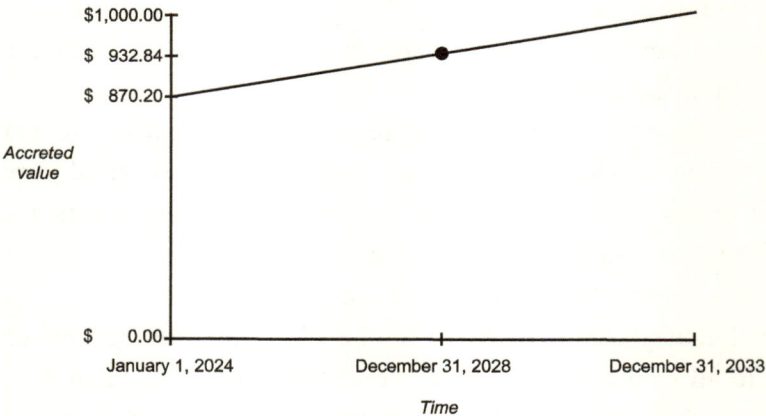

The dot shows accreted value of $932.84 on December 31, 2028.

The accreted value is just one measure of the worth of a zero. Actual worth, and price, can differ. Consider an outstanding zero from an issuer that becomes distressed. The prospect of the zero not performing becomes real. In that case actual worth and price may be less than accreted value.

Zeros have advantages, and disadvantages.

An advantage is that they have no reinvestment risk. A holder doesn't have to scramble to find a productive way to reinvest the coupon payments. There aren't any. That's helpful if interest rates drop after the zero is bought.

The flip side of that is a disadvantage. If interest rates rise, there's no opportunity to invest coupon payments at increased rates.

Another disadvantage is that zeros can trigger tax liabilities before they generate cash. That's because of *imputed interest*. Imputed interest is the amount of income a taxing authority assumes came from a zero, even though no cash flowed. It's the authority's nasty way of dressing up a zero in a coupon bond costume.

This gives zeros a special glow to tax-exempt organizations, like churches and charities. Such entities are immune from imputed interest. And it's why individuals that own zeros sometimes do so in tax-deferred and tax-exempt accounts, like American 401(k)s and Roth IRAs.

A final disadvantage is interest rate risk. It's high. Indeed it's as high as it can be, since a zero's Macauley duration equals its tenor. That means that its modified duration is also high. So the price of an investment grade zero is particularly sensitive to changes in interest rates.

Investment grade zeros can be useful to holders anticipating big, known expenses. A university may buy zeros to make a future scheduled payment on a capital project, for example.

But zeros below investment grade play a different role. Sometimes they're just ignorable trash. But other times they're embroiled in special situations that offer outsized returns, as the following case study shows.

SUMMARY

1. Zeros don't pay interest.
2. The return on a zero comes purely from the discount to par.
3. The accretion rate is the speed at which a zero's worth marches toward par value.
4. Zeros have the highest possible Macauley duration: tenor.
5. An advantage of zeros is that they have no reinvestment risk.
6. Disadvantages of zeros include no chance to reinvest coupons at higher rates, imputed interest tax liabilities, and high interest rate risk.

CASE STUDY
Tyco International Ltd.
Zero Coupon Convertible Debentures due 2020

Tyco International Ltd. was a listed company based in Bermuda. In 2000 it issued zeros. The prospectus is lost to history. But an amendment to Tyco's 2002 10-K describes them well enough for us to take a stab at the 11 parameters of understanding:

http://www.gooddebtcheap.com/ab.htm

First, the *issuer* is a company: Tyco International Ltd.

Second, the *currency* is U.S. dollars.

Third, *par value* isn't stated. But it's probably $1,000 since the issue is a U.S. dollar-denominated corporate.

Fourth, the *issue date* is November 17, 2000. That's from the indenture date given on page 33.

Fifth, *maturity* seems to be November 17, 2020. Footnote seven on page 107 says "November 2020." It's safe to assume that it's on or around the 17th, given the issue date.

Sixth, there are no *payments*. There's no coupon. But the annual accretion rate is 1.5 percent, per page 172.

Seventh and eighth, there's no evidence that the zeros are either *secured* or *senior*.

Ninth, there are *provisions*. Foremost among them is a put provision. It's on page 172. It lets holders sell the zeros back to Tyco at the then-accreted value in November 2003, 2005, 2007, and 2014. The exact day of the month isn't given. But again, we can safely assume that it's on or around the 17th.

There's a conversion provision as well. It's summarized on page 108. Basically, holders can swap the zeros for Tyco common stock if the stock is priced above some threshold, or if Tyco calls the zeros. But conversion isn't central to the opportunity, as we'll soon see.

Incidentally, since the zeros can be converted if called there must be some redemption provision as well. I can't find any details on it. But that's okay, since redemption isn't central to the opportunity either.

Tenth, it's unclear if the zero is subject to *covenants*. Some of the company's debts are, such as one limiting total debt divided by total capitalization to a maximum 52.5 percent. That tidbit is on page 169. But again, it's unclear if that or any other covenant applies to the zero specifically.

Eleventh, the zero doesn't seem to be listed, so it probably wasn't as *liquid* as it could have been.[1] But it traded over-the-counter enough for frightened investors to dump it. One might ask, why would they do that?

In June 2002, Moody's downgraded Tyco to just above junk, with a negative outlook.[2] Then in September 2002 the SEC filed a complaint against three senior executives, accusing them of concealing material information, and of taking out zero interest rate loans from the company to refurbish a ski house:[3]

http://www.gooddebtcheap.com/yt.htm

Tyco subsequently lost its investment-grade credit rating,[4] and the price of the zeros dropped to around 60. That's when some value investors took notice.

The newest report available at that time was the 10-Q for the second quarter of 2002. So we'll use that document to tackle the four *issuer* points:

http://www.gooddebtcheap.com/jj.htm

To start, Tyco obviously doesn't have the *power to coin*.

Regarding *solvency*, the balance sheet and income statement appear on pages one and three.[5] The ratios are simple to calculate:

http://www.gooddebtcheap.com/uf.xlsx

Debt to equity is just over two, twice as high as my benchmark of one. That's bad. *Liabilities to equity* is also too high, but not by as much. It's 2.9 versus my preferred benchmark of two.

The *quick ratio* is more encouraging. It matches my benchmark of one. But the interest coverage ratio is inadequate, since *EBIT* is negative.

Note that I had to calculate EBIT myself. I just added *interest and other financial charges* back to *income before taxes*. And since the company's fiscal year ends September 30, the income statement we're using covers six months. Hence my interest coverage ratio is for a two-quarter period.

So, is Tyco solvent? Not particularly. But the quick ratio seems fine. That's important.

Owners is unclear. That's because a proxy statement from that time period isn't available.

Lastly, Tyco's *credit rating* is in junk territory.[6] That's the result of the recent downgrade.

Moving on to *issue*, it's hard to assess the *performance* of an outstanding zero. That's because there are no coupon payments to miss. So as of late 2002 it can't be said that the zero is nonperforming.

As for *credit rating*, the issue has the speculative status of its issuer. It has no credit enhancements.

With a junk rating, a slashed price, and an issuer run by chalet renovators, *duration* and *convexity* aren't top concerns. In addition, it's tricky calculating duration and convexity for a bond with embedded options.   We explored that in chapter 6 with *effective duration*. But for the record, let's calculate both as if there were no options.

Let's assume that the price of 60 was available on the convenient date of November 17, 2002. That would mean that there are 18 years until maturity. With that we turn again to the online calculator:

http://www.gooddebtcheap.com/pl.htm

If we think of the accretion rate as a coupon rate, our inputs are:

Price	$ 600.00
Par	$1,000.00
Years to maturity	18.00
Annual coupon rate	1.500%
Coupon payment frequency	None

The calculator spits out a Macauley duration of 18. We knew that, since that's tenor. And convexity is a fairly meaningless 193.47.

Moving on to *inexpensiveness*, the online calculator tells us that YTM is 2.879 percent. That's measley.

What about yield to put? Recall that the first put date is November 17, 2003. That's in just a year. And the put price equals the then-accreted value. It's $776.38. We have to calculate that, but it's easy. After all, we know the issue date, maturity date, par value, and accretion rate:

http://www.gooddebtcheap.com/mp.xlsx

To figure yield to put we can use the same online calculator. Just think of the put price as par, and the put date as the maturity date. So only two inputs change:

Price	$ 600.00
Par	$ 776.38
Years to maturity	1.00
Annual coupon rate	1.500%
Coupon payment frequency	None

The calculator tells us that yield to maturity—which we'll read as yield to put—is just over 29 percent.

Twenty-nine percent! Now we're talking.

But we'll only realize that return if Tyco can honor our put. Will the company have enough cash in a year to pay us $776.38 for each bond?

Two facts say yes.

First is the quick ratio. It's one. And its timeline matches our target holding period of a year. That's because current assets—the starting point of the numerator—are defined as assets that could be used within a year. And current liabilities—the denominator—are defined as obligations that have to be settled within a year.

If you think about it, we only need the company to stay alive for a year. And the quick ratio says that it can. Of course if the negative EBIT sustains, the quick ratio will deteriorate. But on the narrow issue of near-term solvency, Tyco seems able to honor a 2003 put.

Second is the SEC complaint. Note that it's targeted at individuals. The defendants are *people*. It's not the company.[7] The issuer is the company, not the people. So while it's conceivable that Tyco could be fined, that doesn't seem to be the likely outcome of this complaint.

Some value investors did indeed put the bonds at the first opportunity. And according to page 95 of the 2003 10-K, Tyco honored the puts:[8]

http://www.gooddebtcheap.com/et.htm

We can't know if the investors' purchase price was exactly $600, or if the purchase date was exactly November 17, 2002. And the accreted value put price cited in the 2003 10-K is actually about a dollar less than the one we modeled. But so what? An annual return of 29 percent in a bond is remarkable. An annual return of 29 percent in *anything* is remarkable.

Note that yield to worst was not an appropriate consideration in this case. That's why we didn't analyze the conversion scenario, or give any weight to yield to maturity. We focused on yield to put because that was the likely outcome.

In retrospect, it's easy to see that this was a good trade. But to see it in advance required uncommon foresight, foresight you've just taken another step to develop.

CHAPTER 10

TREASURYS

Treasurys are fixed income securities issued by the U.S. Department of the Treasury. And they really are pluralized oddly like that: *Treasurys*.

Treasurys aren't thrilling. They're more about capital preservation than returns. Folding laundry offers more drama. But Treasurys are still worth mastering, for four reasons.

First, they're foundational. They're like scales to a musician, or layups to a basketball player. Competent professionals understand them.

Second, they often define the *risk-free rate*. That's the theoretical rate of return available to an investor without taking on credit risk. Many bonds have coupon rates set at some spread over the risk-free rate.

Third, they're the default basis of the *yield curve*. More on that shortly.

Fourth, Treasurys are where investors can park cash awaiting higher-return opportunities. They ably house dry powder. Of course for lesser balances high-yield government-insured savings accounts serve that function just fine. But at scale—like millions of dollars—Treasurys can be more efficient.

Treasurys are thought to carry no credit risk because in a pinch, the U.S. government could simply print the dollars necessary to repay its obligations. The issuer has the power to coin.

Other governments also have the power to coin. India could print more rupees, Japan could print more yen, and Switzerland could print more francs. But the U.S. is considered particularly dependable, giving Treasurys their credit risk-free reputation. Not to gloat, of course.

While Treasurys may be free of credit risk, they're not free of interest rate risk. Recall that that's the chance that interest rates will rise, causing the price of outstanding fixed income securities to fall. Intelligent investors are aware of this distinction. But many folks aren't.

There are different kinds of Treasurys. They change over time. As of this writing there are five: *bills, notes, bonds, TIPS* and *FRNs*.

First are Treasury *bills*. They're zeros with terms of up to 52 weeks. They're commonly called *T-bills*.[1]

Incidentally, a T-bill is a good example of a fixed income security that's of two types. It's both a zero and a Treasury.

Second are Treasury *notes*. They're coupon bonds with terms of between two and 10 years. They pay interest every six months.[2]

Third are Treasury *bonds*. They're coupon bonds with terms exceeding 10 years. They also pay interest semiannually.[3] The 30-year Treasury bond is sometimes called the *long bond.*

Fourth are *TIPS*. TIPS stands for *Treasury Inflation-Protected Securities*. They're coupon bonds with terms of between five and 30 years. Their special feature is that their par value varies with the *Consumer Price Index*, or CPI. So even though their coupon *rates* are fixed, their semiannual coupon *payments* vary because the rate is applied to a floating principal amount.[4]

Fifth are *FRNs*. FRN stands for *Floating Rate Note*. It's a coupon bond with an interest rate that varies with the most recent discount on the 13-week Treasury bill. It pays this interest every three months, in contrast to standard Treasury notes that pay interest every six months. It has a term of two years.[5]

Floating rate notes can be issued by entities other than the U.S. Department of the Treasury. Corporations, for example. So a security called an FRN isn't necessarily backed by the United States. *TIPS* and *T-bills*, by contrast, are. Only America can issue TIPS and T-bills.

We'll cover FRNs in greater detail in chapter 13.

We know that T-bills are zero-coupon securities with terms of up to 52 weeks. But sometimes an investor wants a zero-coupon Treasury with a longer term. For that, there are *STRIPS*.

STRIPS—irritatingly capitalized, I know—are single scheduled interest payments made out of Treasurys. They're created by financial institutions. STRIPS stands for *Separate Trading of Registered Interest and Principal Securities*.

STRIPS share two characteristics with the Treasurys out of which they're made.

First, they're still backed by the government. Even though financial institutions created them, America stands behind them.

Second, interest earned on them is exempt from U.S. state and local taxes. That's relevant even though STRIPS don't pay cash interest. For tax purposes they're seen as paying imputed interest.

Of course imputed interest applies to T-bills too. A T-bill generates taxable interest even though it pays no cash until maturity. But like STRIPS, T-bill imputed interest is taxed only at the federal level.

STRIPS are bought from brokerages.[6] So are Treasurys. But unlike STRIPS, Treasurys can also be bought directly from the government:

http://www.gooddebtcheap.com/mm.htm

The dirty prices of Treasury bonds, Treasury notes, TIPS, Treasury FRNs, and STRIPS use the actual/actual day count convention. But T-bills, like other money market instruments, use actual/360.

Back in chapter 7 we saw how some fixed income securities are quoted in 32nds and 64ths. Remember? That's the antique convention where 101-04+ means 101 plus 4/32 plus 1/64, or 101.140625 percent of face value. Anyway, the Treasury note and

Treasury bond markets are where that happens. So if securities with terms of at least two years and no credit risk are your thing, strap in for some old-timey fun.

The main reason Treasurys ably house dry powder is because they're credit risk-free. They have the highest credit ratings. But another reason is the state and local tax exemption.

Another advantage of Treasurys is that they generally can't be called. There can be exceptions. But there's usually no chance you'll get your Treasury yanked away from you if interest rates plunge.

Because they're credit risk-free and noncallable, Treasurys are often the building materials of choice for *bond ladders*. Bond ladders excite capital-preservation freaks more than they do return hunters. But they're fundamental, and easy to understand.

A bond ladder is a portfolio of fixed income securities designed to create periodic liquidity and minimize interest rate risk. They're built out of *rungs*, identical amounts of money invested in bonds with particular maturity dates. The maturity dates of the rungs are spaced out evenly.

Picture $1,200,000 earmarked for capital preservation, periodic liquidity, and minimal interest rate risk. Say that it's March 1, 2025. The $1,200,000 could be divided into 12 rungs of $100,000 each. The first rung could be invested in Treasurys maturing March 31, 2025. The second rung could be invested in Treasurys maturing April 30, 2025. The third, May 31, 2025. And so on through the 12th rung.

When the first rung matures 30 days later on March 31, 2025, the proceeds could be reinvested in Treasurys maturing March 31, 2026. That investment would, of course, be made at then-prevailing rates. And it's that *then-prevailing rates* thing that minimizes interest rate risk.

When the second rung matures on April 30, 2025, the proceeds could be reinvested in Treasurys maturing April 30, 2026. When the third matures on May 31, 2025, the proceeds could be reinvested in Treasurys maturing May 31, 2026. And so on.

Snoresville? Yes. But that's a bond ladder.

Since Treasurys are often the basis of the yield curve, let's tackle that economic indicator now. It's simple.

The yield curve is a graph of the prices of fixed income securities with the same credit risk but different maturity dates. It's also called the *term structure of interest* rates. The vertical axis is *yield to maturity*. The horizontal axis is *maturity*.

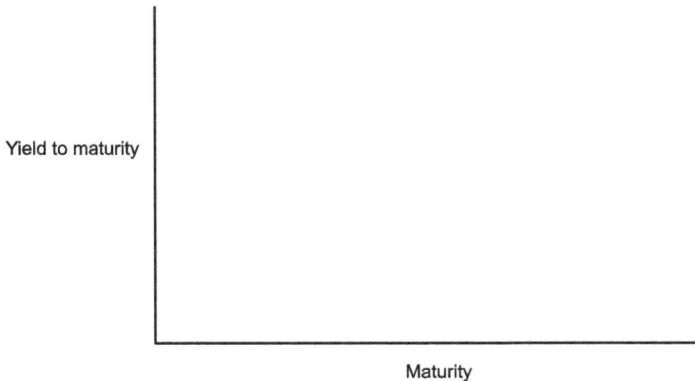

Yield to maturity

Maturity

The axes of the yield curve graph

Note that most yield curve graphs don't label the vertical axis this way. They just say *yield*. But we know that there are several versions of yield, so it's probably best to be specific.

As for the horizontal axis, *maturity* could be read as either *maturity date* or *tenor*.

Because a yield curve holds credit quality constant, it's useful to base it on Treasurys. After all, the perceived credit quality of all Treasurys has been the same. The yield curve can assume different shapes. Each shape is thought to reflect a different market sentiment. There are five shapes.

First is the *normal* yield curve. It's upward-sloping, where long-term yields exceed short-term yields. It's generally taken as a sign of a healthy economy. It's the most common shape.

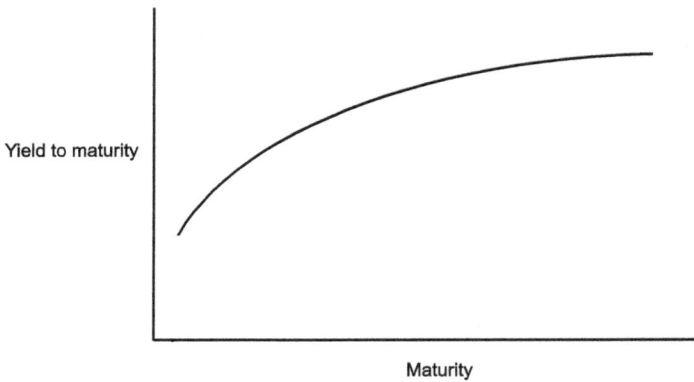

A normal yield curve

Second is the *steep* yield curve. It's even more upward sloping. It's generally taken to suggest a healthy and improving economy.

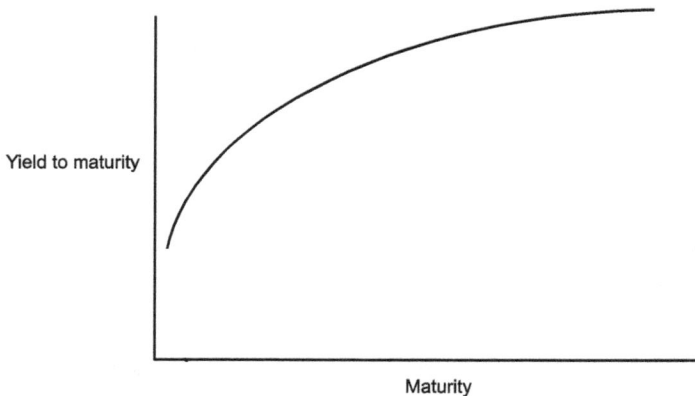

A steep yield curve

Third is a *flat* yield curve. It's horizontal. It's often assumed to indicate economic uncertainty.

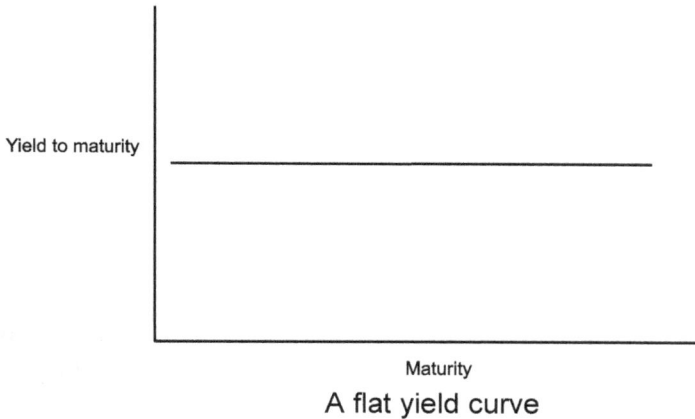

A flat yield curve

Fourth is an *inverted yield curve*. It's downward-sloping, where short-term yields exceed long-term yields. It's often read to forecast a recession.

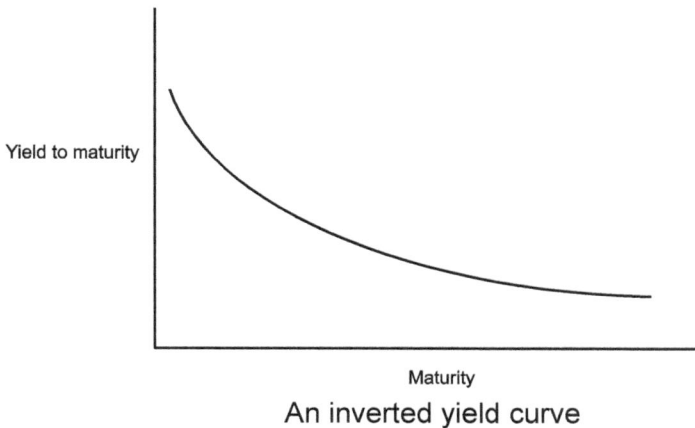

An inverted yield curve

Fifth is a *humped* yield curve. It bulges up in the middle. It shows *medium-term* yields exceeding both *long-term* and *short-term* yields. It's often taken as a sign of a slow economy.

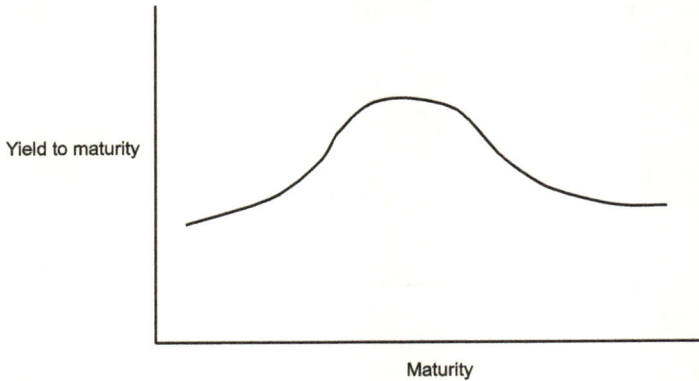

A humped yield curve

In the context of yield curves, *spread* means the distance between yields on securities that vary only in credit quality. It's an indicator of the *risk premium*, the incremental return available by accepting more credit risk. It would be normal, for example, for corporates rated A+ by S&P and Fitch to offer yields that exceed those of Treasurys with the same tenor.

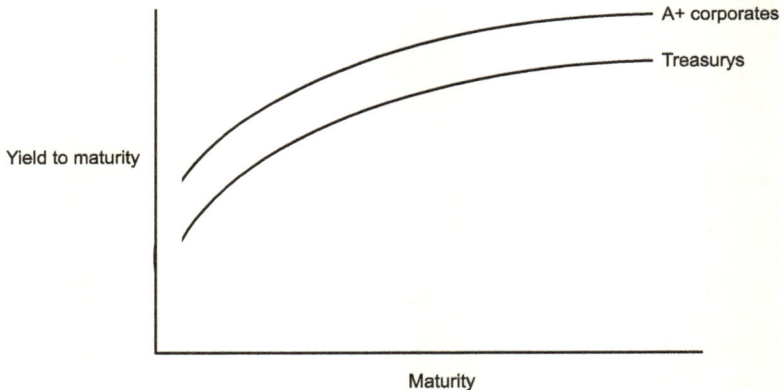

The yield to maturity of A+ corporates set
above a normal yield curve to illustrate spread

The yield curve is not riveting. Soup is more dynamic. But it can shine a bright light on gargantuan risk premiums.

Treasurys matter most to American investors with U.S. dollars. Investors elsewhere, with other currencies, may focus more on bonds from their governments. Like Treasurys, many of those bonds have nicknames. Germany has *Bunds*,[7] India has *G-Secs*,[8] and the UK has *gilts* (which is indeed not capitalized).[9] Others are known by acronyms, like France's *OATs*,[10] Italy's *BTPs*,[11] and Japan's *JGBs*.[12]

From all those securities one can construct bond ladders, plot yield curves, and figure risk premiums. To be clear, they're not equals. They don't all have the same credit risk, and they're not denominated in currencies with the same stability. But in their own countries they can emerge as the most relevant sovereign debt.

SUMMARY

1. Treasurys are worth understanding because they're foundational, define the risk-free rate, underlie the yield curve, and efficiently house dry powder.
2. Treasurys may be free of credit risk, but they're not free of interest rate risk.
3. Types of Treasurys include bills, notes, bonds, TIPS, and FRNs.
4. Interest earned on Treasurys is exempt from American state and local taxes.
5. STRIPS are single scheduled interest payments made out of Treasurys.
6. Treasurys can't be called.
7. A bond ladder is a portfolio designed to minimize interest rate risk.
8. The yield curve is usually based on Treasurys.
9. The yield curve may be normal, steep, flat, inverted, or humped.

CHAPTER 11

MUNIS

While Treasurys are issued by the federal government, *municipal bonds* are issued by state and local governments.

Munis are an important part of the fixed income landscape. They're issued around the world. But they rarely offer big returns. So we'll just briefly address the biggest muni market, the United States.

There are two main types of munis. First is a *general obligation bond*. It's sometimes called a *GO bond*. It's backed by the issuer generally, instead of by particular assets.

Second is a *revenue bond*. It's backed by a specific revenue stream, like bridge tolls.[1]

Munis make up the foremost market for *bond insurance*. We saw in chapter 4 how that external credit enhancement can give an issue a higher credit rating than that of its issuer. It provides for an insurance company to deliver on the promises of the muni if the issuer defaults.

Muni defaults are rare. But they happen. For example in late 1994—right after I graduated from business school, suspiciously— the California city of San Diego defaulted on a muni that had financed the restoration of a river channel.[2]

Unlike Treasurys, munis can have call provisions. But like Treasurys, they have tax advantages. Interest earned on munis is normally tax-free at the federal level. And if the holder is domiciled in the state of the issuer, they're generally tax-free at the state and local level as well. That's their key selling point.

But it complicates comparisons. That's because tax-exempt interest has a benefit that taxable interest does not. So the yield on a muni isn't directly comparable to the yield on, say, a corporate.

The solution is to gross-up the yield on the muni as if it were taxable. That's done with a metric called *tax equivalent yield*. It equals the muni's actual yield to maturity divided by the quantity one minus the tax rate. It can be figured with an online calculator:

http://www.gooddebtcheap.com/pe.htm

To illustrate, say that the yield to maturity on a muni is 3 percent. If the tax rate is 40 percent, the tax equivalent yield is 5 percent. That's just 0.03 divided by the quantity one minus 0.4.

But if the tax rate is only 25 percent, the tax equivalent yield is only 4 percent. That's just 0.03 divided by the quantity one minus 0.025.

So tax equivalent yield is high when the tax rate is high. And the tax rate is high when taxable income is high. That's the nature of a progressive tax system. So munis work best for investors with high taxable incomes.

Such investors can buy individual munis. But those in populous states can also buy low-cost municipal bond funds. VNYUX, for example. That's the *ticker symbol* for the Vanguard New York Long-Term Tax-Exempt Fund. It offers state and local —as well as federal—exemptions to holders domiciled in New York State.[3]

There are similar funds for Massachusetts, New Jersey, Ohio, and Pennsylvania. But not for Florida and Texas. They're both plenty populated. But they have no state income tax. So there's nothing for a state-specific muni fund to shield against.

Investors in Florida and Texas, and those in less populous states that don't want to spend time picking individual munis, still have available to them low-cost funds focused only on the federal exemption. VWIUX, for example. That's the Vanguard Intermediate-Term Tax-Exempt Fund. It owns munis from Colorado, Kentucky, Michigan—all over.[4]

SUMMARY
1. Munis are issued by state and local governments.
2. Muni interest is normally tax-free at the federal level, and at the state and local level if the holder is domiciled in the state of the issuer.
3. Tax equivalent yield makes comparisons between munis and taxable bonds possible.
4. Low-cost municipal bond funds that maximize tax exemptions are available for investors in populous states.

CHAPTER 12

CORPORATES

A *corporate bond* is a fixed income security issued by a corporation. It's commonly called a *corporate*.

We've already seen several corporates. We've seen Berkshire Hathaway notes, Constellation Software debentures, OneMain notes, Tyco debentures, and Santander notes. So we needn't rehash everything we've already learned. But we should emphasize some points, and learn from a new case.

Corporates lack features of some government bonds. Their interest payments aren't automatically tax-exempt. Their issuers have neither the power to coin, nor the power to tax.

Otherwise, corporates and government bonds can have many of the same features. Their terms can be long or short. They can pay coupons or not. And their rates can be floating or fixed.

An American corporate almost always offers a higher yield to maturity than a Treasury of the same tenor. Sometimes the spread is large enough to create an opportunity.

But a better opportunity may come from an embedded option, as in the Tyco case. What mattered there was the chance that a put would be honored. Other times what matters is the chance of a call, as in the following case study.

SUMMARY

1. Corporates lack features of some government bonds.
2. American corporates almost always offer higher yields than comparable Treasurys.
3. Corporates can be attractive for their yields to maturity, but their embedded options may promise higher returns.
4. Intelligent investors gauge the chance that embedded options will be exercised.

CASE STUDY
Amazon.com, Inc.
10% Senior Discount Notes due 2008

Amazon.com, Inc. is based in Seattle. In 1998 it issued notes. The company's 10-Q from the second quarter of 1998 describes them well enough to give us our *understanding*:

http://www.gooddebtcheap.com/ny.htm

First, the *issuer* is a company, Amazon.com, Inc. That's the "exact name of registrant" given on page 1.

Second, the *currency* is U.S. dollars. That's made clear on page 18. That page has most of the other information we need as well.

Third, *par value* isn't stated. But it's probably $1,000 since the note is an American corporate.

Fourth, the *issue date* is May 1, 1998. This isn't immediately obvious. But notice that May 1 is the day of the month when everything important seems to happen, like when the note starts to bear interest, and when the note matures.

Page 18 then says "the company completed the offering" on "May 8, 1998." I'm guessing that that's distinct from the issue date. It's a week later, after everything was finalized. That's a safe assumption for our purposes, anyway.

Fifth, *maturity* is May 1, 2008.

Sixth, *payments* come from a fixed coupon of 10 percent. It's paid semiannually, on May 1 and November 1. But interest doesn't start accruing until May 1, 2003. The first interest payment date is six months later, on November 1, 2003. So the coupon rate for the first five years of the term is nothing.

The note does accrete during that period, however. And while the 10-Q doesn't state the accretion rate, we can easily calculate it.

Page 18 says that the offering had $326,000,000 in "gross proceeds." That's the offering price per note times the number of notes sold. It's how much the company raised. Page 18 also says that the "principal amount at maturity" is $530,000,000.[1] That's par value times the number of notes sold.

The accretion period is five years, since that's the time between the issue date of May 1, 1998 and when interest starts accruing on May 1, 2003. So the accretion rate comes out to just over 10.2 percent:

http://www.gooddebtcheap.com/xk.xlsx

Note that my spreadsheet uses *gross proceeds* and *principal amount at maturity* in the *accreted value* column. We could just as easily divided those numbers by the total number of notes issued. That's 530,000 if we're right that par value is $1,000, since 530,000,000 divided by 1,000 equals 530,000. But for calculating the accretion rate this isn't necessary. The big numbers work just fine.

So to summarize, the note accretes at about 10.2 percent for the first half of the term, and pays a 10 percent coupon for the second half.

Seventh, the notes aren't *secured*.

Eighth, they're *senior*. That's obvious from the name "senior discount notes."

Ninth, there are redemption *provisions*. During the accretion period up to 35 percent of the notes can be called at 110 percent of accreted value. More can be called at accreted value plus a call premium. Unfortunately that premium isn't quantified in the 10-Q.

Once they start to bear interest on May 1, 2003, the notes can be redeemed according to the table on page 18. They can be called at 105 until May 1, 2004; then at 103.333 until May 1, 2005; then at 101.667 until May 1, 2006; and then at par until maturity.

Tenth, there are *covenants*. According to the bottom of page 18, the indenture limits Amazon's ability to do things like take on more debt, pay dividends, and sell assets. But it doesn't say much more.[2]

Eleventh, the notes aren't listed.[3] So like most bonds, any *liquidity* comes from over-the-counter transactions.[4]

In August 2002 an investor bought some of the notes at 90.[5] So let's assess the *issuer* as of then.

As a company, the issuer doesn't have the *power to coin*.

For *solvency*, the most recent financial statements come from the company's 10-Q for the period ending March 31, 2002:

http://www.gooddebtcheap.com/ig.htm

Calculating the ratios is straightforward:

http://www.gooddebtcheap.com/bd.xlsx

Equity is negative. So both *debt-to-equity* and *liabilities-to-equity* are negative. The quick ratio looks better. It's just above the benchmark, at 1.24. But the interest coverage ratio isn't. It's an anemic 0.05.

Amazon is a U.S. consumer retailer. That's clear from page 14 of the 2002 10-Q. So it's sensible that page 31 says "we expect a disproportionate amount of our net sales to be realized during the fourth quarter."[6] Hence the interest coverage ratio should be calculated for a full year, not just the relatively weak first quarter. Maybe that will make it look healthier. Let's check the income statement on pages 43 and 44 of the 2001 10-K:

http://www.gooddebtcheap.com/tx.htm

No dice. Operating income for all of 2001 is -412,257,000. It's negative. And there's no non-operating income to make EBIT higher.[7] So the interest coverage ratio is still light.

The most current information on *owners* is in the 2002 proxy statement:

http://www.gooddebtcheap.com/xs.htm

Page five shows that the founder and CEO owns almost 30 percent of the company.[8] In the summer of 2002 that holding was priced at around $2 billion. Would he inject capital into the company if required? Perhaps. But more generally, the captain of the ship has a strong reason to keep the company afloat. That's good.

Moody's gives Amazon a *credit rating* of B3.[9] That's six levels below investment grade. But notably, it was just raised. In January 2002 Moody's upgraded the company to B3 from Caa1.[10]

Moving on to *issue*, the notes are *performing*. Of course during the accretion period there aren't any interest payments to miss. But the company isn't in default on anything.

As for *credit rating*, the notes share the junk status of their issuer.

Duration and *convexity* aren't central to this case, as will become clear.

Two big things changed between when the notes were issued in May 1998 and when the investment was made in the summer of 2002.

First, interest rates plunged. In May 1998 the *federal funds rate* was around 5.5 percent. But by summer 2002 it was around 1.7 percent.[11] That's a big drop.

The federal funds rate is what banks charge each other for overnight loans.

Second, Amazon's credit rating improved. Remember, the B3 rating was the result of an upgrade.

For these two reasons the company could now borrow for less than the 10.2 percent accretion rate or the 10 percent coupon rate it had to offer in 1998. Its cost of debt capital decreased. So surely it wants to redeem these expensive notes.

Indeed, by the time the investor bought the notes most of them had already been called. The company had redeemed just over half of them.[12]

This impacts how we look at *inexpensiveness*. Specifically, it focuses us on *yield to call*.

Since over 35 percent of the notes have already been called, the current redemption opportunity for the issuer is to buy them at accreted value plus a call premium. We don't know that premium. But call premiums often decline as tenor shortens.

We know that on May 1, 2003 the call price changes to 105. That's probably a drop from a higher number. So let's figure yield to call on that date. Here's our calculator again:

http://www.gooddebtcheap.com/mo.htm

Assume the investor bought the notes on August 1, 2002. There's 10 months between then and the call date of May 1, 2003. In years that's 10 divided by 12, or about 0.83.

Coupon is irrelevant, since if the notes are called on May 1, 2003 interest is never given a chance to accrue. So the inputs for our online calculator are:

Price	$ 900
Par	$1,000
Price to call	$1,050
Years to call	0.83
Coupon rate	0%
Coupon payment frequency	None

The result is a yield to call of around 20 percent. That's astronomical.

Of course the numbers here are so simple we could have figured yield without the online calculator. The return is the call price of $1,050 minus the price of $900. That's $150. Divide that by the cost of $900, and we get almost 0.17. That's 17 percent. Divide that by 0.83 to annualize, and we get around 20 percent.

A month after the investment, Moody's raised Amazon's credit rating from B3 to B2.[13] That made a call even more likely.

On May 28, 2003 the company did in fact call the remaining notes.[14] It took a month longer than we modeled. That added time, decreasing yield. Conversely, it added a month's worth of interest. But who cares? Yield to call still came out at around 19 percent. That's fantastic.

But it wasn't surprising. It was foreseeable. It was foreseeable at the time the investment was made in August 2002, in four ways.

First, interest rates plunged since the company first issued the notes. Had they been floating rate notes, that wouldn't have mattered. But they were fixed, so it did. It created an opportunity to refinance at a lower cost.

Second, the issuer's credit rating improved. That further lowered the company's cost of debt capital.

Third, the company had the resources to pay for the call. Of course it may have paid with money borrowed at a lower rate. But in August 2002 the knowable fact was that the quick ratio was above one.

Fourth, the company had already called most of the notes, proving that it wasn't particularly fond of them.

In chapter 7 we saw how yield to worst is a reasonable basis for gauging a bond's price if it's not clear what will happen. But here, it was clear what would happen. What mattered was the overwhelming likelihood that an embedded option would play out well. Anyone that fell back on yield to worst would have missed the opportunity entirely.

Welcome to not being anyone.

CHAPTER 13

FLOATERS

Know what to do.	→	Do it.	→	Don't do anything else.

Do I understand it?	→	Is it good?	→	Is it inexpensive?

Issuer	Issuer	Yield	Reject choices born of:	
Currency	Power to coin	Current	Affinity	Intermixing
Par value	Solvency	To maturity	Reciprocity	Consistency
Issue date	Owners	To call	Anchoring	Confirmation
Maturity	Credit rating	To put	Authority	Hope
Payments	Issue	To worst	Availability	Lossophobia
Security	Performance	Required margin	Cleverness	Scarcity
Seniority	Credit rating	Dividend yield	Incomprehensibility	Hotness
Provisions	Duration		Consensus	Miscontrast
Covenants	Convexity		Peculiarity	Windfallapathy
Liquidity				

Reject actions born of akrasia:

Impetuosity   Weakness

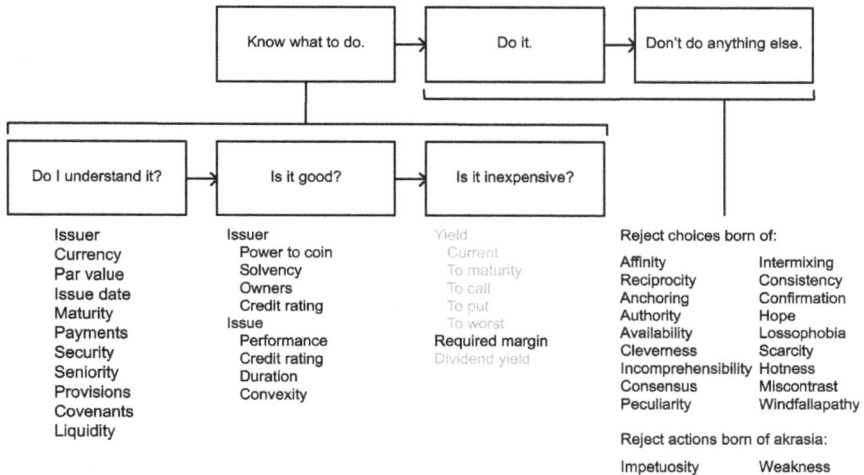

Floaters are coupon bonds with variable interest rates. They're often called *floating rate notes*, *FRNs,* or *floating rate bonds*. This chapter gathers all that we've read about floaters so far, and adds a bit more.

The coupon rate of a floater is a spread over a reference rate. That spread is called a *quoted margin*. It's often referred to as a *QM* or *margin*.

Most bonds have a quoted margin that's fixed. But some change at predetermined intervals.

Many floaters reset their coupon rates when they pay interest. The reset rate determines the amount of the next interest payment. So floaters have durations near zero, since they're not chained to a fixed rate. The more frequently the rate resets, the lower the duration.

Since it has nil duration, a floater that performs and has a stable credit rating often trades at or near par.

Some floaters have a *cap*. That's a maximum that the coupon rate can't exceed no matter how high the reference rate gets. Some also have a *floor*. That's a minimum that the coupon rate can't fall below no matter how low the reference rate gets.

A floater with both a cap and a floor has what's called a *collar*. Collar has other meanings in finance as well. But it always refers to some mechanism for narrowing the range of possible outcomes.

Floaters issued by the U.S. Department of the Treasury are generally called FRNs. Their term is two years. Their reference rate is the most recent discount on the 13-week T-bill.[1]

The reference rate on corporate floaters is usually different. Sometimes it's SOFR. Other times it's the federal funds rate.

Picture a corporate floater. At issuance its quoted margin is sufficient to get investors to accept credit risk in excess of the reference rate.

But say that later, the floater's credit rating drops. Its price subsequently decreases. One could read that decrease as saying that the quoted margin is no longer enough. Investors now demand more compensation.

The quoted margin plus that additional compensation is called the *required margin*. It's also called the *discount margin*. It exceeds the quoted margin when the security trades at a discount, that is, at less than par.

Now picture the opposite. Say that instead of a downgrade, the floater gets an upgrade. Its credit rating increases. Investors that previously shunned the floater now want it. So the required margin becomes less than the quoted margin. The security will then trade at a premium. It trades above par value.

Required margin is easy to calculate. It equals yield to maturity minus the reference rate.

Picture a floater with a two-year tenor with a coupon rate of 200 basis points over SOFR. Say that SOFR is 5 percent. That means the coupon rate is 7 percent. If interest is paid quarterly and the ask on the floater is 94, yield to maturity is 10.36 percent. That comes from our online calculator:

http://www.gooddebtcheap.com/pl.htm

YTM of 10.36 percent minus the reference rate of 5 percent equals 5.36 percent. That's the required margin. It will probably stay at 5.36 percent as long as the issuer's creditworthiness sustains, all while SOFR and the coupon rate bop around.

Required margin is a useful way to think about the inexpensiveness of a floater. It has an advantage over yield to maturity, yield to call, and yield to put in that those measures assume a fixed coupon rate. Floaters don't have that.

Nonetheless, yield is often published for floaters. It's figured by assuming a constant coupon rate, generally the coupon rate established at the last reset. This practice is so institutionalized that YTM based on the next coupon payment is part of the floater's name on many brokerage websites.

But again, the notion that the coupons are fixed is a myth. It makes a present value calculation doable. But it doesn't make it accurate.

That's why I like thinking in terms of required margin. What matters is the gap over the reference rate created by the quoted margin and any changes in creditworthiness. Sometimes a relative idea is more meaningful than a precise number. Often, actually. I'll illustrate.

Picture the open ocean. On it is a cruise ship. In it is you, in a top-floor cabin. Say that right now the floor of that cabin is 50 meters above the waterline, that is, 50 meters above the level where the hull meets the sea.

At this moment you could define your cabin floor as 50 meters high. And you'd be right.

But just briefly. Winds and tides toy with the level of the ocean. The ship pitches and heaves as it sails. Fifty meters becomes 49, and then 48, and then 51. So calling the cabin floor 50 meters high is only temporarily correct.

It might be more useful to just say that you're on the *top floor*. That's imprecise, but more meaningful. No matter what the winds and the tides do, no one on the boat sleeps higher than you.

SUMMARY

1. Floaters are coupon bonds with variable interest rates and —as a result—minimal durations.
2. Floaters often pay interest quarterly, and reset their coupon rates quarterly.
3. A floater may have a cap, a floor, or—if both—a collar.
4. Performing floaters with stable credit ratings often trade at or near par.
5. Required margin is better than yield at capturing a floater's inexpensiveness.
6. Required margin equals yield to maturity minus the reference rate.

CASE STUDY
Mutares SE & Co. KGaA
Floating Rate Notes due 2027

Mutares is based in Munich, Germany. In 2023 it issued floating rate notes. They're described on this webpage:

http://www.gooddebtcheap.com/pp.htm

The links on the webpage include one to a document titled *bond terms*:

http://www.gooddebtcheap.com/vg.htm

As always, we first *understand* the security by nailing down the 11 parameters.

First, the *issuer* is the company Mutares SE & Co. KGaA. That's on the webpage, and on page three of the document.

Second, the *currency* is the euro. That's for everything—the borrowing, the coupon, the principal payment—as shown on document page 24.

Third, *par value* is €1,000. Page 24 calls that the *initial nominal amount*.[2] That's a synonym for par value. The webpage uses a simpler term: *denomination*.[3] Here that word means par value. Other times it can mean currency. Confusing, I know. But context makes things clear.

Fourth, the *issue date* is March 31, 2023. That's both on the webpage and on document page nine.

Fifth, *maturity* is March 31, 2027. That's on document page 10.[4]

Sixth, *payments* come from a coupon of "three-month Euribor plus margin of 850 bps," per the webpage.[5]

Euribor is short for *Euro Interbank Offer Rate*. It's what big European banks charge each other for loans. There are five versions of it, each for a different term. One is three months. So that's the reference rate: three-month Euribor.

Here's the official source for Euribor rates:

http://www.gooddebtcheap.com/aq.htm

Page eight also tells us that the coupon rate is reset quarterly, one day before interest is paid. That's in the paragraph called "interest quotation day."[6]

The coupon is paid quarterly. The webpage says so, using the term "interest dates." And the document says payments are made on March 31, June 30, September 30, and December 31. That's in the "interest payment date" and "interest period" paragraphs on page eight.

As of this writing the floater's last reset was in late June 2024. Three-month Euribor then was 3.722 percent.[7] That made the coupon rate 12.222 percent. That's just the reference rate of 3.722 percent plus the quoted margin of 8.5 percent.

Seventh and eighth, the floater is both *secured* and *senior*. The webpage tells us this, defining "status" as "senior secured."[8]

Ninth, there's a call *provision*. It's described on document page 36, under the heading "Voluntary early redemption - Call Option ." It looks complicated. But it isn't.

Basically the bond can be called for 105.625 until September 30, 2025; then at 103.938 until March 31, 2026; then at 102.250 until September 30, 2026; and then at 100.563 until maturity on March 31, 2027. Summarizing like this requires a little dance through the document to get definitions for "first call date" and "make whole amount." But that's easy.

The floater also has a put provision. It's on document page 37. It lets the holder sell at 101. But only if there's a "put option event," which is defined on page five as a "change in control."

That's a standard clause. It allows the holder to put the security if the issuer gets acquired by some overleveraged monster whose balance sheet fouls the floater's creditworthiness. It's a useful protection. But it's unlikely to take effect. So outside of exceptional circumstances, we can safely ignore it.

Tenth, a handful of *covenants* appear on document page 45. They're *affirmative covenants*, requiring Mutares to do things. The company has to keep at least €10,000,000 in cash; at least 12.5 percent of net debt in cash; net debt divided by total assets under 15 percent; and net debt divided by equity under 150 percent.[9]

Net debt is just *total debt* minus *cash*.

These covenants aren't exceptional. But their presence suggests that Mutares isn't the most creditworthy outfit on earth. After all, it's the dogs of questionable temperament that get leashed.

Eleventh, the floater is relatively *liquid*. That's because it's listed. The webpage states that it's listed on both Open Market and Nordic ABM.[10]

Open Market is a lightly-regulated segment of the Frankfurt Stock Exchange. And *Nordic ABM* is a lightly-regulated part of the Oslo Stock Exchange. Light regulation means that Mutares doesn't have to disclose as much as it would if its floater was on, say, the New York Stock Exchange. That's both good and bad.

It's good in that it gives the issuer lower compliance costs. That leaves it with more money to pay our interest. But it's bad in that such permissiveness can attract dicier issuers, precisely the ones that most investors want to avoid.

Did your high school have a teacher known for turning a blind eye to cheating? Remember the students that took that class? Like that.

For this reason many investors avoid bonds that trade on lightly-regulated exchanges. That leads to lower trading volumes. And that means lower liquidity.

As of this writing Nordic ABM's website says that the floater hasn't traded there for a couple weeks.[11] But it's more active on the Frankfurt. That site shows it trading there daily.[12] So again, it's somewhat liquid.

Moving on to the four points of *issuer*, Mutares obviously lacks the *power to coin*.

Next, *solvency*. As of this writing the company's most recent financial report is for the first quarter of 2024:

http://www.gooddebtcheap.com/zc.htm

The report reflects the light regulations at Open Market and Nordic ABM. Just look at the financial statements. They're mere summaries, and *unaudited*, meaning not examined by a public accountancy. But we can squeeze them for something close to the four solvency metrics that we need:

http://www.gooddebtcheap.com/oi.xlsx

The *debt-to-equity ratio* is 0.6, comfortably under my rough benchmark of one. Note that I've assumed that the bond is the only debt. That's probably right, or close to right.

The denominator, equity, is tougher to nail down. That's because Mutares is an investor in unlisted businesses. Private transactions it makes with those businesses impact its equity account. Those transactions could be designed to fluff up equity. So there's the technical possibility of manipulation. That said, manipulation isn't in evidence. Hence I regard debt-to-equity as okay.

The *liabilities-to-equity ratio* comes in at a comfortable 0.7, well under my benchmark of two.

The *quick ratio* is harder to figure. For the numerator, the balance sheet shows current assets of €495,400,000. But there's no number given for inventory, which is what we need to subtract.[13]

So let's estimate. Look at the most recent annual report. It's got a comprehensive balance sheet on page 117:

http://www.gooddebtcheap.com/lk.htm

The balance sheet says that in 2023 inventory was €673,400,000 and current assets were €2,304,200,000. Some quick division tells us that about 29 percent of current assets was inventory. So 71 percent wasn't.

It also says that 2022 inventory was €560,700,000 and current assets were €1,652,400,000.[14] So that year about 34 percent of current assets was inventory. And 66 percent wasn't.

It's reasonable to think that the composition of current assets in the first quarter of 2024 was something like it was in those years. So I applied the more conservative 2022 figure of 66 percent. That's why on my spreadsheet, in cell B23, you see a quick ratio numerator equal to 66 percent of current assets.

I did something similar with the denominator. The first quarter 2024 balance sheet gives a 2023 total liabilities figure of €284,400,000. But it's mum on current liabilities, which is what we need.[15]

So again we turn to the annual report's balance sheet for guidance. In 2023 non-current liabilities was €1,224,600,000 and current liabilities was €2,004,500,000.[16] Those sum to a total liabilities figure of €3,229,100,000. Dividing current liabilities by that number shows that 62 percent of total liabilities were current.

The prior year was similar. In 2022, 65 percent of total liabilities were current.[17] Again I took the conservative route by adopting the 2022 figure of 65 percent. So on my spreadsheet, cell B23 has a denominator equal to 65 percent of total liabilities.

The result is a quick ratio of 1.8. That's comfortably above my benchmark of one.

The interest coverage ratio isn't as adequate. It's below my benchmark of 10. How below is unclear because of the quarterly report's limitations.

The denominator, interest expense, isn't the problem. Yes, I had to use the cash accounting figure from the cash flow statement, since the accrual accounting figure isn't on the income statement. But as we saw in chapter 2, interest expense often matches interest payments. So I set the denominator at €9,500,000.

Less clear is the numerator, EBIT. It's not on the income statement. What is there is *EBITDA*. That's short for *earnings before interest, taxes, depreciation, and amortization*. From one angle that figure is too big, because unlike EBIT it ignores depreciation and amortization expenses. But if I use it, the interest coverage ratio is 0.8. That's just EBITDA of €7,900,000 divided by €9,500,000.

Further down the income statement is *net income*. Usually I would think that number too small for the numerator since it captures interest and tax expenses. But in this case it's larger than EBITDA. That's because it's boosted by the large, positive *financial result* line. Mutares is an investment company, so there's a view that some things in that line are operations-like. So if we use net income as the numerator, the interest coverage ratio is 5.4. That's just €51,300,000 divided by €9,500,000.[18]

Pages 12 through 26 of the annual report suggest that the businesses Mutares is in—public transportation, car parts, tacos—aren't seasonal. Okay, maybe tacos. But on balance it seems safe to figure an interest coverage ratio for the most recent quarter only.

Indeed, the full year ratio isn't much different. The comprehensive 2023 balance sheet suggests that it's somewhere around five, depending on assumptions. So whatever the time frame and however approximate the inputs, the interest coverage ratio is modest.

So is Mutares solvent? Probably. But in my view the interest coverage ratio is tight.

The next point of issuer is *owners*. Page 30 of the annual report reveals that the CEO and founder owns 25 percent of the company.[19] As of this writing the market capitalization of Mutares is almost €700,000,000.[20] So his stake is priced at almost €175,000,000. We can't know that his net worth is that high because he may have some debt. But investors can take comfort in knowing that the issuer isn't run by some mere hired hand.

Finally, *credit rating*. Mutares seems not to have one. There's no mention of any on the webpage, document, quarterly report, or annual report.

Moving on to the four points of *issue*, the floater seems to be *performing*. As of this writing there's nothing to indicate default or distress, either in the company's own materials or in news reports.

Next, the issue doesn't have a *credit rating*.

A floater with a quarterly rate reset has a *duration* that's effectively zero. It's close enough to zero that we don't have to dwell on it, anyway. And by the same token we can skip *convexity*.

Finally, *inexpensiveness*. We know that traditional measures of yield aren't that helpful with floaters. Third party websites still provide them, of course. They do so by assuming that the most recent coupon rate is fixed. But greater insights come from thinking about *required margin*.

As of this writing the ask on the floater is 106.90.[21] That's the clean price on Open Market. So it trades at a premium.

Today is July 3, 2024. So with maturity on March 31, 2027, time to maturity is 2.74 years. Earlier we noted that the current coupon rate is 12.222 percent. And remember, interest is paid quarterly.

Entering all that data into our online calculator gives us a YTM of 9.339 percent. From that we subtract the three-month Euribor reference rate of 3.722 percent to get the required margin. It's 5.617 percent. Is that enough?

Not quite, in my view. It's not sufficiently above the risk-free rate. Admittedly, that's hard to prove. We can't show that 5.617 percent is less than the required margin on a comparable issuer's floater with the same credit rating, since the Mutares floater doesn't have a credit rating.

Perhaps proof comes instead by envisioning a call. As of this writing Mutares can call at 105.625. That's less than the ask, meaning the issuer could force us to immediately swallow a capital loss. No thank you.

There are things to like about this security. It's senior, secured, liquid, and performing. Its quoted margin is huge. And the CEO owns quite a bit of the issuer, an issuer that's pretty solvent. But at 106.90 it's expensive. The way to buy this floater might have been on the primary market, at par. Alas there was only one opportunity to do so. It's when the floater was first issued.

Notably, that wasn't the only primary market sale. In the Mutares material you may have noticed the term *tap issue*. That's the primary market sale of more of a bond already issued. It's an encore, if you will.

The floater had two tap issues:

http://www.gooddebtcheap.com/em.htm

So this bond was issued three times. The first was in March 2023, at a price of 100. The second was a tap issue in May 2023, at 100.75. And the third was a tap issue in January 2024, at 103.75.[22] All three used the same ISIN, NO0012530965.[23]

To secondary market participants, past tap issues aren't pivotal. They're history. What matters more is some idea of the required margin, a required margin that as of this writing seems too small to merit an investment.

CHAPTER 14

PAPER

Commercial paper is short-term debt issued by established corporations. It's often called *CP* or *paper*.

Paper is more about capital preservation than returns. It rarely provides big opportunities. But it teaches us something about regulation, and something about credit ratings. So we'll glance at it.

As short-term debt, paper is part of the money market. Investors usually hold it to maturity. So there's not much of a secondary market.

Companies issue paper because it's often less expensive than borrowing from banks. It provides a lower cost of debt capital.

In the U.S., paper has a term of up to 270 days. That limit keeps it from needing to be registered with the SEC. And that's why established corporations like it. It's cheaper than bank loans, and skips the regulatory costs of a full-blown bond offering.

Paper usually doesn't pay interest. Instead, it's sold at a discount. The return comes from that discount.

Normally, paper is unsecured. But not always. Take *ABCP*. That's short for *asset-backed commercial paper*. It's collateralized, often by the issuer's receivables.

Credit rating agencies grade paper as they do other fixed income securities. But they use different scales. Rather than the long-term debt scales we saw back in chapter 5, they use short-term debt scales.

The short-term debt scales for the three major NRSROs don't line up neatly with one another. For example Fitch's F1 isn't exactly equivalent to Moody's P-2, which isn't exactly equivalent to S&P's A-1. Plus there are internal inconsistencies. Fitch,[1]

Moody's,[2] and S&P[3] allow some overlap in their investment grade categories.

All this makes it hard to capture the short-term debt scales of the three major NRSROs in a single table. So here's a simplified version:

	Fitch	Moody's	S&P
	F1+	P-1	A-1+
	F1		A-1
Investment grade		P-2	
	F2		A-2
	F3	P-3	A-3
	B		B
Non-investment grade	C	Not prime	C
	D		D

A simplified presentation of the short-term debt
rating scales from the three major NRSROs

Recall that paper is only issued by established corporations. Established means investment grade. So paper really only uses the upper part of the scales.

That said, junk does emerge. For example in 1997 a Chicago auto lender called Mercury Finance Co. defaulted on most of its commercial paper.[4] But such events are so rare that the paper holder doesn't think much about the lower part of the scales.

Current U.S. commercial paper rates are easy to find:

http://www.gooddebtcheap.com/ma.htm

Outside of the U.S., commercial paper characteristics can be different. For example in India,[5] Australia,[6] and elsewhere, paper can be issued with terms of up to one year. But the basic function of CP is the same all over.

The way commercial paper is most likely to enter your life is as dry powder, liquid reserves waiting for higher return opportunities. You may own it directly, or you may own it indirectly through a money market fund. That alone makes paper worth understanding.

But sometimes the commercial paper market malfunctions, as it did during the 2008 financial crisis.[7] One could imagine a situation where that creates an opportunity. The contours of that opportunity are hard to predict. But they'll be easier to recognize for those well-versed in CP's basics.

SUMMARY
1. Commercial paper is short-term debt issued by established corporations.
2. In the U.S., commercial paper has a maximum term of 270 days, which spares it from mandatory SEC registration.
3. Commercial paper is rated on short-term debt scales.

CHAPTER 15

PREFERREDS

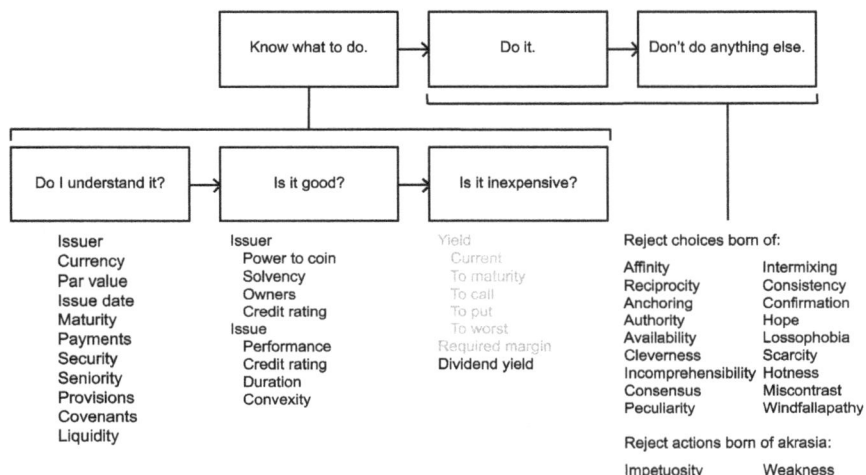

Preferred stock is a *hybrid*. It has characteristics of debt, and characteristics of equity. It's also called *preferred equity, preference shares*, or simply *preferred*.

Preferred stock is like debt in five big ways.

First, it makes regular payments. Like a coupon bond, the amount and timing of those payments is predetermined. Further, they're expressed as a percentage of par.

Second, preferred stock is usually callable. To call, the issuer normally has to pay par value plus a premium, as with debt.

Third, it's senior to common stock. That means that in the cheerless event that the issuer hits trouble, it has to pay preferred stock dividends before it can pay common stock dividends. It also means that if the issuer liquidates, preferred stockholders get cash before common stockholders.

In reality, both often get zilch. But at least it's clear who gets zilch first.

Fourth, it generally carries no voting rights. Preferred shareholders don't have much say in how the company is run. While this often has no practical effect, it puts preferred shareholders in the same boat as bondholders.

Fifth, preferred stock is often rated by credit rating agencies.

Preferred stock is also like equity. It's like equity in three big ways.

First, its regular payments are dividends. They're not interest. This has tax implications, since dividends are often taxed at a lower rate than interest.

It also has credit rating implications. If an issuer unexpectedly fails to pay interest on a debt, its credit rating is likely to suffer. But if it skips a dividend payment, it may not.

Even though they're dividends, preferred stock payments usually don't increase if the issuer thrives. This is a difference between preferred stock dividends and common stock dividends. Preferreds have a ceiling that common stock doesn't.

A second way preferred stock is like equity is that it's subordinate to debt. While an issuer has to pay preferred stock dividends before it can pay common stock dividends, it has to pay interest before both. And if the issuer liquidates, debtholders have priority over preferred shareholders.

Third, preferred stock isn't secured. That's also like equity.

In the U.S., preferred stock often pays dividends quarterly. If it's aimed at retail investors, it usually has a $25 par value. It's higher if it's aimed at institutional investors.

A preferred is defined largely by the amount of its dividend. But it's defined by three other things as well.

First, it can be either *perpetual* or *nonperpetual*. A perpetual preferred pays dividends indefinitely, or at least for as long as the issuer exists. It has no maturity date. But a nonperpetual preferred does. Eventually its dividends end and holders are paid par value.

Second, a preferred stock can be either *cumulative* or *noncumulative*. If it's cumulative, any unpaid dividends remain owed to the investor. If it's noncumulative, they don't.

Third, preferred stock is often *convertible* into the common stock of the issuer. The *conversion ratio* and other conditions are generally set when the preferred is first issued.

If a preferred is expected to act like a fixed income security, it can be analyzed with our model. But there are a couple of twists.

One twist is that a relevant solvency metric becomes the *preferred dividend coverage ratio*. That figure equals *net income* divided by the *preferred dividend*. It takes the place of the *interest coverage ratio*.

Another twist is that the most relevant *inexpensiveness* metric becomes the *dividend yield*. It equals the annual dividend divided by the preferred stock's purchase price.

As with bonds, sometimes yield is the goal. Dividends are what the investor wants. But other times a capital gain is the goal. The prize is the money made by selling the preferred after it increases in price.

Some preferreds are odd. Take Brødrene A & O Johansen A/S. It's a Danish wholesaler of construction materials. Its preference shares have annual dividend payments set at 6 percent. But that percentage can be higher under some circumstances. That's rare. Plus, the preference shares carry voting rights.[1] That's also unusual.

Or consider Eniro Group AB. It's a Swedish online media company. Until recently it had a series A preferred that also carried voting rights.[2]

In the U.S., preferreds are often issued by financial services companies. But they can be issued by other kinds of companies too, including ones that are in trouble. That's illustrated in the following case.

SUMMARY
1. Preferred stock is like debt in some ways, and like equity in some ways.
2. A preferred issue is characterized primarily by its dividend.
3. A solvency metric for preferreds is the preferred dividend coverage ratio.
4. An inexpensiveness metric for preferreds is the dividend yield.

CASE STUDY
Fat Brands Inc.
Series B Cumulative Preferred Stock

Fat Brands is a restaurant franchisor based in Los Angeles. I know its brands—Fatburger, Johnny Rockets, Round Table Pizza—from growing up in Southern California in the 1980's. So when the yield to maturity on its preferred shot through the roof, I noticed.

The prospectus gives us everything we need to understand the security:

http://www.gooddebtcheap.com/vv.htm

First, the *issuer* is a corporation, Fat Brands Inc. That's made clear at the top of page eight.

Second, the *currency* is the U.S. dollar, as evidenced by the monetary amounts given on page eight.

Third, *par value* is effectively $25. Yet again, that's hard to see. After all, a page headed "EXHIBIT A.1" refers to "the Company's Series B Cumulative Preferred Stock, par value $0.0001 per share." But what matters more is the line on page eight that says that if the company liquidates, preferred shareholders have the "right to receive $25.00 per share." More on that later.

Fourth, the *issue date* seems to be sometime in July 2020. The date of the prospectus is July 10, 2020. That's in bold red type towards the beginning of the document. And using the ticker symbol given on page nine—FATBP—I see that brokerages started quoting the preferred in July 2020.

Fifth, there's no *maturity*. FATBP is perpetual. That's clear because the prospectus makes no reference to any end date.

Sixth, *payments* come from a monthly dividend that page eight describes as "8.25 percent per annum of the $25.00 liquidation preference," or "$2.0625 per share each year."

Incidentally, that's why it's best to think of par value as $25. That amount times 8.25 percent equals $2.0625.

Seventh, there's no *security*. That's as expected.

Eighth, *seniority* is spelled out on page nine. FATBP is junior to any debt, and senior to the company's common stock. That's also as expected.

But it's also senior to "Series A-1 Preferred Stock." So apparently there was an earlier preferred that FATBP pushed down.

Then there's another preferred—the Series A Preferred Stock —that's *pari passu* with FATBP. We met pari passu in chapter 4. Here it means that series A and B holders must be treated equally.

There's something else to note about seniority. It's on page six. The company "may issue additional indebtedness and series of preferred stock with rights that are senior to the Series B Preferred Stock." That means that today's series B holders could wind up demoted, as today's series A-1 holders are.

Ninth, there are *provisions*. To start, the preferred is cumulative. That's mentioned throughout page eight. And if the company misses a year of dividend payments, the annual dividend hops up to $2.50. The rate increases from 8.25 percent to 10 percent.

In addition, FATBP is redeemable. It can be called for $25 plus a call premium that seems to start out at 10 percent. So the call price is $27.50.

It's also mentioned that each preferred comes with five *warrants*. A warrant is a call option issued by the issuer of the *underlier*, the security that the warrant can be used to buy. Here each warrant is the right to buy a common share for $5.   So the underlier is Fat Brands common stock. It trades on NASDAQ under the ticker symbol FAT.

But the warrants went only to those that bought FATBP on the primary market. It's history. So that *equity kicker*—that stock-based bonus—is no longer available.

Notably, the preferred isn't convertible. That's uncommon, but not unheard of.

Tenth, there are *covenants*. But they're not special. They start on page 19 of the *underwriting agreement* part of the prospectus. They require Fat Brands to obey securities laws, prepare financial statements, and do other things that one would hope it does anyway. So let's not get hung up on them.

Eleventh, there's reasonable *liquidity* since the preferred is listed on NASDAQ. This is enhanced by the relatively low liquidation preference. A $25 preferred will tend to trade more than a $1,000 preferred.[3]

Moving on to *issuer*, the corporation clearly doesn't have the *power to coin*.

Next, our primary *solvency* metric is the preferred dividend coverage ratio. That's net income divided by the preferred dividend. As I write this in the summer of 2024 the most current financial statements are in the first quarter 2024 10-Q:

http://www.gooddebtcheap.com/om.htm

Page five shows that net income for the first quarter of 2024 was -$38,316,000. It was negative. It was also negative for the first quarter of 2023.[4] And this isn't some seasonal quirk. The most recent 10-K shows negative net income for each of the last two full years.[5] That's on page F-7:

http://www.gooddebtcheap.com/bx.htm

So there's really *no* dividend coverage. Do other solvency metrics provide any reassurance?

No. The debt-to-equity and liabilities-to-equity ratios don't, since equity is negative. And neither does the quick ratio, which comes in at less than half of my benchmark of one. It's 0.4:

http://www.gooddebtcheap.com/ha.xlsx

For *owners*, we turn to the most recent proxy statement:

http://www.gooddebtcheap.com/cx.htm

Page 29 reveals that about half of the business is owned by an outfit called Fog Cutter Holdings LLC. Pages 14 and 16 show that Fog Cutter is run by five Fat Brands directors, four of whom have the same last name. Page 32 then reveals that three of them are grandsons of the fifth director. So if all those family members own Fog Cutter, about half of Fat Brands is effectively owned by five directors.[6]

Is that good? Usually, yes. But pages 19-21 of the 10-Q suggest that some of those folks are involved in some scrapes. There's a lawsuit brought by shareholders, and a federal government investigation. Both Fog Cutter and Fat Brands are named in those cases as well.[7]

Lastly, I can't find any *credit rating* for Fat Brands, either through a brokerage or in any of the company's materials.

Next is *issue*. *Performance* is easy to gauge, since each month the company either pays the dividend or doesn't. According to the NASDAQ website, it pays. It has done so every month since August of 2020. Its last dividend was paid two days ago, right on schedule.[8]

As for *credit rating*, again there doesn't seem to be one.

Fat Brands seems so troubled that *duration* and *convexity* are the least of our concerns. Plus the lack of a maturity date makes those metrics hard to even think about. So we'll skip them.

Inexpensiveness is what interested me in FATBP in the first place. As of this writing the ask is $13.21.[9] So the dividend yield is 15.6 percent. That's just $2.0625 divided by $13.21. So, is FATBP inexpensive?

Well, 15.6 percent is high. And the preferred has performed for a long time. Plus if it gets called, the return will be astronomical. It will be 108 percent. That's just the call price of $27.50 minus the ask of $13.21, all divided by the ask of $13.21.

But there's nothing to suggest that the call will happen, and plenty to suggest that it won't. Fat Brands needs the cash. It's flirting with insolvency. Plus the legal exposure of the company and of some of the people behind it are unfortunate.

I'd rather take my $13.21 to the Fatburger in Santa Monica and have lunch.

PART IV

EXTREMES

CHAPTER 16

ARGENTINA

In 1998 Argentina issued fixed income securities called *floating rate accrual notes*, or *FRANs*. Most of the information we need to *understand* them is available online.

The *issuer* is a country, Argentina. The *currency* is the U.S. dollar. *Par value* isn't clear, so we'll just think in percentages. The *issue date* is April 1998, and *maturity* is in 2005.[1]

Regarding *payments*, the FRANs have a variable interest rate. That's like the FRNs we saw in chapter 13. But unlike the FRNs, the FRANs don't pay a coupon. Instead, their interest accumulates. It adds up until it's paid along with principal at maturity.

The quoted margin is unclear. But the reference rate is based on the yield to maturity of Argentina's outstanding benchmark bonds due in 2006 and 2027.[2] Those are Argentine Treasurys, if you will.

The FRANs are neither *secured* nor *senior*. But there is a *provision* that permits holders to put the securities in the event of any default.

Covenants and *liquidity* aren't clear. But like par value and quoted margin, we don't need them to grasp this situation.

The year the FRANs were issued, 1998, Argentina slipped into a recession.[3] Exports and foreign investment slowed, and rising borrowing costs forced many businesses to close.[4]

In 2001 Argentina descended into a depression. A fifth of Argentines were unemployed, and half lived in poverty.[5] In an attempt to safeguard the banking system, the government restricted deposit withdrawals.[6] This led to widespread demonstrations and a political crisis that saw the country cycle through five presidents in 10 days.[7]

In late December 2001 Argentina defaulted on its debt. This included the 2006 and 2027 benchmark bonds. Their prices plunged, and their yields—however fictitious, given the default— soared. So the reference rate on the FRANs went through the roof.

In 2003 a group of American investors started buying defaulted Argentine bonds. They bought various issues at various prices on various dates. For example they bought some FRANs at 35.5 on October 16, 2008. That may have added to a position established earlier at a higher price. But let's assess the *issuer* as of that date.

Argentina has the *power to coin*. But only Argentine pesos. That's not particularly helpful, since the FRANs are denominated in U.S. dollars.

Solvency means the same basic thing for a country as it does for a company. But the financial statements are different, and the metrics are different. So suffice it to say that Argentina isn't particularly solvent at this time.

I don't mean to gloss over this. Government accounting is an important topic. But it's a big topic, and it isn't central to the investment thesis of this case.

Neither is *owners*, since countries don't really have them.

As for *credit rating*, it's junk. In August 2008 Moody's rated Argentina B3, just six levels from the bottom of its 21-level scale. That same month S&P rated it B, eight levels from the bottom of its 22-level scale.[8]

Moving on to *issue*, the FRANs are *non-performing*. True, scheduled interest payments haven't ceased. But that's because there aren't any. FRANs are *accrual* notes. Nonetheless, they're subject to Argentina's overall default.

Credit rating is unclear. But it's probably the same for the issue as it is for the issuer.

With non-performing junk we can safely skip *duration* and *convexity* because they're innessential.

Regarding *inexpensiveness*, we have imperfect information. We know that some FRANs were bought for 35.5. But purchases made earlier at higher prices may have made the average price higher. We don't know the quoted margin, so we can't know the required margin. And any yield measures—misleading with floaters anyway—are myths, given the default. But that's okay. That's okay because yield wasn't the investors' focus. Their focus was a capital gain.

In 2005 Argentina offered to exchange its defaulted bonds for new bonds at about 30 percent of face value. This was standard procedure for an emerging economy in default. And it was standard procedure for creditors to accept. Here, most did. But not our group of investors. They held out.[9]

Historically, country issuers were protected by sovereign immunity. That's a legal principle that protects nations from being sued in the courts of other nations. So if a country defaulted on a bond, foreign holders had little recourse. That's why they routinely accepted exchange offers.

By the 1970s this protection had weakened. Investors started suing deadbeat republics. Sometimes they won, paving the way for them to seize debtor country assets in order to get their investment capital back. The mere threat of this process, and the disruption it would cause, was often enough to force a debtor nation to settle. Our investor group clearly had this in mind. But they also had in mind something new.[10]

Argentina's indentures had a standard *pari passu* clause. As we know, that requires an issuer to treat all bondholders equally.

Our investor group's take on pari passu was that as holdouts, they needed to be treated the same as creditors that accepted the exchange offer. Their argument was that if Argentina serviced the new bonds it would have to service any old, unexchanged bonds.

This was gutsy. A UK court dismissed the argument as "novel and unprecedented." A prominent American legal magazine described it as "a goofball legal theory" that many considered "nuts." But the investors took their argument to a New York court, and in October 2012 won. Argentina appealed.

The ARA *Libertad* is the flagship of the Argentine navy. It's a 103 meter long windjammer, a tall ship that around this time was docked at the African port city of Tema. It once set the world speed record for crossing the Atlantic by sail. But it didn't look too speedy on October 2, 2012 when agents representing the investors seized it.

The grab didn't last long. The International Tribunal for the Law of the Sea ordered the ship's release. But it worked. As a part of the investors' global hunt for Argentine assets, it was a visible disruption that made organizations reluctant to work with the country. Argentina flew the ship's 300 crew members back to Buenos Aires on a French charter jet for fear that if it used one of its own planes it would be seized.

The country found itself increasingly isolated. In the summer of 2014 a clearing house stopped transmitting funds that Argentina needed to service the new bonds. Later that year a new Argentine bond offering was undersubscribed. In early 2015 another bond offering was scrapped entirely.

Shut out of capital markets, in March 2016 Argentina agreed to pay the investors 79 cents on the dollar.[11] The settlement reportedly included a compensatory interest rate of 9 percent, plus reimbursement for legal expenses.

How well the investor group did is a matter of some speculation. One media outlet said it earned a "total return of 1,180 percent."[12] Another said it got back "10 to 15 times its original investment." I estimate the annualized return at about 22 percent. But by any measure, it was a lot. It was enough for the investors' law firm to win the award for Global Dispute of the Year.[13]

Now: you are not going to buy defaulted sovereigns, commandeer frigates, and muscle a troubled republic to the negotiating table. I appreciate that.

Further, no thinking investor could miss the real human suffering in this case. People just like you and me but for their passports were hungry and scared. Some died in the demonstrations.[14] One could have a moral posture against investing in securities tarnished by such catastrophe, no matter how great the financial reward. That's reasonable.

But it's not reasonable to ignore the lessons that this case shows us. There are four.

First, this case is a reason *collective action* clauses are now standard in sovereign indentures. They let a *supermajority* of bondholders bind all bondholders in a restructuring negotiation. Holdouts no longer have the disruptive leverage that they once did.

A supermajority is a specified percentage of holders above 50 percent.

Second, it shows how a command of the law is essential in distressed debt investing. The deep legal knowledge of the investor group enabled their outsized return. Investing in a non-performing bond without understanding the law is like reading a balance sheet without understanding accounting.

Third, not all reference rates are the same. It's one thing to base a variable interest rate on SOFR, Euribor, or the prime rate. Those are established indexes that fluctuate within bounds. But it's another thing to base it on the yield of the sovereign debt of an emerging market economy. That's a wilder ride.

Most importantly, this case shows how a debt everyone finds revolting can have worth. That ethos powers all value investments in bonds, at least in part. Unpopularity by itself doesn't make a debt attractive. But widespread repulsion can lead to the price drops that pave the way for outperformance.

SUMMARY

1. Collective action clauses have become standard in sovereign debt indentures.
2. A command of the law is essential in distressed debt investing.
3. Nonstandard reference rates act differently than standard reference rates.
4. Value investors see merit in securities that others reject.
5. Unpopularity by itself doesn't make a security attractive.

CHAPTER 17

CPI

CPI Property Group S.A. is based in Luxembourg. It owns hotels, office buildings, and other real estate in Europe. Like many property companies, it has significant debt in its capital structure. Part of that debt is two bonds.

One bond matures in 2026. The other matures in 2028. So for simplicity, let's refer to them as the 26 and the 28.

The ISIN of the 26 is XS2171875839. For the 28 it's XS2106589471.

CPI issued the bonds as part of its *euro medium-term note*—or *EMTN*—program. *Euro* means outside of the U.S. and Canada. *Medium-term* here means between one and five years.

An EMTN program lets a company issue a series of securities over time under a base prospectus. The details of a single issue are in a final terms document. The final terms document for the 26 is here:

http://www.gooddebtcheap.com/qa.htm

The final terms document for the 28 is here:

http://www.gooddebtcheap.com/ds.htm

The *issuer* of both bonds is a company, CPI Property Group S.A. That's in the first pages of both final terms documents, as is most of the information we need for our *understanding*.

The *currency* of the 26 is euros. For the 28 it's British pounds.

Par value for the 26 is €1,000. For the 28 it's £1,000.

The *issue date* for the 26 is May 12, 2020. For the 28 it's January 22, 2020.

Maturity for the 26 is May 12, 2026. For the 28 it's January 22, 2028.

Regarding *payments*, both bonds have a coupon rate of 2.75 percent, paid annually. The 26 pays on May 12. The 28 pays on January 22.

Neither bond is *secured*. But both are *senior*.

As for *provisions*, both bonds are callable. The 26 can be redeemed through February 12, 2026 at a 0.5 percent call premium. The 28 can be redeemed through October 27, 2027 at a 0.35 percent call premium.[1]

The base prospectus was updated between the two issuances. But the *covenants* stayed the same. Here's the base prospectus in effect for the 26:

http://www.gooddebtcheap.com/fz.htm

Here's the base prospectus in effect for the 28:

http://www.gooddebtcheap.com/kj.htm

One covenant says that debt divided by assets can't exceed 0.6. Another says that secured debt divided by assets can't exceed 0.45.

Of course the prospectuses use fancier language. Instead of saying *debt divided by assets*, for example, they say *consolidated total indebtedness divided by consolidated adjusted total assets*. But my shorthand is probably accurate.

There's another covenant, however, that I can't summarize as crisply. It's a minimum *consolidated leverage ratio*. The numerator is EBITDA—a bloated measure of earnings that we first saw back in chapter 13—excluding any revaluations, financial income, financial expenses, and a handful of other non-recurring, non-cash items.   The denominator is all finance expenses except subordinated shareholder debt interest, minus interest income. Complicated, yes. But anyway, this ratio can't go below 1.9.[2]

Both bonds are listed on the Frankfurt Stock Exchange. That's the largest stock exchange in Germany. So they're relatively *liquid*.[3]

In November 2023 an American investment firm announced that it had shorted CPI's debt.[4] Which exact debt is unclear. But the 26 and the 28 are both listed, which makes them good candidates. We'll assume it's them. But first, let's understand *shorting*.

Shorting is betting that the price of a security will go down. It involves selling a security without actually owning it, by borrowing it through a broker from someone who does, with the goal of profiting when the price falls.

The other cases in this book are *long*. To be long is to own a security. An investor that is long essentially believes that the return from that security—through appreciation, periodic payments, or both—will be positive. Most investing is long.

Shorting is less common. Shorting bonds is particularly uncommon. But it can be done.

Short selling has four steps.

First, the investor pays a fee to a broker to borrow the security. The shares may be owned by the broker, or they may be owned by a *securities lender*.

Second, the investor sells the borrowed securities to a buyer through the broker. The broker withholds some of the sales proceeds as collateral for the securities loan.

Third, the investor *covers* by buying the securities it owes to the broker in the open market, hopefully after the price has declined.

Fourth, the investor returns the securities to the broker, who then releases the withheld sales proceeds to the investor.

The gain to the investor is the proceeds from the sale of step two, minus the cost of the purchase of step three, minus the borrow fee of step one.

Sale proceeds
− Cost of covering
− Borrow fee
= Gain

Calculation of the gain from shorting a security

Shorting is seductive. It promises a way to benefit from a finding that a security is overpriced, or that the issuer is troubled. But it's hard to do. Specifically, six issues can emerge.

First, securities to borrow can be hard to locate. This is particularly true when the shorting idea is obvious. That's because many short sellers will try to borrow the same security all at once.

Second, security borrowing costs can be high. This also happens when the shorting idea is obvious.

Third, the price of covering can be high. If many investors short the same security at the same time, demand for that security can soar. This can cause the price of a security fit to fall to actually rise. This is called a *short squeeze*. It's terrifying.

Fourth, if a short position *moves against* the investor—that is, if the price of the shorted security spikes instead of diving—the broker may close the position. Stated differently, the broker can force the investor to lose money.

The fifth issue involves periodic payments. With stocks those are dividends, and with bonds they're interest. If a security generates a periodic payment while borrowed, the investor is required to make that payment to the securities lender as if the lender still held the security. This is generally handled by the broker, who makes such payments from the investor's account.

Sixth, short selling is viewed negatively. Sometimes it's even banned.

There's a seventh issue with shorted bonds that doesn't apply to shorted stocks. It's that debt is senior to equity. We saw this in chapter one. In liquidation, bondholders may get something while stockholders get nothing. So if an issuer fails, the price of the equity charges downward more forcefully than the price of the debt. That's inconvenient if the security you're short is a bond.

The outfit that shorted CPI's debt is an *activist short seller*. It shorts securities and then publicizes issuers' problems in order to drive the securities' prices down. If that sounds uncharming, that's because it is. But it can work. More selflessly, it can expose wrongdoing that rightly alerts regulators.

Our model can apply to activist short selling. But it requires two tweaks. Both tweaks are obvious.

The first involves the question *is it good?* If we're betting that the price will decrease, we don't want it to be good. We want it to be bad. *Durably* bad. We want it to be so bad that the issuer can't fix the problem. An intractable miserableness weighs on a price like an anchor on a feather.

Further, we want it to be durably bad *for an unpublicized reason*. We want to be the one that reveals the disaster to the market. That's because if the disaster is already exposed, the price may have already done all of the dropping it's going to do.

The second tweak involves the question *is it inexpensive?* If we're betting that the price will decrease, we don't want it to be inexpensive. We want it to be *expensive*. We want yield to be as slim as a twig. That sets up a steep vertical cliff from which the price can then dive.

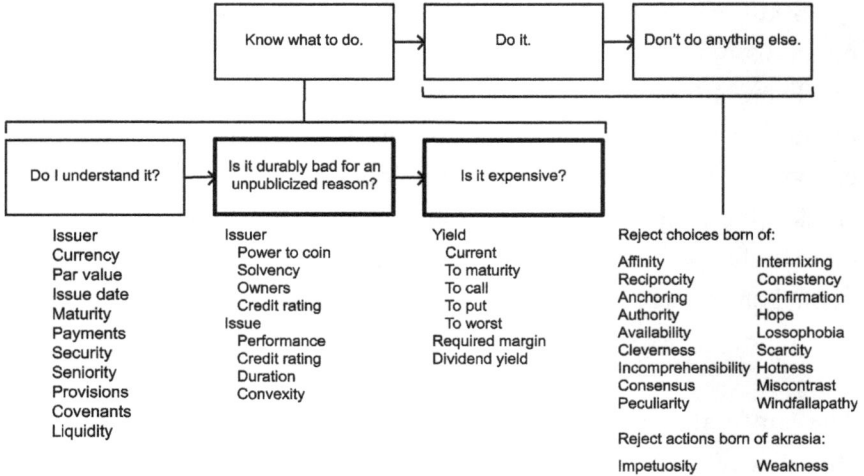

| Know what to do. → | Do it. → | Don't do anything else. |

| Do I understand it? → | Is it durably bad for an unpublicized reason? → | Is it expensive? |

Issuer	Issuer	Yield	Reject choices born of:
Currency	Power to coin	Current	Affinity — Intermixing
Par value	Solvency	To maturity	Reciprocity — Consistency
Issue date	Owners	To call	Anchoring — Confirmation
Maturity	Credit rating	To put	Authority — Hope
Payments	Issue	To worst	Availability — Lossophobia
Security	Performance	Required margin	Cleverness — Scarcity
Seniority	Credit rating	Dividend yield	Incomprehensibility — Hotness
Provisions	Duration		Consensus — Miscontrast
Covenants	Convexity		Peculiarity — Windfallapathy
Liquidity			

Reject actions born of akrasia:

Impetuosity   Weakness

The Value Investing Model for
Short Fixed Income Activist Investing

On November 21, 2023 the activist published a report criticizing CPI. It boils down to two allegations: accounting irregularities and undisclosed related party transactions. It makes those serious claims with pointed language. And it promises a second report on other misdeeds.[5]

Let's assess the *issuer* as of November 20, 2023. That's right before the activist published its report.

Clearly the company doesn't have the *power to coin*.

For *solvency*, the most recent financial statements available were in the 2023 half-year management report:

http://www.gooddebtcheap.com/rg.htm

The financial statements start on page 87. But remember, the activist claims that the accounting is irregular. If it is, calculating solvency metrics from the financial statements could be as useless as calculating them from tide tables.

But if an issuer misrepresents its financials, it's likely to do so in a way that makes it look better. So let's trust CPI for the moment. If solvency looks bad, it's unlikely to look any better with truer accounting.

http://www.gooddebtcheap.com/rc.xlsx

Debt-to-equity seems a little heavy, at 1.21. But *liabilities-to-equity* looks manageable at 1.48. The *quick ratio* is fine at about two. But the *interest coverage ratio* is weak at 0.85.

One could reasonably argue that real estate companies are entitled to more leverage than my benchmarks permit. After all, property is routinely purchased with borrowed money. When an industry has its own word for debt—*mortgage*—you know that leverage is in its DNA.

That said, CPI's solvency doesn't strike me as exemplary. And if the accounting is irregular, it could be even less exemplary.

For *owners*, page 66 of the 2023 half-year management report shows that over 88 percent of the company is owned by CPI's multibillionaire founder. Interestingly, he seems not to be an officer or director of the company. So while he might have capital to inject, he might feel less fiduciary pressure to do so.

I'm speculating here. Fiduciary obligations under Luxembourg law are surely different from the U.S. law that I'm more familiar with. Plus fiduciaries don't have obligations to debtholders like they do to shareholders. Most importantly, no standard I know of requires fiduciaries to inject their own money into an entity. But it's relevant, I think, that the big owner seems to be a step removed from responsibility.

Credit rating is addressed on page 57 of the management report. Moody's rates CPI Baa3, and S&P rates it BBB-.[6] Both are the lowest investment-grade levels on their respective scales. The notch below each is junk.

Moving on to *issue*, both bonds are *performing*. The 26 faithfully paid its €27.50 on May 12, 2023;[7] and the 28 paid its £27.50 on January 22, 2023.[8]

As for *credit rating*, Moody's gives the same rating to the bonds as it does to the issuer: Baa3.[9] S&P does the same with a BBB-.[10] Again, both NRSROs pick the level just above junk.

Yet again *duration* and *convexity* aren't essential here. But for the record, we'll calculate them.

On November 20, 2023 the 26 traded at around 82, and the 28 traded at around 72. The tenors of the two bonds can be figured with the years-between-two-dates calculator we used earlier:

http://www.gooddebtcheap.com/gg.htm

So the information we need is:

	26	28
Price	€ 820	£ 720
Par	€1,000	£1,000
Years to maturity	2.475	4.175
Annual coupon rate	2.75%	2.75%
Coupon payment frequency	Annually	Annually

That all goes into our online calculator:

http://www.gooddebtcheap.com/pl.htm

For the 26, modified duration is 1.834, and convexity is 6.618. For the 28, modified duration is 3.460, and convexity is 16.115.

Next, *inexpensiveness*. The *current ratio* for the 26 is approximately 3.4 percent. That's just 27.50 divided by 820. For the 28, it's 3.8 percent. That's just 27.50 divided by 720.

Those seem low, don't they? I think so. In the Europe of late 2023 one could get rates like that from government-insured bank accounts, all without having to fret over hotel and office building vacancies.

The *yield to maturity* figures come out of our duration calculation. For the 26 it's 11.517 percent, and for the 28 it's 11.583 percent.

Since the bonds are redeemable, we should also calculate *yield to call*:

http://www.gooddebtcheap.com/mo.htm

Since the call premium on the 26 is 0.5 percent, the call price is €1,005. The call premium on the 28 is 0.35 percent, so the call price there is £1,003.50.

For call date, let's assume that it's the last possible date for each bond. For the 26 that's February 12, 2026. For the 28, it's October 27, 2027. We can use our years-between-two-dates calculator to figure the time from November 20, 2023 until those dates. Then we have the information we need:

	26	28
Price	€ 820.00	£ 720.00
Par	€1,000.00	£1,000.00
Call price	€1,005.00	£1,003.50
Years to call	2.230	3.934
Annual coupon rate	2.75%	2.75%
Coupon payment frequency	Annually	Annually

The online calculator spits out a yield to call for the 26 of 12.73 percent. For the 28, it's 12.205 percent.

But remember that the bonds can be called sooner. That would make the call premiums come sooner. And since the coupon rate is low, that would make the yield to call higher. Indeed if the time to call was only a year, yield to call for the 26 would be almost 26 percent. For the 28, it would be 43 percent.

If the call was today, yield to call might not be the best metric to use. Simple return might be better. If the 26 was called now, the return would be 22.5 percent. That's just the call price of €1,005 minus the price of €820, all divided by the price of €820. Similarly, the return on a 28 called now would be over 39 percent.

So as is commonly the case, yield to worst here equals yield to maturity. But remember, that's not what our investor is after. Our investor is *short*. It wants the bonds to be *expensive*. Are they?

Yes, a bit. Most of the yields seem modest for an issuer barely hovering above junk.

The day the activist report was published, the price of both bonds went down. That's typical. But they didn't go down by much. The 26 dropped from 82 to 77,[11] and the 28 dropped from 72 to 66.[12]

Then the bond prices started rising. By April 2024 the 26 hit 90,[13] and the 28 hit almost 80.[14]

In May 2024 S&P downgraded CPI from BBB- to BB+ with a negative outlook.[15] Two months later Moody's downgraded the company from Baa3 to Ba1, also with a negative outlook.[16] Both NRSROs now saw CPI as junk. And yet the bond prices continued to rise. As I write this in the summer of 2024 the 26 is at 93,[17] and the 28 is at 86.[18]

As promised, the activist published an additional report. And then several more reports. As of this writing the most recent one came out in June 2024.[19]

It's conceivable that the activist covered right after the initial price drop, closed positions, and made money. But the drops might not have been sufficient to cover the borrow fees. Plus the activist continued to publish reports, suggesting that the positions remain at least partly open.

As in the Argentina case, there's much information we don't have. That's largely because the investors were private funds, exempt from some reporting requirements. So we don't know which exact securities were used. We don't know the exact prices at which positions were established. And we don't know the exact timing of events.

Nonetheless, this case teaches us something.

The activist seems smart to have targeted an issuer at the bottom of the investment grade scale. Many bond funds are prohibited by charter from owning junk. Their world is strictly investment grade. So one notch downward and the price of the bonds could tumble as big funds rushed for the exits.

Of course that downgrade is exactly what happened. And yet the prices of the bonds didn't plunge. Why?

Maybe they didn't plunge because of a short squeeze.

Maybe they didn't plunge because the company took steps to fix its problems. If the company was bad, perhaps it wasn't *durably* bad.

Maybe they didn't plunge because the market knew about the issuer's problems back in late 2023. If the company was bad, perhaps it wasn't bad for an *unpublicized* reason. As a result, the securities might not have been sufficiently *expensive*.

But maybe it was simpler than all that. Maybe they didn't plunge for the fundamental reason that debt is senior to equity.

I never explored a short bond case before this one. I didn't even know that one existed. That's one reason why discovering this situation surprised me. Another is that the native seniority of fixed income securities would seem to make them poor candidates for shorting.

But I'm not certain about that. This case is still playing out. So I'm watching it. Like you, I'm still learning.

SUMMARY

1. Good activist short sellers seek expensive securities that are durably bad for an unpublicized reason.
2. Shorting is hard.
3. Shorting bonds is particularly hard, since debt is senior to equity.

GLOSSARY

^
Caret, the math symbol meaning *raised to the power of*. Also called *circumflex* or *hat*.

7-day effective yield
Annualized yield based on *income* from the last seven days, with the effect of *compounding*; as with a *money market fund*. Also called *effective yield*.

7-day yield
Annualized yield based on *income* from the last seven days, without the effect of *compounding*; as with a *money market fund*.

8-K
A report of *material* corporate events filed with the *SEC* by U.S. companies that have issued *listed securities*.

10-K
An annual report filed with the *SEC* by U.S. companies that have issued *listed securities*.

10-Q
A quarterly report filed with the *SEC* by U.S. companies that have issued *listed securities*.

30-day SEC yield

A *fund* performance ratio. The *numerator* equals *dividends* and *interest* received by the fund, minus the fund's operating expenses; based on the most recent full month, *annualized*. The denominator is the highest price of the fund's *shares* on the last day of that month.

30/360

The *day count convention* that assumes 30 days in a month and 360 days in a year, commonly used in the American *corporate* and *muni* markets.

30/365

The *day count convention* that assumes 30 days in a month and 365 days in a year.

30E/360

The *day count convention* that assumes 30 days in all months except for February, where the actual number of days is used; and assumes 360 days in a year.

1099-DIV

An annual form issued by financial institutions to investors and the *IRS* that reports *dividends* and other distributions, including *preferred stock* dividends.

1099-INT

An annual form issued by financial institutions to investors and the *IRS* that reports *interest*, including interest on *bonds*.

AAR

The rate of *return* that, had it been achieved each year, would have delivered the same end result that the more *volatile* annual returns actually did. Short for *average annual return*.

ABCP

Commercial paper that's *collateralized*, often by the *issuer's receivables*. Short for *asset-backed commercial paper*.

ABS

A *fixed income security* backed by specified *assets*, often *debts* that generate *cash flow*. *MBSs* and other *CDOs* are examples of ABSs. Commonly sold in *tranches*. Short for *asset-backed security*.

AIM

A lightly-regulated segment of the London Stock Exchange, comparable to the *Open Market* of the Frankfurt Stock Exchange or *First North* of Nasdaq Nordic. Includes *fixed income securities*. Short for *Alternative Investment Market*.

A.M. Best

An *NRSRO* and *credit rating agency*, generally viewed as less prominent than *Fitch*, *Moody's*, and *S&P*.

APR

Yearly *interest* divided by balance excluding *compounding*. Short for *annual percentage rate*.

APY

The yearly *yield* of an *asset* including intra-year *compounding*. Short for *annual percentage yield*.

ARM

A *loan secured* by *real estate* whose *interest* rate is *fixed* for an initial period and *floating* thereafter. Short for *adjustable-rate mortgage*. An alternative to a *fixed-rate mortgage*.

AT1

A *hybrid* that converts into *equity* under certain circumstances, issued primarily by European *banks*. Short for *additional tier 1*. Also called *contingent convertible*, *CoCo*, *enhanced capital note*, or *ECN*.

AUM

The total market value of *assets* managed, in a *fund* or otherwise. Short for *assets under management*.

Absolute

A basis for assessing investment returns by *benchmarking* to a *fixed* percentage. An alternative to *relative*.

Accelerated

A method of accounting for *depreciation* or *amortization* whereby more is expensed in early periods than in later periods. An alternative to *straight-line*.

Accounts payable

Money owed to vendors. An item in the *liabilities* section of the *balance sheet*. Also called *trade payable*.

Accounts receivable

Money expected from customers. An item in the *assets* section of the *balance sheet*. Also called *trade receivables* or just *receivables*.

Accreted value

The worth of a *zero-coupon bond* at any point in time between issuance and when it reaches *par value* at *maturity*.

Accretion

The process by which a *zero-coupon bond* increases in worth over time, ultimately reaching *par value* at *maturity*.

Accretion rate

The speed at which a *zero-coupon bond* increases in worth, ultimately reaching *par value* at *maturity;* expressed as an annual percentage of *par value*. Equal to *yield to maturity* at issuance.

Accrual basis

An accounting standard based on rules of *revenue* and expense recognition, as opposed to *inflows* and *outflows*. The alternative to *cash basis*.

Accrual bond

A *fixed income security* that defers *interest* payments, generally until *maturity*. Distinct from a *zero*.

Accrual period

The time between a *bond's coupon* payments.

Accrued expenses

Periodic amounts owed but not yet paid, like salaries. An item in the *liabilities* section of the *balance sheet*.

Accrued interest

Interest earned but not yet paid on a *fixed income security*. Equal to the *dirty price* minus the *clean price* of that security.

Acid-test ratio

The quantity *current assets* minus *inventory*, divided by *current liabilities*. A higher acid-test ratio means an *issuer* is better able to meet its *short-term* obligations. A *liquidity ratio* that's stricter than the *current ratio*. Also called the *quick ratio*.

Active

The characteristic of a *fund* that means it's based on *security selection* instead of an *index*. The alternative to *passive*.

Activism

An investment approach that involves agitating for change in a company in which one has a financial interest.

Activist short seller

An investor that *shorts* a *security* and then publicizes the *issuer's* problems in order to drive the security's price down.

Actual/360

The *day count convention* that uses the actual number of days in a month and assumes 360 days in a year, commonly used in the *money market*.

Actual/365

The *day count convention* that uses the actual number of days in a month and assumes 365 days in a year.

Actual/365L

The *day count convention* that uses the actual number of days in a month and assumes 365 days in all years except leap years, where it assumes 366 days.

Actual/actual

The *day count convention* that uses the actual number of days in a month and the actual number of days in a year, commonly used in the market for *Treasury bonds* and *Treasury notes*.

Additional tier 1

A *hybrid* that converts into *equity* under certain circumstances, issued primarily by European *banks*. Shortened to *AT1*. Also called *contingent convertible*, *CoCo*, *enhanced capital note*, or *ECN*.

Adjustable-rate mortgage

A loan *secured* by real estate whose *interest* rate is *fixed* for an initial period and *floating* thereafter. Shortened to *ARM*. An alternative to a *fixed-rate mortgage*.

Affirmative covenant

A clause in an *indenture* that requires the *issuer* to do something, like publish *audited financial statements* or keep the *debt-to-equity ratio* below a specified level. Also called a *positive covenant*. The counterpart to a *negative covenant*.

Agency

An *issuer* that is either a division of a federal government or a *government-sponsored enterprise*. Distinct from a *credit rating agency*.

Agency bond

A *fixed income security* issued by a division of a federal government or, in the U.S., a *government-sponsored enterprise*. Also called *agency debt*.

Agency debt

A *fixed income security* issued by a division of a federal government or, in the U.S., a *government-sponsored enterprise*. Also called *agency bond*.

Agg

Short for the Bloomberg U.S. Aggregate Bond Index, a *benchmark* for *fixed income securities* that are *investment grade*.

Alpha

A measure of investment outperformance, generally attributed to the *active* management skill of the investor.

Alternative Investment Market

A lightly-regulated segment of the London Stock Exchange, comparable to the *Open Market* of the Frankfurt Stock Exchange or *First North* of Nasdaq Nordic. Includes *fixed income securities*. Shortened to *AIM*.

Alternative trading system

A *securities* trading venue other than a traditional exchange like NYSE or NASDAQ.

Amortization

The process of reducing the *principal* on a loan by making periodic payments. Separately, the decreasing of the *book value* of an intangible, *noncurrent asset* by recognizing periodic expenses on the *income statement*.

Amortization schedule

A table showing how much of each periodic payment on a *loan* reduces *principal*, and how much is *interest* expense.

Amortized bond

A *fixed income security* with scheduled payments that are a changing mix of *principal* and *interest*. Also called an *amortizing bond*. An alternative to a *bullet bond* or a *sinkable bond*.

Amortizing

The characteristic of a loan meaning that its *principal* is fully repaid by *maturity*, generally enabling the borrower to make equal payments over the *term*. One of several principal repayment structures, others being *balloon* and *bullet*.

Amortizing bond

A *fixed income security* with scheduled payments that are a changing mix of *principal* and *interest*. Also called an *amortized bond*. An alternative to a *bullet bond* and a *sinkable bond*.

Annual percentage rate

Yearly *interest* divided by *balance* excluding compounding. Shortened to *APR*.

Annual percentage yield

The yearly *yield* of an *asset* including intra-year compounding. Shortened to *APY*.

Annualized

Stated in yearly terms but based on data from a different period, as with a quarterly *dividend* multiplied by four.

Annuity

A series of payments made at regular intervals, like *interest* on a *coupon bond*. Relatedly, an investment product offered by insurance companies that promises such payments.

Appreciation

The increase in market price relative to purchase price.

Arithmetic mean

The sum of a set of numbers divided by the number of numbers in the set.

Ask

The price offered to a potential buyer of a *security*. Also called *offer*. The counterpart to *bid*.

Asset

Something owned that has value. Often used as a synonym for investment, holding, or *security*. Separately, a *balance sheet* section that includes things that have value that an entity owns.

Asset allocation

The process of apportioning wealth among different *asset classes*. Happens before any *security selection*.

Asset-backed commercial paper

Commercial paper that's *collateralized*, often by the *issuer's receivables*. Shortened to *ABCP*.

Asset-backed security

A *fixed income security* backed by specified *assets*, often *debts* that generate cash flow. *Mortgage-backed securities* and other *collateralized debt obligations* are examples of asset-backed securities. Commonly sold in *tranches*. Shortened to *ABS*.

Asset class

A group of *assets* with similar characteristics, such as *fixed income securities* or *stocks*.

Assets under management

The total market value of *assets* managed, in a *fund* or otherwise. Shortened to *AUM*.

At par

Equal to *face value*.

At the money

The state of an *option* with a *strike price* equal to the market price of the *underlier*.

Audited

Examined by a public accountancy, as with a *listed* company's *financial statements*. The opposite of *unaudited*.

Available-for-sale

An accounting term that describes a *security* that a *holder* intends to sell, generally after a year. The alternative to *held-for-trading* and *held-to-maturity*.

Average annual return

The rate of *return* that, had it been achieved each year, would have delivered the same end result that the more *volatile* annual returns actually did. Shortened to *AAR*.

BEY

Short for *bond-equivalent yield*. The *annualized* rate of return from a *fixed income security*, commonly calculated for *zeros* like *T-bills* as the quantity *par* minus price divided by price, all times the quantity 365 divided by *tenor* in days:

$$((par - price) / price) \times (365 / tenor \ in \ days)$$

BTP

A sovereign *debt* obligation of Italy, comparable to a U.S. *Treasury*. Short for *Buoni del Tesoro Poliennali*.

Backtest

To test an investment strategy model with historical data.

Balance sheet

A *financial statement* that measures a business at a single point in time by subtracting *liabilities* from *assets* to produce *equity*.

Balanced

The characteristic of a *fund* that means it contains both *stocks* and *fixed income securities*.

Balloon

The characteristic of a loan meaning that it isn't fully *amortized* by *maturity*, requiring the borrower to make a large final payment. One of several *principal* repayment structures, others being *amortizing* and *bullet*.

Balloon payment

The large final amount paid by a borrower who takes out a loan with a *balloon* structure.

Bank

A regulated financial institution that accepts deposits and makes loans.

Bank for International Settlements

An organization that serves and is owned by *central banks*.

Bank guarantee

An *external credit enhancement* that calls for a financial institution to assume the obligations of a *debt* if the *issuer defaults*.

Bank of Japan

The *central bank* of Japan.

Bank rate

The *interest* rate a *central bank* charges financial institutions for *short-term* loans. Also called *discount rate*.

Banker's acceptance

A *money market security* representing a promised future payment by a *bank*, generally to *settle* an international trade *account payable*.

Bankruptcy

A legal state in which a *distressed* entity obtains relief from creditors. Distinct from the financial state of *insolvency*.

Barbell

The investment strategy of holding *short-term* and *long-term bonds*, but not *medium-term* bonds.

Basic shares

Stock in a company held by *shareholders*. Does not include *shares* that could become outstanding from the conversion of a *convertible bond* or a convertible *preferred*, or from the exercise of an *option* or a *warrant*. Also called *shares outstanding*.

Basis point

One one hundredth of 1 percent. Also called *BPS*.

Bayesian

Of or related to a statistical method of assigning probabilities.

Bearer bond

An *unregistered fixed income security* that conveys ownership rights to whoever physically holds the certificate. An alternative to a *registered bond*.

Bearer share

Unregistered stock that conveys ownership rights to whoever physically holds the *stock certificate*. An alternative to a *registered share*.

Benchmark

A quantitative standard, often based on an *index*.

Beta

A measure of the expected change in the price of a *listed security* given a change in an *index*.

Bias

A flawed mental shortcut.

Bid

The price offered by a potential buyer of an *asset*. The counterpart to *ask*.

Bid-ask spread

The difference between *bid* and *ask*, expressed in either money, a percentage, or *basis points*.

Block

A large amount of a single *security* meant to be bought or sold.

Blue-chip

Large and established, as with *corporations* that issue *commercial paper*.

Bond

A *fixed income security* with a longer *term* than a *note*. Relatedly, a type of *Treasury* with a term of over 10 years and up to 30 years. More generally, a synonym for fixed income security or *debt*.

Bond-equivalent yield

Shortened to *BEY*. The *annualized* rate of return from a *fixed income security*, commonly calculated for *zeros* like *T-bills* as the quantity *par* minus price divided by price, all times the quantity 365 divided by *tenor* in days:

$$(\, (\, par - price \,) \, / \, price \,) \; x \; (\, 365 \, / \, tenor \; in \; days \,)$$

Bond insurance

An *external credit enhancement* that calls for an insurance company to assume the obligations of a *debt* if the *issuer defaults*. Also called *default insurance* and *financial guarantee insurance*.

Bond ladder

A portfolio of *fixed income securities* that *mature* on different dates, creating periodic *liquidity* and reducing *interest rate risk*. Shortened to *ladder*.

Bondholder

The owner of a *fixed income security*.

Book-entry

The electronic registration of *security* ownership, without the issuance of physical certificates.

Book value

Assets minus *liabilities*. Also called *equity, net assets, owners' equity*, or *shareholders' equity*. Separately, the cost of a *fixed asset* net of adjustments like *depreciation*.

Borrowing

A financial *liability* that generally incurs *interest* and must be paid back. Also called *debt* or *leverage*.

Broker

A person or company that intermediates the sale and purchase of *assets* like *bonds*. When a company, also called a *brokerage*.

Broker-dealer

A person or company that intermediates the sale and purchase of *securities*, and that buys and sells securities for its own account.

Brokerage

A company that intermediates the sale and purchase of *assets* like *bonds*. Also called *broker*.

Bullet

The investment strategy of holding *bonds* that share a *maturity date*. Separately, the characteristic of a loan meaning that *principal* is repaid at *maturity*. In that context one of several principal repayment structures, others being *amortizing* and *balloon.*

Bullet bond

A *fixed income security* that's meant to pay *principal* back all at once at *maturity*, without provisions like *callability* or *convertibility*. Also called a *plain vanilla bond* or a *straight bond*. An alternative to an *amortizing bond* or a *sinkable bond*.

Bund

A sovereign *debt* obligation of the German federal government, comparable to a U.S. *Treasury*. Aways starts with a capital B.

Buy-side

Investors, as a broad group. The counterpart to *sell-side*.

Buyback

The purchase by an *issuer* of its own *securities* for cash. Also called *repurchase*.

CAGR

The *annualized* rate of return of an investment given an initial value, final value, and time between the two. Short for *compound annual growth rate*. Equal to final value divided by initial value, all raised to the power of one divided by the number of time periods, minus one:

$$((\text{ final value } / \text{ initial value }) \wedge (1 / \text{ time })) - 1$$

CBO

A *bond*, generally *investment grade*, backed by *non-investment grade bonds*. Generally sold in *tranches*. Short for *collateralized bond obligation*.

CD

An *interest*-bearing *bank* deposit that cannot be withdrawn without penalty before a predetermined *maturity date*. Short for *certificate of deposit*.

CDO

A *fixed income security* backed by *debt*, like a *mortgage-backed security*. Generally sold in *tranches*. Short for *collateralized debt obligation*.

CDS

A contract where a buyer pays cash to a seller that promises to pay a specified amount to the buyer if a specified *debt defaults*. Short for *credit default swap*. Distinct from *CDs*, the plural acronym for *certificates of deposit*.

CLO

A *collateralized debt obligation* backed by business loans. Short for *collateralized loan obligation*.

CMO

A *mortgage-backed security* sold in *tranches*. Short for *collateralized mortgage obligation*.

CP

Debt issued by established *corporations* that is generally *unsecured* and has a *term* of less than nine months. Short for *commercial paper*. Also called *paper*.

CPI

A standard measure of *inflation*, sometimes used as an *index* for *floating rate notes*. Short for *Consumer Price Index*.

CRISIL

A major *credit rating agency* in India. An acronym for the original name *Credit Rating Information Services of India Limited*.

CUSIP

A nine-character combination of numbers and possibly letters that represents a *listed security* in the U.S. or Canada. Short for *Committee on Uniform Securities Identification Procedures*.

Call

An *option* that gives the *holder* the right to purchase an *asset* on predetermined terms.

Call date

A date on which a *security* can be *called*.

Call premium

The amount over *par value* paid to *call* a *fixed income security*. Equal to *call price* minus par value.

Call price

The amount paid to *call* a *fixed income security*. Equal to *par value* plus *call premium*.

Call risk

The chance that an investor won't be able to redeploy the proceeds from a *redeemed fixed income security* at an attractive rate of return. A form of *reinvestment risk*.

Callable

The characteristic of a *fixed income security* that gives the *issuer* the right to *retire* the obligation prior to *maturity* by paying the *holder*. Also called *redeemable*. The opposite of *putable*.

Cancel

To end the existence of a *security* after buying it back, as with a *redeemed bond* or a *repurchased preferred*. Also called *retire*.

Cap

The maximum possible *coupon rate* of a *floater*, regardless of how high the *reference rate* rises. Can be combined with a *floor* to create a *collar*.

Capex

The purchase of *assets* of *material* cost that will last for more than one year. An item in the *cash flow from investments* section of the *cash flow statement*. Short for *capital expenditure*. Also called *purchase of property, plant, and equipment*.

Capital expenditure

The purchase of *assets* of *material* cost that will last for more than one year. An item in the *cash flow from investments* section of the *cash flow statement*. Shortened to *capex*. Also called *purchase of property, plant, and equipment*.

Capital gain

The sale price minus the purchase price of a *security*, when positive. The opposite of *capital loss*.

Capital loss

The sale price minus the purchase price of a *security*, when negative. The opposite of *capital gain*.

Capital market

The market for *equity* and *long-term fixed income securities*. Distinct from the *money market*.

Capital preservation

An investment posture that prioritizes not losing money as opposed to return.

Capital structure

The mix between *debt* and *equity* on a company's *balance sheet*.

Capitalized

Recognized as a *noncurrent asset* on the *balance sheet*.

Capped

The characteristic of a *floater* or a *coupon* that sets a maximum coupon amount.

Caret

A math symbol meaning *raised to the power of*. Denoted ^.
Also called *circumflex* or *hat*.

Carry trade

An investment in *bonds* with relatively high *coupon* rates made
with money borrowed at relatively low *interest* rates.

Cash basis

An accounting standard based on *inflows* and *outflows*. The
alternative to *accrual basis*.

Cash equivalent

A *money market instrument* with a *term* of three months or
less.

Cash flow

A movement of money, in or out.

Cash flow from financing

The section of the *cash flow statement* concerned with
borrowings, *dividends*, and the sale and *repurchase* of an
issuer's own *securities*, like *preferred stock*. Also called *cash
flow from financing activities*.

Cash flow from investments

The section of the *cash flow statement* concerned with the
purchase and sale of *long-term assets*. Also called *cash flow
from investing activities*.

Cash flow from operations

The section of the *cash flow statement* concerned with a company's core activities. Also called *operating cash flow* or *cash flow from operating activities*.

Cash flow matching

The *immunization* strategy of buying a portfolio of *fixed income securities* that generate cash when needed, like *zeros* that mature precisely when the *principal* is needed to make a *capital expenditure*. Also called *dedication*.

Cash flow statement

A *cash basis financial statement* that describes a business over a period of time.

Cat bond

A *fixed income security* issued by an insurance company that *performs* if a specified natural disaster does not occur. Short for *catastrophe bond*.

Catalyst

A reason that the price of a *security* could change, particularly in the *short-term*.

Catastrophe bond

A *fixed income security* issued by an insurance company that *performs* if a specified natural disaster does not occur. Shortened to *cat bond*.

Central bank

A governmental institution that manages the currency of a country or group of countries, like the *Bank of Japan*, *European Central Bank*, or *Federal Reserve*.

Century bond
   A *fixed income security* with a *term* of 100 years.

Certificate of deposit
   An *interest*-bearing *bank* deposit that cannot be withdrawn without penalty before a predetermined *maturity date*. Also called a *CD*, a *guaranteed investment contract* in Canada, and a *time deposit* or *term deposit* elsewhere.

Change of control
   A *material* change in the ownership of an *issuer*, sometimes letting the *holder* of a *fixed income security* exercise a *put*.

Circumflex
   A math symbol meaning *raised to the power of*. Denoted ^. Also called *caret* or *hat*.

Class
   A tier of *preferred stock* or *common stock*, often distinguished by voting rights.

Clean price
   The price of a *fixed income security* excluding any *accrued interest*. Also called the *flat price*. The alternative to the *dirty price*.

Clearing
   Intermediating the *settlement* of a financial transaction, often by a *clearing house*. Relatedly, the activities that occur between a *trade date* and a *settlement date*.

Clearing house

A specialized entity that intermediates the *settlement* of a financial transaction.

Clearstream

A major *clearing house* in Europe.

CoCo

A *hybrid* that converts into *equity* under certain circumstances, issued primarily by European *banks*. Short for *contingent convertible*. Also called *AT1*, *additional tier 1*, *enhanced capital note*, or *ECN*.

Collar

A *floor* and a *cap* together, as with a *floater*. More generally, a mechanism for narrowing the range of possible outcomes.

Collared

The characteristic of a *floater* meaning it has a *cap* and a *floor*. Also used to describe a *coupon* payment from such a floater.

Collateral

Assets pledged to back a *secured debt*.

Collateral trust bond

A *fixed income security* that is *secured* by financial *assets* such as *stock* or other *bonds*. Also called a *collateral trust certificate* or a *collateral trust note*.

Collateral trust certificate

A *fixed income security* that is *secured* by financial *assets* such as *stock* or other *bonds*. Also called a *collateral trust bond* or a *collateral trust note*.

Collateral trust note

A *fixed income security* that is *secured* by financial *assets* such as *stock* or other *bonds*. Also called a *collateral trust bond* or a *collateral trust certificate*.

Collateralization ratio

With a *secured debt*, the value of the *collateral* divided by the amount of the debt.

Collateralized bond obligation

A *bond*, generally *investment grade*, backed by *non-investment grade bonds*. Generally sold in *tranches*. Shortened to *CBO*.

Collateralized debt obligation

A *fixed income security* backed by *debt*, like a *mortgage-backed security*. Generally sold in *tranches*. Shortened to *CDO*.

Collateralized loan obligation

A *collateralized debt obligation* backed by business loans. Shortened to CLO.

Collateralized mortgage obligation

A *mortgage-backed security* sold in *tranches*. Shortened to *CMO*.

Collective action

An *indenture* clause that lets a *supermajority* of *bondholders* bind all bondholders in a *restructuring*.

Commercial paper
  Debt issued by established *corporations* that is generally *unsecured* and has a *term* of less than nine months. Shortened to *paper* or *CP*.

Commercial surety bond
  A *surety bond* used in an industry other than construction. An alternative to a *contract surety bond*.

Common code
  A nine-digit identifier of a *listed security*, comparable to *CUSIP* or *ISIN*.

Common stock
  An ownership interest in a *corporation*, *subordinate* to *preferred stock*. Also called *ordinary shares*.

Compound annual growth rate
  The *annualized* rate of return of an investment given an initial value, final value, and time between the two. Shortened to *CAGR*. Equal to final value divided by initial value, all raised to the power of one divided by the number of time periods, minus one:

$$((\text{final value} / \text{initial value}) \wedge (1 / \text{time})) - 1$$

Compounding
  The effect of one period's return increasing the amount on which the next period's return is based.

Concentration
  The commitment of capital to a limited number of *assets*. Also called *focus*. The opposite of *diversification*.

Conduit
> A *muni* issued to raise capital that the *issuer* channels to a non-governmental entity like a developer of affordable housing.

Conforming
> The characteristic of a *mortgage* that means it meets *Federal Housing Finance Agency* guidelines.

Consumer price index
> A standard measure of *inflation*, sometimes used as an *index* for *floating rate notes*. Shortened to *CPI*.

Contingent convertible
> A *hybrid* that converts into *equity* under certain circumstances, issued primarily by European *banks*. Shortened to *CoCo*. Also called *AT1*, *additional tier 1*, *enhanced capital note*, or *ECN*.

Contract surety bond
> A *surety bond* used in the construction industry. An alternative to a *commercial surety bond*.

Conventional gilt
> A sovereign *debt* obligation of the UK government with a *fixed semiannual coupon* and fixed *principal*. An alternative to an *index-linked gilt*.

Conversion premium
> The amount by which the price of a *convertible fixed income security* exceeds the *conversion price*.

Conversion price
> The *par value* of a *convertible fixed income security* divided by the number of *shares* received if converted.

Conversion ratio

The predetermined amount of an *asset* like *common stock* that will be received if a *convertible security* is exchanged for that asset.

Convertible

The characteristic of a *security* like a *bond* or *preferred stock* that enables it to be exchanged for a predetermined amount of another *asset*, generally *common stock*; and generally at the option of the *holder*.

Convexity

An estimate of the change in *duration* of a *fixed income security*, or a portfolio of fixed income securities, to a change in *interest* rates.

Corporate

A *fixed income security* issued by a *corporation*. More generally, of or related to a corporation.

Corporation

A common type of business entity, where ownership is represented by *shares* of *stock*. Can be either *public* or *private*. An alternative to *partnership*.

Correlation

The degree to which two *assets'* prices move together.

Correlation coefficient

A number between negative one and one that measures the degree to which the prices of two assets moved together.

Cost of capital

The amount an *issuer* pays to finance itself, expressed as an annual percentage. With *debt*, generally equal to the *interest* rate.

Cost of goods sold

Expenses that a business incurred specifically in producing *revenue* during a period. An *income statement* item. Also called *cost of revenue*.

Cost of revenue

Expenses that a business incurred specifically in producing *revenue* during a period. An *income statement* item. Also called *cost of goods sold*.

Counterparty

The other entity involved in a transaction.

Counterparty risk

The chance that the other party in a transaction will be unable to fulfill its obligation.

Country ceiling

The *credit rating* of a country serving as the maximum credit rating an *issuer* in that country can receive.

Coupon

Interest paid on a *fixed income security*, expressed either in currency or as an annual percentage of *par value*.

Coupon bond

A *fixed income security* that pays *interest*.

Coupon rate

Interest paid on a *fixed income security*, expressed as an annual percentage of *par value*. Also called *nominal yield*.

Covariance

A measure of how two *assets'* prices have moved in relation to one another.

Covenant

A clause in an *indenture* that requires the *issuer* to do something, or prohibits the issuer from doing something. The former is an *affirmative covenant*. The latter is a *negative covenant*.

Cover

To buy a *security* owed to a *broker* in a *short*.

Cover pool

The group of *assets* that *collateralize* a *covered bond*.

Coverage ratio

A measure of an *issuer's* ability to *service* its *fixed income securities*, like the *interest coverage ratio* or *preferred dividend coverage ratio*.

Covered bond

A *fixed income security* that is *collateralized*, usually by *mortgages*. Conveys less *credit risk* to *holders* than do *mortgage-backed securities*. Common in Europe. Also called a *Pfandbrief*.

Credit default swap

A contract where a buyer pays cash to a seller that promises to pay a specified amount to the buyer if a specified *debt defaults*. Shortened to *CDS*.

Credit enhancement

The reduction of the *credit risk* of a *fixed income security* by an *issuer* with an *internal* tool like *seniority* or an *external* tool like *financial guaranty insurance*. Relatedly, that internal or external tool.

Credit fund

A *pooled investment vehicle* focused on *corporate debts*.

Credit rating

An assessment of *credit risk* by a *credit rating agency*, generally represented by one to three capital letters, up to two lower case letters, up to one number, and up to one plus or minus sign.

Credit rating agency

An organization paid by *issuers* of *fixed income securities* to assess *credit risk*, such as *Fitch*, *Moody's*, and *S&P*.

Credit risk

The chance that a *fixed income security* will fail to *perform*. Also called *default risk*.

Credit spread

The difference in *yield* between two *fixed income securities* with different *credit risks* that are otherwise similar, often expressed in *basis points*. Also called *yield spread*.

Credit watch

A *credit rating agency* reassessing a *credit rating* because of an event impacting the *issuer*. Shortened to *watch*.

Cross acceleration

A *covenant* that permits *bondholders* to demand immediate repayment if the *issuer defaults* on a different *debt*.

Cross default

A *covenant* that puts an *issue* in *default* if another of the *issuer's debts* goes into default.

Cumulative

The characteristic of a *preferred stock* meaning that any unpaid *dividends* remain owed to the *holder*. The alternative to *noncumulative*.

Currency option bond

A *fixed income security* that gives *holders* the right to choose the currencies in which they receive *interest* and *principal*.

Current assets

Assets that could be used within a year. A *balance sheet* subsection.

Current liabilities

Obligations that must be *settled* in one year or less. A *balance sheet* subsection.

Current ratio

Current assets divided by *current liabilities*. A higher current ratio means an *issuer* is better able to meet its *short-term* obligations. A *liquidity ratio* that's not as strict as the *quick ratio*.

Current yield

Annualized payments received from a *security* divided by the current price of that security. Also called *running yield*. Distinct from *nominal yield*.

Custodian

A financial institution that holds *assets* on a client's behalf.

DBRS

An *NRSRO* and *credit rating agency*, generally viewed as less prominent than *Fitch*, *Moody's*, and *S&P*.

DEF 14A

An annual filing with the *SEC* made by American companies that includes information on ownership. Also called a *proxy statement*.

DM

The *quoted margin* of a *floater* adjusted for price, presumably to capture a change in *credit risk* since issuance. Calculated as *yield to maturity* minus the *reference rate*. Short for *discount margin*. Also called *required margin*.

DTCC

A major American *clearing house*. Short for *Depository Trust & Clearing Corporation*.

DV01

A measure of the sensitivity of a *fixed income security's* price to a single *basis point* change in *interest* rates, expressed in money. Calculated as *dollar duration* divided by 10,000. A one basis point change in interest rates is estimated to change a *bond's* price in the opposite direction by DV01. Also called *DVBP* or *dollar value of a basis point*.

DVBP

A measure of the sensitivity of a *fixed income security's* price to a single *basis point* change in *interest* rates, expressed in money. Calculated as *dollar duration* divided by 10,000. A one basis point change in interest rates is estimated to change a *bond's* price in the opposite direction by DVBP. Short for *dollar value of a basis point*. Also called *DV01*.

Dated date

The date that a *fixed income security* starts accruing *interest*. Distinct from the *issue date*.

Day count basis

The standard a *fixed income security* market uses to calculate the *accrued interest* in a *dirty price*, such as *30/360* with *munis* and *corporates, actual/actual* with *Treasury bonds* and *Treasury notes,* and *actual/360* with *money market instruments* like *commercial paper*. Also called the *day count convention*.

Day count convention

The standard a *fixed income security* market uses to calculate the *accrued interest* in a *dirty price*, such as *30/360* with *munis* and *corporates, actual/actual* with *Treasury bonds* and *Treasury notes,* and *actual/360* with *money market instruments* like *commercial paper*. Also called the *day count basis*.

Deal flow
> The amount and character of opportunities an investor can access over time.

Dealer
> A person or company that buys and sells *securities* for its own account. Similar to, but distinct from, *market maker*.

Death spiral
> The circumstance of a company financed with *convertible fixed income securities* that lead to an excessive increase in the number of *shares outstanding*. Also used to describe such convertible securities.

Debentures
> *Fixed income securities* that are generally *unsecured* when issued in the U.S., but often *secured* when issued in the UK.

Debt
> A financial *liability*, generally *interest*-bearing. Relatedly, a synonym for *fixed income security*.

Debt-to-equity ratio
> A measure of the manageability of a company's *debt* load. Calculated as financial debt divided by *equity*. A debt-to-equity ratio maximum is a common *covenant*. Also called the *leverage ratio*.

Debtor-in-possession financing
> A *loan* to a *bankrupt* company, generally *senior* to other *debt* and with a high *interest* rate.

Default

An *issuer's* failure to pay *interest* or *principal* on its *debt*.

Default insurance

An *external credit enhancement* that calls for an insurance company to assume the obligations of a *debt* if the *issuer defaults*. Also called *bond insurance* and *financial guarantee insurance*.

Default risk

The chance that a *fixed income security* will fail to *perform*. Also called *credit risk*.

Deferred income

Advance payments received by a company for products not yet delivered to customers. An item in the *liabilities* section of the *balance sheet*.

Deflation

A decline in the general level of prices.

Delist

To remove from a *stock exchange*, as with *stock* in a company taken *private*.

Demotech

An *NRSRO* and *credit rating agency*, generally viewed as less prominent than *Fitch*, *Moody's*, and *S&P*.

Denomination

A currency, such as pounds or yen. Alternately, the minimum amount of something. Sometimes also used to mean *par value*.

Denominator
    The bottom of a fraction, under the *numerator;* like *interest expense* in the *interest coverage ratio.*

Depository Trust & Clearing Corporation
    A major American *clearing house.* Shortened to *DTCC.*

Depreciation
    Decreasing the *book value* of a tangible, *noncurrent asset* by recognizing periodic expenses on the *income statement.*

Derivative
    A *security* whose worth comes from another *asset.*

Developing outlook
    A *credit rating agency's* admission that it doesn't know whether it will notch a *credit rating* up or down in the *medium-term.* The alternative to *positive outlook, negative outlook,* and *stable outlook.*

Direct method
    A way of preparing the *cash flow from operations* section of the *cash flow statement* that begins with *inflows.* The alternative to *indirect method.*

Dirty price
    The price of a *fixed income security* including *accrued interest.* The alternative to the *clean price.*

Discount
    An amount under some standard, as with the price of a *bond* below *par value.* The opposite of *premium.*

Discount bond

A *fixed income security* issued for less than *par value*.

Discount margin

The *quoted margin* of a *floater* adjusted for price, presumably to capture a change in *credit risk* since issuance. Calculated as *yield to maturity* minus the *reference rate*. Shortened to *DM.* Also called the *required margin*.

Discount rate

The percentage used to calculate a *present value*. Separately, the *interest* rate a *central bank* charges financial institutions for *short-term* loans. Also called *bank rate* in that context.

Distress

The state of a troubled *issuer* of a *fixed income security*.

Diversification

The commitment of capital to a broad range of different *assets* or multiple *asset classes*. The opposite of *concentration*.

Dividend

A payment made by an *issuer* to its *shareholders*, generally in cash, and often quarterly or annually.

Dividend payout ratio

Dividends divided by *net income*, generally on an annual basis.

Dividend yield

Current annual *dividend* divided by current *stock* price.

Dollar duration

A measure of the sensitivity of a *fixed income security's* price to a change in *interest* rates, expressed in money. Calculated as *modified duration* times price. A 1 percent change in interest rates is predicted to change a *bond's* price in the opposite direction by dollar duration. Also called *money duration*.

Dollar value of a basis point

A measure of the sensitivity of a *fixed income security's* price to a single *basis point* change in *interest* rates, expressed in money. Calculated as *dollar duration* divided by 10,000. A one basis point change in interest rates is estimated to change a *bond's* price in the opposite direction by the dollar value of a basis point. Shortened to *DVBP*. Also called *DV01*.

Domestic bond

A *fixed income security* denominated in the currency of, and traded in, the *issuer's* home country. The alternative to an *international bond*.

Downgrade

To change from one *credit rating* to a lower one. The opposite of *upgrade*.

Downtick

A just-occurred decrease in the price of a *security*. The opposite of *uptick*.

Drawdown

A measure of historic price movement. Calculated as the decline in historic price from peak to trough during a specified period, divided by peak during that same period.

Dry powder

Cash waiting to be invested in higher-return *assets*.

Dual currency bond

A *fixed income security* involving two currencies, generally with one used for *interest* and another for *principal*.

Duration

One of several measures based on the *weighted average* time until cash *inflows* from a *fixed income security*, including *effective duration*, *Macaulay duration*, *modified duration*, and *money duration*.

Duration risk

The chance that the price of a *fixed income security* will fall because of a rise in *interest* rates. Also called *interest rate risk* or *price risk*.

EBIT

Operating income plus *non-operating income*. An *income statement* item. Short for *earnings before interest and taxes*.

EBITDA

EBIT with *depreciation* and *amortization* added back. Short for *earnings before interest, taxes, depreciation, and amortization*.

EBT

EBIT minus *interest* expense. Short for *earnings before taxes*.

ECN

A *hybrid* that converts into *equity* under certain circumstances, issued primarily by European *banks*. Short for *enhanced capital note*. Also called *AT1*, *additional tier 1*, *contingent convertible*, or *CoCo*.

ECP

Commercial paper issued in a currency other than that of the *issuer's* home country. Short for *eurocommercial paper*.

EMTN

A *fixed income security* issued outside of the U.S. and Canada, generally with a *term* of less than five years. Short for *euro medium-term notes*.

ETF

A *fund* that invests in *securities* and that trades throughout the day on a *stock exchange*. Short for *exchange-traded fund*. An alternative to a *mutual fund*.

Earnings before interest and taxes

Operating income plus *non-operating income*. An *income statement* item. Shortened to *EBIT*.

Earnings before interest, taxes, depreciation, and amortization

Earnings before interest and taxes with *depreciation* and *amortization* added back. Shortened to *EBITDA*.

Earnings before taxes

Earnings before interest and taxes minus *interest* expense. Shortened to *EBT*.

Effective duration

A version of *duration* for *bonds* with *provisions* like *calls* or *puts*.

Efficient market hypothesis

A proposition from economics that holds that the price of something equals its worth.

Egan-Jones

An *NRSRO* and *credit rating agency*, generally viewed as less prominent than *Fitch*, *Moody's*, and *S&P*.

Embedded option

A right contained in a *fixed income security*, such as a *call* or a *put*. Also called a *provision*.

Enhanced capital note

A *hybrid* that converts into *equity* under certain circumstances, issued primarily by European *banks*. Shortened to *ECN*. Also called *AT1*, *additional tier 1, contingent convertible*, or *CoCo*.

Equipment trust certificate

A *fixed income security* that is *collateralized* by tangible *noncurrent assets* such as aircraft.

Equity

A *balance sheet* section that equals *assets* minus *liabilities*. Also called *book value, net assets, owners' equity*, or *shareholders' equity*. Separately, a synonym for *shares* or *stock.*

Equity kicker
Equity or *warrants* attached to a *fixed income security* that generally result in a lower *interest* rate for the *issuer*. Shortened to *kicker*.

Euribor
The *interest* rate that European *banks* charge each other for loans. Reset daily and available for one week, one month, three month, six month, and 12 month terms. A common *index* for *debt*. Short for *Euro Interbank Offer Rate*.

Euro area
The countries of the European Union that use the euro as their currency.

Euro Interbank Offer Rate
The *interest* rate that European *banks* charge each other for loans. Reset daily and available for one week, one month, three month, six month, and 12 month terms. A common *index* for *debt*. Shortened to *Euribor*.

Euro medium-term notes
A *fixed income security* issued outside of the U.S. and Canada, generally with a *term* of less than five years. Shortened to *EMTN*.

Eurobond
A *fixed income security* issued in a currency other than that of the issuer's home country. Alternatively, a fixed income security issued by a European government.

Euroclear
A major *clearing house* in Europe.

Eurocommercial paper

Commercial paper issued in a currency other than that of the *issuer's* home country. Shortened to *ECP*.

Eurodollar bond

A *fixed income security denominated* in U.S. dollars but issued outside of the U.S.

European Central Bank

The *central bank* of the European Union.

Euroyen bond

A *fixed income security* denominated in Japanese yen but issued outside of Japan.

Excess spread

The *internal credit enhancement* of *collateralizing* a *fixed income security* with *debt assets* that generate *interest* above that paid on the security. Also used to mean the amount of that excess.

Exchange-traded fund

A *fund* that invests in *securities* and that trades throughout the day on a *stock exchange*. Shortened to *ETF*. An alternative to a *mutual fund*.

Exercise price

The amount that must be paid to convert an *option, warrant,* or other *security* into *equity*. Also called the *strike price*.

Expected return

The sum of the potential outcomes of an investment, each times the probability of that outcome. For example an investment with a 25 percent chance of returning 8 percent and a 75 percent chance of returning 4 percent has an expected return of 5 percent.

External credit enhancement

The reduction of the *credit risk* of a *fixed income security* by an *issuer* with a tool from a *guarantor* like *financial guaranty insurance*. An alternative to *internal credit enhancement*. Also used to describe the tool itself.

FHFA

A U.S. government agency that oversees parts of the *mortgage* market. Short for *Federal Housing Finance Agency*.

FHLMC

A U.S. *government-sponsored enterprise* that issues *mortgage-backed securities*. Short for *Federal Home Loan Mortgage Corporation*. Also called *Freddie Mac*. Distinct from *FNMA*.

FICC

A unit of the *Depository Trust & Clearing Corporation* that deals with *fixed income securities*. Short for *Fixed Income Clearing Corporation*.

FNMA

A U.S. *government-sponsored enterprise* that issues *mortgage-backed securities*. Short for *Federal National Mortgage Association*. Also called *Fannie Mae*. Distinct from the *FHLMC*.

FRN

A *coupon bond* with a *variable interest* rate. When issued by the U.S. Department of the Treasury, has a *term* of two years, pays interest every three months, and bases interest on the most recent *discount* on the 13-week *Treasury bill*. Short for *floating rate note*. Also called *floater* or *floating rate bond*.

Face value

The amount that the *issuer* of a *fixed income security* is meant to pay to the *holder* at *maturity*. Also called *par value* or *principal*.

Fair value

An accounting method where *assets* and *liabilities* reflect current market values as opposed to amounts paid. Also called *mark-to-market* accounting. The alternative to *historical cost* accounting.

Fallen angel

An *issuer* or a *fixed income security* with a *credit rating* *downgraded* from *investment grade* to *non-investment grade*.

Fannie Mae

A U.S. *government-sponsored enterprise* that issues *mortgage-backed securities*. Short for *Federal National Mortgage Association*. Also called *FNMA*. Distinct from *Freddie Mac*.

Federal funds rate

The *interest* rate that U.S. *banks* charge each other for overnight loans.

Federal Home Loan Mortgage Corporation
A U.S. *government-sponsored enterprise* that issues *mortgage-backed securities*. Shortened to *FHLMC* and *Freddie Mac*. Distinct from *Federal National Mortgage Association*.

Federal Housing Finance Agency
A U.S. government agency that oversees parts of the *mortgage* market. Shortened to *FHFA*.

Federal National Mortgage Association
A U.S. *government-sponsored enterprise* that issues *mortgage-backed securities*. Shortened to *FNMA* and *Fannie Mae*. Distinct from *Federal Home Loan Mortgage Corporation*.

Federal Reserve
The *central bank* of the United States. Shortened to *the Fed*.

Fiduciary
A party that is obligated to act in the best interests of another party.

Financial guaranty insurance
An *external credit enhancement* that calls for an insurance company to assume the obligations of a *debt* if the *issuer* defaults. Also called *bond insurance* and *default insurance*.

Financial instrument
A monetary contract between parties, such as a *security*. Shortened to *instrument*.

Financial statement
A quantitative description of an entity, such as an *income statement*, *cash flow statement*, or *balance sheet*.

First lien

A *senior* right to *collateral*.

First North

A lightly-regulated segment of Nasdaq Nordic, comparable to the *AIM* of the London Stock Exchange or the *Open Market* of the Frankfurt Stock Exchange. Includes *fixed income securities*.

Fitch

An *NRSRO* and one of the three leading *credit rating agencies*.

Fixed

Unchanging, as with the *coupon rate* on a *bond*. The alternative to *variable*. Also used to mean tangible and *noncurrent* in the context of *assets*, as with a building or a machine.

Fixed income

A type of *security* that promises to pay set amounts, such as a *bond*, *debenture*, or *Treasury*.

Fixed Income Clearing Corporation

A unit of the *Depository Trust & Clearing Corporation* that deals with *fixed income securities*. Shortened to *FICC*.

Flat price

The price of a *fixed income security* when it does not capture the worth of any accrued, unpaid *interest*. Also called *clean price*. The alternative to *dirty price*.

Flat yield curve

A horizontal *yield curve*, where *long-term* yields are the same as *short-term* yields. Often taken as a sign of economic uncertainty. An alternative to *humped, inverted, normal,* and *steep* yield curves.

Flight-to-quality

A market condition characterized by an increased focus on *capital preservation*, often evidenced by decreasing *yields* on *investment-grade fixed income securities*.

Floater

A *coupon bond* with a *variable interest* rate. When issued by the U.S. Department of the Treasury, has a *term* of two years, pays interest every three months, and bases interest on the most recent *discount* on the 13-week *Treasury bill*. Short for *floating rate note*. Also called *FRN* or *floating rate bond*.

Floating

A characteristic of a *fixed income security* where the *coupon rate* moves with a specified *reference rate*. Also called *variable*. The alternative to *fixed*.

Floating rate bond

A *coupon bond* with a *variable interest* rate. Shortened to *floater*. Also called *FRN* or *floating rate note*.

Floating rate note

A *coupon bond* with a *variable interest* rate. When issued by the U.S. Department of the Treasury, has a *term* of two years, pays interest every three months, and bases interest on the most recent *discount* on the 13-week *Treasury bill*. Shortened to *floater* or *FRN*. Also called a *floating rate bond*.

Floor

The minimum possible *coupon rate* of a *floater*, regardless of how low the *reference rate* drops. Can be combined with a *cap* to create a *collar*.

Floored

The characteristic of a *floater* or a *coupon* that sets a minimum amount of a coupon payment. Relatedly, the state of having a *floor*.

Focus

The commitment of capital to a limited number of *assets*. Also called *concentration*. The opposite of *diversification*.

Forbearance

An agreement by a lender to postpone the collection of *interest* or *principal* owed, or the seizing of *collateral* owned, by a borrower in *distress*.

Foreign exchange risk

The chance of an unfavorable change in the price of a currency expressed in a different currency.

Forward interest rate

The *interest* rate on a *debt* issued at some time in the future. Also called the *forward rate*. The alternative to the *spot interest rate*.

Forward rate

The *interest* rate on a *debt* issued at some time in the future. Also called the *forward interest rate*. The alternative to the *spot rate*.

Freddie Mac

A U.S. *government-sponsored enterprise* that issues *mortgage-backed securities*. Short for *Federal Home Loan Mortgage Corporation*. Also called *FHLMC*. Distinct from *Fannie Mae*.

Free cash flow

The amount of cash that a company produces by operating. Generally calculated as *cash flow from operations* minus *capital expenditures*.

Fully diluted shares

Shares outstanding plus the number of *shares* that could become outstanding upon exercise or conversion of other *securities*, such as *convertible bonds*.

Fund

A portfolio of capital from different sources meant to be invested according to some theme or strategy. Also called a *pooled investment vehicle* in that context. Separately, to finance or pay for.

Fundamental analysis

A method of evaluating *securities* that focuses on individual *issuers* and *issues* as opposed to macroeconomics or security price trends. A linchpin of *value investing*. An alternative to *technical analysis*.

Future value

The worth of an *asset* at a specified forthcoming time, such as the *principal* of a *zero* at *maturity*. The alternative to *present value*.

G-Sec

A sovereign *debt* obligation of India, comparable to a U.S. *Treasury*. Short for *Government Security*.

GAAP

The U.S. accounting standard. Short for *Generally Accepted Accounting Principles*. An alternative to *IFRS*.

GIC

The Canadian term for an *interest*-bearing deposit at a financial institution that cannot be withdrawn without penalty before a predetermined *maturity date*. Short for *guaranteed investment certificate* in that context. Separately, a *CD*-like *financial instrument* issued by an insurance company. Short for *guaranteed investment contract* in that context.

GO bond

A *muni* backed by the *issuer* generally as opposed to a specific *asset* or revenue stream. Short for *general obligation bond*. An alternative to a *revenue bond*.

GSE

A financial services *corporation* created by the U.S. government, like *Fannie Mae* and *Freddie Mac*. Short for *government-sponsored enterprise*.

Gearing

Debt, or the prominence of debt in a *capital structure*. Also called *leverage*.

General obligation bond

A *muni* backed by the *issuer* generally as opposed to a specific *asset* or revenue stream. Shortened to *GO bond*. An alternative to a *revenue bond*.

Generally Accepted Accounting Principles

The U.S. accounting standard. Shortened to *GAAP*. An alternative to *IFRS*.

Geometric mean

A type of average better suited to growth rates than *arithmetic mean*. Also called the *compound annual growth rate*.

Gilt

A sovereign *debt* obligation of the UK Government, comparable to a U.S. *Treasury*.

Going concern

An accounting term that describes a business able to meet its obligations and continue operating.

Goodwill

Acquisition price in excess of the *fair value* of the *equity* of the acquired entity. An intangible *asset* on the acquirer's *balance sheet*.

Government-sponsored enterprise

A financial services *corporation* created by the U.S. government, like *Fannie Mae* and *Freddie Mac*. Shortened to *GSE*.

Growth capital expenditures

Capital expenditures made to expand a business. Also called *growth capex*. The counterpart to *maintenance capital expenditures*.

Growth investing

An *active* strategy that emphasizes buying *assets* that are likely to increase in value over time.

Guaranteed investment certificate

The Canadian term for an *interest*-bearing deposit at a financial institution that cannot be withdrawn without penalty before a predetermined *maturity date*. Comparable to a *certificate of deposit*, *term deposit*, and *time deposit*. Shortened to *GIC*.

Guaranteed investment contract

A *CD*-like *financial instrument* issued by an insurance company. Shortened to *GIC*.

Guarantor

An entity that assumes the obligations of a *debt* if the *issuer* *defaults*. Also called a *surety*.

HR Ratings

An *NRSRO* and *credit rating agency*, generally viewed as less prominent than *Fitch*, *Moody's*, and *S&P*.

Haircut

A reduction in worth, for example of the *face value* of outstanding *bonds* in a *restructuring*.

Handle

The whole-number portion of the price of a *security*. If the *ask* on a *bond* is 101.125, the handle is 101.

Hat

A math symbol meaning *raised to the power of*. Denoted ^. Also called *caret* or *circumflex*.

Held-for-trading

An accounting term that describes a *security* that a *holder* intends to sell in the *short-term*. The alternative to *available-for-sale* and *held-to-maturity*.

Held-to-maturity

An accounting term that describes a *security* that a *holder* does not intend to sell. The alternative to *available-for-sale* and *held-for-trading*.

High-net-worth individual

An affluent person, generally with financial *assets* exceeding $1,000,000.

High water mark

The maximum market price reached by a portfolio or *fund*, commonly referenced in the compensation plans of money managers.

High-yield

The characteristic of a *fixed income security* suggesting that *interest* and *principal* may not be paid as promised. Indicated by *credit ratings* of Ba1 or lower from *Moody's* and BB+ or lower from *Fitch* and *S&P*. Also called *junk, non-investment grade*, or *speculative*. The opposite of *investment grade* in that context. Separately, the characteristic of a *bank* account that means it offers a high *interest* rate.

Historical cost

An accounting method where *assets* and *liabilities* reflect amounts paid as opposed to current market values. The alternative to *mark-to-market* accounting.

Holder

The owner of a *security*.

Holding period

The time an *asset* is owned by an investor.

Holding period return

The *total return* during a *holding period*.

Humped yield curve

An upward-bulging *yield curve*, where *medium-term yields* exceed both *long-term* and *short-term* yields. Often taken as a sign of a slow economy. An alternative to *flat, inverted, normal*, and *steep* yield curves.

Hybrid

A *security* that has both *debt* and *equity* characteristics, such as *preferred stock*.

IFRS

An accounting standard common outside of America. Short for *International Financial Reporting Standards*. An alternative to *GAAP*.

IPA

A financial institution that administers payments like *interest* and *dividends* on behalf of an *issuer*. Short for *Issuing and Paying Agent*.

IPO

The original sale of *securities* on a *public* exchange. Short for *initial public offering*.

IRR

A measure of the profitability of an investment that, unlike *CAGR*, captures *cash flows* during the *holding period*. Short for *internal rate of return*.

IRS

The U.S. federal *tax* agency. Short for *Internal Revenue Service*.

ISIN

A combination of 12 letters and numbers that represents a *listed security*. Short for International Securities Identifier Number.

Illiquid

Not readily convertible into cash, as with *bonds* issued in a *private placement* that are *held to maturity*. The opposite of *liquid*.

Immunization

One of several strategies for keeping *interest* rate changes from compromising a *fixed income security* portfolio's ability to serve its purpose, such as *cash flow matching*.

Imputed interest

The *interest*-like amount assumed for tax purposes to be made on a *zero* bought at a *discount*.

In arrears

After becoming due, as with *interest* payments from a *fixed income security*.

In the money

The state of an *option* with positive *intrinsic value*. The opposite of *out of the money*.

Income

Cash paid periodically by a *security*, like *interest* on a *coupon bond* or *dividends* on a *preferred stock*. Separately, an *income statement* item of which there are several variants, generally equal to *revenue* minus some measure of expenses. Also called *earnings* in that context.

Income statement

An *accrual basis financial statement* that describes a business over a period of time. Also called a *consolidated statement of operations*, a *profit and loss statement*, or a *P&L*.

Increment

A minimum amount. Like *integral multiple*, often used to mean *face value* or *par value*.

Indenture
> The contract between the *issuer* and the *holder* of a *fixed income security*.

Index
> A benchmark or standard, such as *SOFR* for the *coupon rate* on a *debt*.

Index-linked gilt
> A sovereign *debt* obligation of the UK government with a *floating semiannual coupon* and floating *principal*. An alternative to a *conventional gilt*.

Indexed bond
> A *fixed income security* whose payments vary with some *index*, such as the rate of *inflation*.

Indirect method
> A way of preparing the *cash flow from operations* section of the *cash flow statement* that begins with *net income*. The alternative to *direct method*.

Inflation
> A rise in the general level of prices.

Inflow
> Cash entering an entity. The counterpart to *outflow*.

Initial public offering
> The original sale of *securities* on a *public* exchange. Shortened to *IPO*.

Insolvent

Unable to meet financial obligations, most basically because *liabilities* exceed *assets*. The opposite of *solvent*. Distinct from *bankrupt*.

Instrument

A monetary contract between parties, such as a *security*. Short for *financial instrument*.

Integral multiple

A minimum amount. Like *increment*, often used to mean *face value* or *par value*.

Interest

An amount periodically received by a holder of a *fixed income security*, or paid by a borrower on a *debt*. Separately, an ownership stake in an entity, particularly a *fund* or a *partnership*. Sometimes called *unit* in that context.

Interest coverage ratio

A measure of an *issuer's* ability to *service* its *debt*. Generally equal to *earnings before interest and taxes* divided by *interest* expense. An interest coverage ratio minimum is a common *covenant*.

Interest rate risk

The chance that the price of a *fixed income security* will fall because of a rise in *interest* rates. Also called *duration risk* or *price risk*.

Interest rate swap

An exchange of future streams of *interest* payments between parties.

Intermarket spread swap

An exchange of different *bonds* between parties, generally
motivated by the perception that a *yield spread* is too big or too
small.

Internal credit enhancement

The reduction of the *credit risk* of a *fixed income security* by an
issuer with a tool like *seniority, overcollateralization*, or
excess spread. An alternative to *external credit enhancement*.
Also used to describe the tool itself.

Internal rate of return

A measure of the profitability of an investment that, unlike the
compound annual growth rate, captures *cash flows* during the
holding period. Shortened to *IRR*.

Internal Revenue Service

The U.S. federal *tax* agency. Shortened to *IRS*.

International bond

A *fixed income security* not denominated in the currency of, or
not traded in, the *issuer's* home country. The alternative to a
domestic bond.

International Financial Reporting Standards

An accounting standard common outside of America.
Shortened to *IFRS*. An alternative to *GAAP*.

Intrinsic value

The market price of the *underlier* minus the *strike price* of an
option, when positive. The counterpart to *time value* in that
context. Separately, worth as determined by *fundamental
analysis* as opposed to market price.

Inventory

A *current asset* poised to become a *cost of goods sold*. Also called *stock-in-trade*. Subtracted from *current assets* in the calculation of the numerator of the *quick ratio*.

Inverted yield curve

A downward-sloping *yield curve*, where *short-term* yields exceed *long-term* yields. Often taken as a sign of an unhealthy economy. An alternative to *flat*, *humped*, *normal*, and *steep* yield curves.

Investment grade

The characteristic of a *fixed income security* suggesting that *interest* and *principal* are expected to be paid as promised. Indicated by credit ratings of Baa3 or higher from *Moody's* and BBB- or higher from *Fitch* and *S&P*. The opposite of *non-investment grade*.

Investor relations

The department of an *issuer*, usually *listed*, that fields questions from investors.

Issue date

The first date a *security* could be bought. Distinct from the *dated date*.

Issuer

An entity that offers for sale its own *securities*.

Issuing and Paying Agent

A financial institution that administers payments like *interest* and *dividends* on behalf of an *issuer*. Shortened to *IPA*.

JGB

> A sovereign *debt* obligation of Japan, comparable to a U.S. *Treasury*. Short for *Japanese Government Bond*.

Japan Credit Rating Agency

> An *NRSRO* and *credit rating agency*, generally viewed as less prominent than *Fitch*, *Moody's*, and *S&P*.

Junior

> The characteristic of a *fixed income security* that has it *perform* only after *senior* fixed income securities from the same *issuer* do. Also called *subordinated*.

Junk

> The characteristic of a *fixed income security* suggesting that *interest* and *principal* may not be paid as promised. Indicated by *credit ratings* of *Ba1* or lower from *Moody's* and BB+ or lower from *Fitch* and *S&P*. Also called *high-yield*, *non-investment grade*, or *speculative*. The opposite of *investment grade*.

KBRA

> An *NRSRO* and *credit rating agency*, generally viewed as less prominent than *Fitch*, *Moody's*, and *S&P*.

Kicker

> *Equity* or *warrants* attached to a *fixed income security* that generally result in a lower *interest* rate for the *issuer*. Short for *equity kicker*.

LEI

A 20-character code that identifies a *corporation*, government, or other entity in a financial transaction. Short for *legal entity identifier*.

LIBOR

The *interest* rate that big international *banks* charged each other for *short-term* loans. An old *index* for *debt*. Short for *London Interbank Offered Rate*. Replaced by *SOFR*.

Ladder

A portfolio of *fixed income securities* that *mature* on different dates, creating periodic *liquidity* and reducing *interest rate risk*. Short for *bond ladder*.

Law of large numbers

A principle from probability that says that the more times an experiment is run, the closer the average result will be to the expected result.

Lead

The head lender in a *syndicate*.

Legal entity identifier

A 20-character code that identifies a *corporation*, government, or other entity in a financial transaction. Shortened to *LEI*.

Leverage

Debt, or the prominence of debt in a *capital structure*. Also called *gearing*.

Leverage ratio

A measure of the manageability of a company's *debt* load.
Calculated as financial debt divided by *equity*. A leverage ratio
maximum is a common *covenant*. Also called the *debt-to-
equity ratio*.

Leveraged loan

Debt assumed by high *credit risk* borrowers, generally *secured*
and with a *floating* rate of *interest*.

Levered free cash flow

A measure of *free cash flow* that captures *interest* payments.

Liabilities

Obligations, calculated as *assets* minus *equity*. A *balance sheet*
section.

Liabilities-to-equity ratio

A measure of the manageability of a company's obligations.
Generally calculated as total *liabilities* divided by *equity*. A
liabilities-to-equity ratio maximum is a common *covenant*.

Lien

The right that a lender has to *collateral*.

Limit order

An investor's instruction to a *broker* to buy a *security* at or
below a specified price, or to sell a security at or above a
specified price. An alternative to a *market order*.

Line of credit

A standing opportunity to repeatedly borrow and repay money up to some limit, often tapped by businesses as an alternative to issuing *fixed income securities*.

Liquid

Readily convertible into cash without penalty. The opposite of *illiquid*.

Liquidation

The process of a business converting *assets* into cash in anticipation of ceasing operations.

Liquidation accounting

A financial presentation standard used for entities in *liquidation* characterized by *mark-to-market* accounting. Also called *liquidation basis of accounting*.

Liquidation basis of accounting

A financial presentation standard used for entities in *liquidation*, characterized by *mark-to-market* accounting. Also called *liquidation accounting*.

Liquidation value

The amount paid to holders of *preferred stock* in a company undergoing *liquidation* before *common stock* holders get anything.

Liquidity

The degree to which an *asset* is convertible into cash without penalty.

Liquidity premium
>The additional amount in the price of a *security* that's *liquid* relative to a similar security that isn't.

Liquidity ratio
>One of several measures of a company's ability to meet its *short-term* obligations, including the *current ratio* and *quick ratio*.

Listed
>Traded on an exchange, as with an *ETF*. Also called *public*.

Loan to own
>Lending to an entity with the aim of converting *debt* into *equity*, generally to take control of a *distressed* business.

London Interbank Offered Rate
>The *interest* rate that big international *banks* charged each other for *short-term* loans. An old *index* for *debt*. Shortened to *LIBOR*. Replaced by the *Secured Overnight Financing Rate*.

Long
>The state of owning outright, as with *bonds*. The opposite of *short*.

Long bond
>The 30-year *Treasury bond*.

Long squeeze
>An accelerated decrease in the price of a *listed security* caused by excess selling while the price is falling. The opposite of a *short squeeze*.

Long-term

An extended period, generally more than a year; as in time to *maturity*. Distinct from *short-term*.

Long-term assets

Assets that take more than a year to use. Also called *noncurrent assets*.

Lot

A quantity of something, often used to define the minimum amount of a *security* that can be traded.

MBS

A *fixed income security* that is *collateralized* by *mortgages*. Conveys more *credit risk* to *holders* than do *covered bonds*. Short for *mortgage-backed security*.

Macaulay Duration

The *weighted average* time until cash *inflows* from a *fixed income security*, including repayment of *principal*, measured in years. Shortened to *duration*, as are—confusingly—*effective duration*, *modified duration*, and *money duration*.

Maintenance capital expenditures

Capital expenditures made to replace *assets* wearing out. Shortened to *maintenance capex*. The counterpart to *growth capital expenditures*.

Make Whole Call Provision

A *redemption provision* that gives an *issuer* the right to *redeem* a *fixed income security* at the greater of *par value* or the *present value* of the *bond's* remaining payments.

Management information circular
A Canadian filing similar to an American *proxy statement*.

Management's discussion and analysis
A Canadian filing similar to an American *10-K* or *10-Q*. Relatedly, a common section in a 10-K or 10-Q.

Mandatory convertible
A *fixed income security* that automatically becomes *equity*, generally *common stock*.

Margin
A loan made by a *brokerage, collateralized* by the borrower's own capital at the brokerage. Also used to mean the amount of that collateral or the account in which it sits. Separately, a ratio or amount, as in *quoted margin*.

Margin of safety
The outsized *discount* to worth that *value investors* demand before buying an *asset*. First appeared with this meaning in the 1934 book *Security Analysis*.

Mark-to-market
An accounting method where *assets* and *liabilities* reflect current market values as opposed to amounts paid. Also called *fair value* accounting. The alternative to *historical cost* accounting.

Market cap
The theoretical price for all of the *equity* of a *public* company, calculated as *shares outstanding* times the current *share* price. Short for *market capitalization*.

Market capitalization

The theoretical price for all of the *equity* of a *public* company, calculated as *shares outstanding* times the current share price. Shortened to *market cap*.

Market maker

A person or company that buys and sells *securities* for its own account to provide *liquidity* to clients. Similar to, but distinct from, *dealer*.

Market order

An investor's instruction to a *broker* to buy or sell a *security* at the best available price. An alternative to a *limit order*.

Marketable

The characteristic of a *security* meaning that it can be readily bought and sold on a *public* exchange.

Material

Sufficiently significant, as in the cost of a *noncurrent asset* fit to be *depreciated* or *amortized* instead of expensed all at once at purchase.

Maturity

The time when the *principal* of a *fixed income security* is meant to be repaid. Short for *maturity date*.

Maturity date

The time when the *principal* of a *fixed income security* is meant to be repaid. Shortened to *maturity*.

Maximum drawdown

A measure of the historic price movement of an *asset*. Calculated as the greatest decline in historic price from the peak to the trough during a period, divided by the peak during that period.

Mean reversion

The view that an *asset's* price tends to equal its *long-term* average price.

Medium-term

A period of intermediate length, often between one and five years; as with time to *maturity*. Distinct from *short-term*. Overlaps somewhat with *long-term*. In the context of *credit rating outlooks*, between six months and two years.

Mezzanine

A type of hybrid financing. Relatedly, a type of *fund* focused on such financings.

Modified duration

A measure of the sensitivity of a *fixed income security's* price to a change in *interest* rates. A 1 percent change in interest rates is predicted to cause a bond's price to change in the opposite direction by its modified duration. Shortened to *duration*, as are—confusingly—*effective duration*, *Macaulay duration* and *money duration*.

Momentum investing

An *active* strategy that emphasizes buying *securities* that have recently increased in price, based on the view that they'll continue to increase in price.

Money duration

A measure of the sensitivity of a *fixed income security's* price to a change in *interest* rates, expressed in money. Calculated as *modified duration* times price. A 1 percent change in interest rates is predicted to change a *bond's* price in the opposite direction by its money duration. Also called *dollar duration*, particularly when the security's currency is the U.S. dollar. Shortened to *duration*, as are—confusingly—*effective duration*, *Macaulay duration* and *modified duration*.

Money market

The segment of the *fixed income securities* market consisting of *marketable, short-term,* low *credit risk* securities like *Treasury bills, certificates of deposit*, and *commercial paper*. Distinct from the *capital market*.

Money market fund

A *mutual fund* that invests in *marketable, short-term,* low *credit risk* securities like *Treasury bills, certificates of deposit*, and *commercial paper*.

Moody's

An *NRSRO* and one of the three leading *credit rating agencies*.

Mortgage

A loan *secured* by real estate.

Mortgage-backed security

A *fixed income security* that is *collateralized* by *mortgages*. Conveys more *credit risk* to *holders* than do *covered bonds*. Shortened to *MBS*.

Muni

A *fixed income security* issued by a local government, often with *interest* exempt from some *taxes*. Short for *municipal bond*.

Municipal bond

A *fixed income security* issued by a local government, often with *interest* exempt from some *taxes*. Shortened to *muni*.

Mutual fund

A *fund* that trades once a day at its *net asset value* on a *stock exchange*, and is generally *actively* managed. An alternative to an *ETF*.

NAV

The *assets* minus *liabilities* of a *fund*, generally expressed on a per-*share* basis. Short for *net asset value*.

NRSRO

An entity recognized by the *SEC* to score the creditworthiness of *issuers* and *fixed income securities*. Short for *Nationally Recognized Statistical Rating Organization*.

Naked shorting

Selling *securities short* without having borrowed them. Often prohibited.

Nationally Recognized Statistical Rating Organization

An entity recognized by the *SEC* to score the creditworthiness of *issuers* and *fixed income securities*. Shortened to *NRSRO*.

Negative convexity
The characteristic of a *bond* with *duration* that increases as *interest* rates increase. The opposite of *positive convexity*.

Negative covenant
A clause in an *indenture* that prohibits the *issuer* from doing something, like selling *assets* or paying *dividends*. Also called a *restrictive covenant*. The counterpart to an *affirmative covenant*.

Negative outlook
An assessment by a *credit rating agency* that may notch a *credit rating* down in the *medium term*. The alternative to *positive outlook*, *stable outlook*, and *developing outlook*.

Negative pledge
A *covenant* that restricts an *issuer* from using its *assets* as *collateral* for another *debt*.

Negotiable instrument
Cash, or a cash-like *financial instrument* such as a *promissory note*.

Net asset value
The *assets* minus *liabilities* of a *fund*, generally expressed on a per-*share* basis. Shortened to *NAV*.

Net assets
Assets minus *liabilities*. Also called *book value*, *equity*, *owners' equity*, or *shareholders' equity*.

Net debt

> Total *debt* minus cash. A net debt maximum is a common *covenant*.

Net income

> The bottommost measure of *income* on the *income statement*. Calculated as *revenue* minus all expenses, including *interest* and *tax*. Also called *profit* or *net profit*.

Net profit

> The bottommost measure of *income* on the *income statement*. Calculated as *revenue* minus all expenses, including *interest* and *tax*. Also called *net income* or *profit*.

Nominal

> Not adjusted for price, *tax*, or *inflation*. In the context of inflation, the opposite of *real*.

Nominal yield

> *Interest* paid on a *fixed income security*, expressed as an annual percentage of *par value*. Also called *coupon rate*. Distinct from *current yield*.

Non-current liabilities

> Obligations meant to be settled in more than one year. A *balance sheet* subsection.

Non-investment grade

> The characteristic of a *fixed income security* suggesting that *interest* and *principal* may not be paid as promised. Indicated by *credit ratings* of *Ba1* or lower from *Moody's* and BB+ or lower from *Fitch* and *S&P*. Also called *high-yield*, *junk*, or *speculative*. The opposite of *investment grade*.

Non-operating income

Earnings from peripheral activities. An *income statement* item.

Non-performing

The characteristic of a *fixed income security* that means it has failed to pay *interest* or *principal*. The opposite of *performing*.

Nonconforming

The characteristic of a *mortgage* meaning that it doesn't meet *Federal Housing Finance Agency* guidelines.

Noncumulative

The characteristic of a *preferred stock* meaning that any unpaid *dividends* are not owed to the *holder*. The alternative to *cumulative*.

Noncurrent assets

Assets that take more than a year to use. A *balance sheet* subsection. Also called *long-term assets*.

Nonperpetual

The characteristic of a *preferred stock* that means it pays *dividends* for a limited time. The alternative to *perpetual*.

Nonrecourse

The characteristic of a *secured debt* that lets the lender seize only *collateral* in the event of *default*. The alternative to *recourse*.

Nordic ABM

A lightly-regulated segment of the Oslo Stock Exchange that includes *fixed income securities*.

Normal yield curve

An upward-sloping *yield curve*, where *long-term* yields exceed *short-term* yields. Often taken as a sign of a healthy economy. An alternative to *flat*, *humped*, *inverted*, and *steep* yield curves.

Notching

The practice by *credit rating agencies* of assigning a *credit rating* to a *fixed income security* that differs from that of the *issuer* or other fixed income securities from that issuer.

Note

A *fixed income security* that generally has a shorter *term* than a *bond*. Relatedly, a *Treasury* with a term of between two and 10 years. Separately, an explanation of part of a *financial statement*.

Numerator

The top of a fraction, above the *denominator*; like *debt* in the *debt-to-equity ratio*.

OAT

A sovereign *debt* obligation of France, comparable to a U.S. *Treasury*. Short for *Obligation assimilable du Trésor*.

OTC

Not listed on an organized *securities* exchange. Short for *over-the-counter*.

OTR

The characteristic of a *Treasury* meaning that it's the most recently issued one of a particular *maturity*. Short for *on-the-run*. Distinct from *off-the-run*.

Obligee

A party that is owed something, as the *holder* of a *zero-coupon bond* is owed *par value*. The counterpart to *obligor*.

Obligor

A party that owes something, as the *issuer* of *zero-coupon bond* owes *par value*. The counterpart to *obligee*.

Odd lot

A nonstandard quantity of a *security* for trades on an exchange. The opposite of *round lot*.

Off-the-run

The characteristic of a *Treasury* meaning that it's not the most recently issued one of a particular *maturity*. Distinct from *on-the-run*.

Offer

The price presented to a potential buyer of a *security*. Also called *ask*. The counterpart to *bid*.

Offering memorandum

An information document provided to potential investors in a *private placement*. The alternative to a *prospectus*.

On-the-run

The characteristic of a *Treasury* meaning that it's the most recently issued one of a particular *maturity*. Shortened to *OTR*. Distinct from *off-the-run*.

Open Market
> A lightly-regulated segment of the Frankfurt Stock Exchange, comparable to the *AIM* of the London Stock Exchange or *First North* of Nasdaq Nordic. Includes *fixed income securities*.

Operating earnings
> *Revenue* minus *cost of goods sold* and *operating expenses*. Also called *operating income* and *operating profit*. An *income statement* item.

Operating expenses
> Expenses recognized by a business regardless of what was sold during a period. An *income statement* item. Also called *selling, general and administrative expenses*, or *SG&A*.

Operating income
> *Revenue* minus *cost of goods sold* and *operating expenses*. Also called *operating earnings* and *operating profit*. An *income statement* item.

Operating profit
> *Revenue* minus *cost of goods sold* and *operating expenses*. Also called *operating earnings* and *operating income*. An *income statement* item.

Option
> A *derivative* that conveys a right to buy or sell an *asset* on predetermined terms.

Ordinary dividends

Payments made by an *issuer* to its *shareholders* that do not qualify for relatively low U.S. federal *long-term capital gains tax* rates. *Preferred stock dividends* can be ordinary dividends, but are often *qualified dividends*.

Ordinary shares

An ownership *interest* in a *corporation*, *subordinate* to *preferred stock*. Also called *common stock*.

Out of the money

The state of an *option* with a *strike price* above the market price of the *underlier*. The opposite of *in the money*.

Outflow

Cash leaving an entity. The counterpart to *inflow*.

Outlook

A *credit rating agency's* characterization of the *medium-term* future of a *credit rating* as *positive*, *negative*, *stable*, or *developing*. Short for *rating outlook*.

Over-the-counter

Not listed on an organized *securities* exchange. Shortened to *OTC*.

Overcollateralization

The *internal credit enhancement* of *securing* a *debt* with *assets* worth more than the amount of the debt.

Overnight repo

A *repurchase agreement* with a *term* of one day.

Owners' equity
Assets minus *liabilities*. Also called *book value, equity, net assets,* or *shareholders' equity*.

PERCS
Mandatory convertibles issued as *preferred stock* that automatically become a different *asset* later, usually *common stock*. Short for *preferred equity redemption cumulative stock*.

Paper
Debt issued by established *corporations* that is generally *unsecured* and has a *term* of less than nine months. Short for *commercial paper*. Also called *CP*.

Par value
The *nominal* value of a *security*. With *fixed income securities*, the amount meant to be paid by the *issuer* to the *holder* at *maturity*. Also called *face value* or *principal* in that context. With *common stocks*, a minimum value that is often stated for regulatory reasons and is unrelated to market price. With *preferred stock*, a minimum value on which *dividends, calls*, and *liquidation values* are generally based.

Parent
A business that owns a *subsidiary*.

Pari passu
Ranking the same, as with different *fixed income securities* from the same *issuer* that have equal *seniority*.

Parity
The state of being neither *subordinated* nor *unsubordinated*, as with two *bonds* of equal *seniority*.

Partners' capital

A section of the *balance sheet* of a *partnership* that equals *assets* minus *liabilities*. Similar to *equity* on the balance sheet of a *corporation*.

Partnership

A type of business entity, where ownership is represented by *units* or *interests*. Can be either *public* or *private*. An alternative to *corporation*.

Passive

The characteristic of a *fund* that means it's based on an *index* like the *Agg*. The opposite of *active*.

Payee

An entity paid, or meant to be paid.

Performing

The characteristic of a *fixed income security* that means it's paying *interest* and *principal* as scheduled. The opposite of *non-performing*.

Perpetual

The characteristic of a *fixed income security* that means it makes payments forever, such as a *preferred stock* that pays *dividends* indefinitely. The alternative to *nonperpetual*.

Pfandbrief

A *fixed income security* that is *collateralized*, usually by *mortgages*. Conveys less *credit risk* to *holders* than do *mortgage-backed securities*. Common in Europe. Also called a *covered bond*.

Plain vanilla bond

A *fixed income security* that's meant to pay *principal* back all at once at *maturity*, without provisions like *callability* or *convertibility*. Also called a *bullet bond* or a *straight bond*. An alternative to an *amortizing bond* or a *sinkable bond*.

Pooled investment vehicle

A portfolio of capital from different sources meant to be invested according to some theme or strategy. Also called a *fund*.

Positive convexity

The characteristic of a *bond* with *duration* that increases as *interest* rates decrease. The opposite of *negative convexity*.

Positive covenant

A clause in an *indenture* that requires the *issuer* to do something, like publish *audited financial statements* or keep the *debt-to-equity ratio* below a specified maximum. Also called an *affirmative covenant*. The counterpart to a *negative covenant*.

Positive outlook

An assessment by a *credit rating agency* that may notch a *credit rating* up in the *medium-term*. The alternative to *negative outlook*, *stable outlook*, and *developing outlook*.

Preference shares

A *hybrid* that is *senior* to *common stock* and *junior* to *debt*, and that generally pays a stable *dividend*. Also called *preferred equity*, *preferred stock*, or simply *preferred*.

Preferred
> A *hybrid* that is *senior* to *common stock* and *junior* to *debt,* and that generally pays a stable *dividend.* Also called *preference shares*, *preferred equity*, or *preferred stock.*

Preferred dividend coverage ratio
> A measure of an *issuer's* ability to *service* its *fixed income securities.* Equal to *net income* divided by the *preferred dividend.*

Preferred equity
> A *hybrid* that is *senior* to *common stock* and *junior* to *debt,* and that generally pays a stable *dividend.* Also called *preference shares*, *preferred stock*, or simply *preferred.*

Preferred equity redemption cumulative stock
> *Mandatory convertibles* issued as *preferred stock* that automatically become a different *asset* later, usually *common stock.* Shortened to *PERCS.*

Preferred stock
> A *hybrid* that is *senior* to *common stock* and *junior* to *debt,* and that generally pays a stable *dividend.* Also called *preference shares*, *preferred equity*, or simply *preferred.*

Premium
> An amount over some standard, as with the price of a *bond* in excess of *par value.* The opposite of *discount.*

Present value
> A stream of future *cash flows* discounted back at some rate such that they can be expressed as a single amount in current terms. The alternative to *future value.*

Price risk

>The chance that the price of a *fixed income security* will fall because of a rise in *interest* rates. Also called *duration risk* or *interest rate risk*.

Primary dealer

>A financial institution that buys *securities* directly from a government with the aim of reselling them.

Primary market

>Where a *security* is first issued, before it can trade on the *secondary market*. A conception, as opposed to an actual place like the London Stock Exchange.

Prime rate

>The *interest* rate that *banks* charge their most creditworthy borrowers. A common *index* for *debt*.

Principal

>The amount that the *issuer* of a *fixed income security* is meant to pay to the *holder* at *maturity*. Also called *face value* or *par value* in that context. Relatedly, a total amount borrowed or invested. Separately, a borrower.

Private

>Not *listed* on an exchange, as with many *fixed income securities*. Short for *privately held* in that context. Separately, not related to a government. The alternative to *public* in both contexts.

Private placement

The *primary market* sale of *unlisted securities*, as with *high-net-worth individuals* buying *commercial paper*. The alternative to a *public offering*.

Privately held

The characteristic of a company indicating that its *stock* is not traded on an exchange. Shortened to *private*.

Profit

The bottommost measure of *income* on the *income statement*. Calculated as *revenue* minus all expenses, including *interest* and *tax*. Also called *net income* or *net profit*. More generally, to make money.

Promissory note

A written *negotiable instrument* that obligates one party to pay another party on set terms.

Proprietary capital

A section on the *balance sheet* of an *agency* that equals *assets* minus *liabilities*. Similar to *equity* on the balance sheet of a *corporation*.

Prospectus

An information document provided to potential investors in a *public offering*. The alternative to an *offering memorandum*.

Provision

A right contained in a *fixed income security*, such as a *call* or a *put*. Also called an *embedded option*.

Proxy statement

An annual filing with the *SEC* made by American companies that includes information on ownership. Also called a *DEF 14A*.

Public

Of or related to government. Separately, traded on an exchange, as with an *ETF*. Also called *listed* in that context. The alternative to *private* in both contexts.

Public offering

The broad sale of *securities*, as in an *IPO*. The alternative to a *private placement*.

Public sector covered bonds

Covered bonds with a *cover pool* of *public* sector loans. Common in Europe.

Purchase of property, plant, and equipment

The purchase of *assets* of *material* cost that will last for more than one year. An item in the *cash flow from investments* section of the *cash flow statement*. Also called *capital expenditure* or *capex*.

Pure discount bond

A *fixed income security* that pays no interest. Also called a *ZCB*, *zero*, or *zero-coupon bond*.

Pure yield pickup swap

The sale of lower *yield*, shorter *tenor bonds*; and concurrent purchase of higher yield, longer tenor bonds.

Put

> An *option* that gives the *holder* the right to sell an *asset* on predetermined terms.

Put date

> A date on which a *security* can be *put*.

Put price

> The predetermined price at which a *security* can be sold back to its *issuer*, as with a *putable bond*.

Putable

> The characteristic of a *fixed income security* that gives the *holder* the right to sell the obligation back to the *issuer* prior to *maturity*. The opposite of *callable*.

QM

> The *spread* over a *reference rate* that determines the *coupon rate* of a *floater*. Short for *quoted margin*.

Qualified dividends

> Payments made by an *issuer* to its *shareholders* that are subject to the relatively low U.S. federal *long-term capital gains tax* rate. *Preferred stock dividends* are often qualified dividends. Distinct from *ordinary dividends*.

Quick ratio

> The quantity *current assets* minus *inventory*, divided by *current liabilities*. A higher quick ratio means an *issuer* is better able to meet its *short-term* obligations. A *liquidity ratio* that's stricter than the *current ratio*. Also called the *acid-test ratio*.

Quoted margin

The *spread* over a *reference rate* that determines the *coupon rate* of a *floater*. Shortened to *QM*.

Rate anticipation swap

The sale of some bonds and the purchase of other bonds in order to change a portfolio's *duration*, with the aim of profiting from an expected change in *interest* rates.

Rating outlook

A *credit rating agency's* characterization of the *medium-term* future of a *credit rating* as *positive*, *negative*, *stable*, or *developing*. Shortened to *outlook*.

Real

Adjusted for *inflation*. The opposite of *nominal*. Separately, the currency of Brazil.

Realized

Actualized through a sale or an investment return. The opposite of *unrealized*.

Rebalancing

Maintaining target allocations among *assets* or *asset classes* in a portfolio through periodic buying and selling.

Receivables

Money expected from customers. An item in the *assets* section of the *balance sheet*. Also called *accounts receivable* or *trade receivables*.

Recourse

The characteristic of a *secured debt* that lets the lender seize more than just *collateral* in the event of *default*. The alternative to *nonrecourse*.

Recovery rating

An assessment by a *credit rating agency* of the chance *holders* will get back their investment in a *fixed income security* in the event of *default*.

Redeemable

The characteristic of a *fixed income security* that gives the *issuer* the right to *retire* the obligation prior to *maturity* by paying the *holder*. Also called *callable*. The opposite of *putable*.

Redemption provision

A *call* option embedded in a *fixed income security*.

Reference rate

The *interest* rate of an *index* used as the basis of other interest rates, as with *SOFR* plus a *quoted margin* equaling a *coupon rate*.

Refinance

To replace an old *debt* with a new debt.

Registered

Cataloged with an authority, as with *listed securities*. The opposite of *unregistered*.

Registered bond

A *fixed income security* that conveys ownership rights to its cataloged owner. An alternative to a *bearer bond*.

Registered share

Stock that conveys ownership rights to its cataloged owner. An alternative to a *bearer share*.

Reinvestment risk

The chance that an investor won't be able to redeploy *coupon* payments, or proceeds from a *redeemed fixed income security*, at attractive rates of return.

Relative

A basis for assessing investment returns by *benchmarking* to an *index*. An alternative to *absolute*.

Reopening

The *primary market* sale of more of a *bond* already issued. Also called a *tap issue*.

Reorganization

An *issuer's* merger, recapitalization, or other transformative event. Also called a *reorg*.

Repo

A *short-term debt* in the form of the sale and subsequent *buyback* of *securities*. Short for *repurchase agreement*.

Repurchase

The buying by an *issuer* of its own *securities* for cash. Also called a *buyback*.

Repurchase agreement

A *short-term debt* in the form of the sale and subsequent *buyback* of *securities*. Shortened to *repo*.

Required margin

The *quoted margin* of a *floater* adjusted for price, presumably to capture a change in *credit risk* since issuance. Calculated as *yield to maturity* minus the *reference rate*. Also called the *discount margin*.

Reset

To change a number, like the *coupon rate* of a *floating rate note*.

Restrictive covenant

A clause in an *indenture* that prohibits the *issuer* from doing something, like selling *assets* or paying *dividends*. Also called a *negative covenant*. The counterpart to an *affirmative covenant*.

Restructuring

Changing the obligations of an *issuer* in *distress*, like delaying the *maturity dates* of the issuer's *bonds*.

Retained earnings

Net income not paid out as *dividends*. An item in the *equity* section of the *balance sheet*.

Retire

To end the existence of a *security* after buying it back, as with a *redeemed bond* or a *repurchased preferred*. Also called *cancel*.

Return of capital
    Money received that is characterized as an original investment
    coming back, and as such is generally not *taxed*.

Revaluation
    A change in the *book value* of an *asset* made to reflect market
    prices.

Revenue
    The sum of sales during a period reported on an *income
    statement*. Also called *turnover*.

Revenue bond
    A *muni* backed by a specific revenue stream instead of by the
    issuer generally. An alternative to a *general obligation bond*.

Risk
    The chance of a bad outcome. Conventionally quantified by
    variance, *volatility*, *beta*, or *premium*.

Risk-free rate
    The theoretical rate of return available to an investor without
    taking on any *credit risk*.

Risk off
    A market condition characterized by a preference for *securities*
    with lower historic returns and lower historic *volatility*.

Risk on
    A market condition characterized by a preference for *securities*
    with higher historic returns and higher historic *volatility*.

Risk premium

A return in excess of the *risk-free rate*, like the *YTM* of a *corporate* minus the YTM of a *Treasury* with the same *tenor*.

Risk-return tradeoff

The notion that higher potential returns are achieved by accepting greater *risk*.

Roll down

The practice of selling *bonds* before *maturity* to profit from an increase in price that happens as *tenors* shorten.

Rollover

Investing funds released by the *maturity* of one *asset* into another, similar asset.

Round lot

A standard quantity of a *security* for trades on an exchange. The opposite of *odd lot*.

Rung

An investment in *bonds* of one *maturity date* that, along with investments in bonds of other maturity dates, makes up a *bond ladder*.

Running yield

Annualized payments received from a *security* divided by the current price of that security. Also called *current yield*. Distinct from *nominal yield*.

S&P

An *NRSRO* and one of the three leading *credit rating agencies*. Short for *Standard and Poor's*.

SEC

The American federal agency that regulates *stock* and *bond* trading. Short for *U.S. Securities and Exchange Commission.*

SEDOL

A seven-character alphanumeric code that represents a *listed security* in the UK. Short for *Stock Exchange Daily Official List*. Comparable to *CUSIP* in the U.S. and Canada.

SG&A

Expenses recognized by a business regardless of what was sold during a period. Short for *selling, general and administrative expenses*. Also called *operating expenses*.

SOFR

The *interest* rate that *banks* charge each other for overnight loans. A new *index* for *debt*. Short for *Secured Overnight Financing Rate*. Replaced *LIBOR*.

STEP

Fixed income securities issued in Europe with a *term* of up to one year that meet certain standards. Relatedly, an EU initiative to encourage the issuance of such securities. Short for *Short-Term European Paper*.

STIBOR

The *interest* rate that *banks* in Sweden charge each other for *short-term* loans. An *index* for *debt*. Short for *Stockholm Interbank Offered Rate*.

STRIPS

Stripped bonds made from *Treasurys*. Short for *Separate Trading of Registered Interest and Principal Securities*. Also called *Treasury STRIPS*.

Sampling

A *passive fund* management tactic of including only some components of an *index* without causing too much *tracking error*. Practical for *fixed income funds* based on indexes composed of thousands of securities, such as the *Agg*.

Screen

To search for *securities* meeting certain parameters, like *issue date* or *yield to call*.

Secondary market

Where a *security* trades for the second and subsequent times, after issuance on the *primary market*. A conception, as opposed to an actual place like the London Stock Exchange.

Secondary offering

A *public* offering of *securities* that have already had an *IPO*.

Secured

The characteristic of *debt* that means it's backed by specific *assets*, as with *Pfandbriefe*. The alternative to *unsecured*.

Secured Overnight Financing Rate

The *interest* rate that *banks* charge each other for overnight loans. A new *index* for *debt*. Shortened to *SOFR*. Replaced the *London Interbank Offered Rate*.

Securities and Exchange Commission

> The American federal agency that regulates *stock* and *bond* trading. Short for *U.S. Securities and Exchange Commission*. Shortened to *SEC*.

Securities lender

> The owner of a *security* used in a *short sale*.

Securitization

> The creation of a new *security* backed by a pool of *debt assets*, as with a *collateralized debt obligation* or other *asset-backed security*.

Security

> A tradable *financial instrument* like a *bond* or *preferred stock*. Separately, the degree to which a *debt* is *collateralized*.

Security selection

> The apportioning of capital among individual *securities* within an *asset class*. Happens after *asset allocation*. Part of an *active* strategy, but not part of a *passive* strategy.

Sell-side

> *Issuers*, as a broad group. The counterpart to *buy-side*.

Selling, general and administrative expenses

> Expenses recognized by a business regardless of what was sold during a period. An *income statement* item. Shortened to *SG&A*. Also called *operating expenses*.

Semiannual

> Twice a year.

Senior

A characteristic of *debt* set to be *serviced* before *subordinated* debt from the same *issuer* in the event of *distress*. Also called *unsubordinated*.

Separate Trading of Registered Interest and Principal Securities

Stripped bonds made from *Treasurys*. Shortened to *STRIPS*.

Serial bond

A *fixed income security* with one *issue date* but staggered *maturity dates*.

Series

Part of a category of *securities* from the same *issuer*, as in *series A preferred stock*. Separately, the designation of a financial securities license in the U.S., including Series 7 and Series 63.

Service

To make the payments required by a *debt*, as with an *issuer* paying *interest* to a *holder*.

Settlement

The end of a transaction, generally marked by the delivery of *securities* to the buyer and the delivery of money to the seller. Relatedly, the full payment of *principal* on a *debt* by a *borrower*.

Settlement date

The date a transaction ends, generally marked by the delivery of *securities* to the buyer and the delivery of payment to the seller. Follows the *trade date* by a standard period, often one business day.

Shareholder
>An owner of *stock*.

Shareholders' equity
>*Assets* minus *liabilities*. A *balance sheet* section. Also called *book value, equity, net assets*, or *owners' equity*.

Shares
>Ownership stakes in *corporations*. Also called *stocks* or *equity*.

Shares outstanding
>*Stock* in a company held by *shareholders*. Does not include *shares* that could become outstanding from the conversion of a *convertible bond* or a convertible *preferred*, or from the exercise of an *option* or a *warrant*. Also called *basic shares*.

Short
>The state of having sold a *security* that was rented rather than owned, in an effort to profit from a drop in that security's price. Also used to describe an investment of that nature. The opposite of *long*.

Short interest
>The quantity of a *security* sold short but not *covered*, generally expressed as a percentage of the quantity of that security outstanding.

Short squeeze
>An accelerated increase in the price of a *listed security* caused by *short* sellers *covering*. The opposite of a *long squeeze*.

Short-term

A brief period, often one year or less; as with time to *maturity*. Distinct from *medium-term* and *long-term*.

Short-Term European Paper

Fixed income securities issued in Europe with a *term* of up to one year that meet certain standards. Relatedly, an EU initiative to encourage the issuance of such securities. Shortened to *STEP*.

Sinkable bond

A *fixed income security* backed by a *sinking fund*. An alternative to an *amortizing bond* or a *bullet bond*.

Sinking fund

Money set aside by an *issuer* to *redeem* portions of a *sinkable bond* according to a predetermined schedule.

Solvent

Able to meet financial obligations. The opposite of *insolvent*.

Speculative

The characteristic of a *fixed income security* suggesting that *interest* and *principal* may not be paid as promised. Indicated by *credit ratings* of *Ba1* or lower from *Moody's* and BB+ or lower from *Fitch* and *S&P*. Also called *high-yield, junk,* or *non-investment grade*. The opposite of *investment grade*.

Spot interest rate

The *interest* rate on a *debt* issued now. Also called the *spot rate*. The alternative to the *forward interest rate*.

Spot rate

The current price of an *asset* delivered now. With *fixed income securities*, the *interest* rate on a *debt* issued now. Also called the *spot interest rate* in that context. The alternative to the *forward rate*.

Spread

The distance between two amounts, as with *bid* and *ask*, or with *SOFR* and a *coupon rate*.

Stable outlook

An assessment by a *credit rating agency* that it probably won't change a *credit rating* in the *medium-term*. The alternative to *positive outlook*, *negative outlook*, and *developing outlook*.

Standard and Poor's

An *NRSRO* and one of the three leading *credit rating agencies*. Shortened to *S&P*.

Standard deviation

The square root of the *variance*. Also called *volatility*.

Steep yield curve

A very upward-sloping *yield curve*, where *long-term* yields exceed *short-term* yields by more than they do in a *normal yield curve*. Often taken as a sign of a healthy and improving economy. An alternative to *flat*, *humped*, *inverted*, and normal yield curves.

Stock

An ownership stake in a *corporation*. Also called *shares* or *equity*.

Stock certificate

A physical piece of paper that represents ownership in a *corporation*.

Stock exchange

An organized *securities* market such as the New York Stock Exchange.

Straight bond

A *fixed income security* that's meant to pay *principal* back all at once at *maturity*, without any special features like *callability* or *convertibility*. Also called a *bullet bond* or a *plain vanilla bond*. An alternative to an *amortizing bond* or a *sinkable bond*.

Straight-line

A method of accounting for *depreciation* or *amortization* whereby the same amount is expensed each period. An alternative to *accelerated* in that context. Relatedly, a method of accounting for *accretion* whereby the same amount is added to the worth of a *zero-coupon bond* each period.

Strike price

The amount that must be paid to convert an *option*, *warrant*, or other *security* into *equity*. Also called *exercise price*.

Strip

A single scheduled *interest* payment parceled out from a *fixed income security* by a financial institution for individual sale. Short for *stripped bond*.

Stripped bond
    A single scheduled *interest* payment parceled out from a *fixed income security* by a financial institution for individual sale. Shortened to *strip*.

Stripper
    A financial institution that creates *stripped bonds*.

Subordinated
    The characteristic of a *fixed income security* that has it *perform* only after *senior* fixed income securities from the same *issuer* do. Also called *junior*.

Subprime
    A characteristic of a *debt* indicating a high *credit risk*.

Subsidiary
    A distinct legal entity owned at least in part by, and controlled to some extent by, a business.

Substitution swap
    The sale of lower *yield bonds* and concurrent purchase of higher yield bonds that are otherwise similar.

Sukuk
    Sharia-compliant *securities* that, while not paying *interest*, do have some *fixed income security*-like characteristics.

Supermajority
    A specified percentage of *holders* in excess of 50 percent.

Surety

An entity that assumes the obligations of a *debt* if the *issuer defaults*. Also called a *guarantor*.

Surety bond

A *credit enhancement* tool that calls for a *guarantor*—usually an insurance company—to assume the obligations of a *debt* if the *issuer defaults*.

Swap

A general term for a contract between two parties that calls for the exchange of some combination of *assets* and *liabilities*, such as a *credit default swap* or an *interest rate swap*.

Swaption

A contract that conveys the right to engage in a specified *swap*.

Syndicate

A group of lenders that *fund* a single loan made to a single borrower.

T+1

Short for "trade date plus one day," a predetermined number of business days between *trade date* and *settlement date* in a securities market. The current standard in North America and elsewhere.

T+2

Short for "trade date plus two days," a predetermined number of business days between *trade date* and *settlement date* in a securities market. Recently replaced by *T+1* in North America and elsewhere.

T+3

Short for "trade date plus three days," a predetermined number of business days between the *trade date* and *settlement date* in a securities market.

T-bill

A *Treasury* with a *term* of up to 52 weeks. Short for *Treasury bill*.

TIGER or TIGR

A *Treasury stripped* of its *coupons* such that it's effectively a *zero*. Short for *Treasury Investment Growth Receipts*.

TIPS

Treasury coupon bonds with a *par value* that moves with the *Consumer Price Index*. Short for *Treasury Inflation Protected Securities*.

TTM

Short for *trailing 12 months*.

Take private

To acquire all of the *publicly*-traded *stock* in a company and *delist* it.

Tap issue

The *primary market* sale of more of a *bond* already issued. Also called a *reopening*.

Tax

A required payment to a government, often calculated as a percentage of a larger number like a *long-term capital gain*.

Tax-deferred

Not subject to *tax* until some specified time or event. Distinct from *tax-exempt*.

Tax-equivalent yield

The hypothetical pre-tax *yield* of a *tax-exempt fixed income security* like a *muni*. Calculated as actual yield divided by the quantity one minus the *tax* rate.

Tax-exempt

Never subject to *tax*. Distinct from *tax-deferred*.

Tax swap

The sale of *bonds* at a *capital loss* and concurrent purchase of similar bonds for the purpose of receiving a *tax* benefit.

Technical analysis

A method of evaluating *securities* that focuses on historic security prices. An alternative to *fundamental analysis*.

Tender

To sell a *security* to a buyer—often the *issuer*—who has made a broad, formal offer.

Tenor

The time left until the end of a financial contract. With *fixed income securities*, the time left until *maturity*.

Term

The time between the *issue date* and the *maturity date* of a *fixed income security*. Separately, a facet of a contract such as an *indenture*.

Term deposit

An *interest*-bearing *bank* deposit that cannot be withdrawn without penalty before a predetermined *maturity date*. Also called a *certificate of deposit* or *time deposit*.

Term repo

A *repurchase agreement* with a *term* of more than one day.

Term spread

The difference in *yield* between two *fixed income securities* with different *maturities* that are otherwise similar, often expressed in *basis points*. Also called the *yield curve spread*.

Term structure of interest rates

A graph of the prices of *fixed income securities* with the same *credit risk* where the vertical axis is *yield to maturity* and the horizontal axis is time to *maturity*. Also called the *yield curve*.

The Fed

The *central bank* of the United States. Short for *Federal Reserve*.

Tick

The minimum amount that the price of a *listed security* can change. Varies by market.

Ticker symbol

A short combination of letters and sometimes numbers that represents a *security* on a particular *stock exchange*. Distinct from *CUSIP*, *ISIN*, and *SEDOL*.

Tight spread

A small distance between a *bid* and an *ask*, often indicating high *liquidity*.

Time deposit

An *interest*-bearing *bank* deposit that cannot be withdrawn without penalty before a predetermined *maturity date*. Also called a *certificate of deposit* or *term deposit*.

Time value

The worth of an *option* that comes from the option not having expired. The counterpart to *intrinsic value*.

Time value of money

The principle that cash obtained now is worth more than the same amount of cash obtained later.

Tombstone

A printed summary announcement of a transaction such as the *issuance* of a *bond*.

Total return

A measure of investment performance that sums *appreciation* and *income* like *dividends* and *interest*, often stated as a percentage of purchase price, and often *annualized*.

Tracking error

The degree to which the price of an *index fund* deviates from the price of its index. Can be caused by *sampling*.

Trade date

The date a sale of *securities* is executed. Precedes the *settlement date* by a standard period, often one business day.

Trade payable

> Money owed to vendors. An item in the *liabilities* section of the *balance sheet*. Also called *accounts payable*.

Trade receivables

> Money expected from customers. An item in the *assets* section of the *balance sheet*. Also called *accounts receivable* or just *receivables*.

Trading volume

> The amount of one or more *securities* that changed hands during a period, often used as a measure of *liquidity*. Also called *volume*.

Tranche

> One of several editions of a *fixed income security* that may vary by *seniority*, *credit rating*, or other characteristics, as with *collateralized debt obligations*. From the French word for *slice*.

Treasury

> A sovereign *debt* obligation of the U.S. Department of the Treasury. Starts with a capital T, and pluralized as *Treasurys*. Separately, the figurative place where an organization keeps its money. Pluralized as *treasuries* in that case.

Treasury bill

> A *zero-coupon Treasury* with a *term* of up to 52 weeks. Shortened to *T-bill*.

Treasury bond

> A *Treasury coupon bond* with a *term* of over 10 years.

Treasury Inflation Protected Securities
Treasury coupon bonds with a *par value* that moves with the *Consumer Price Index*. Shortened to *TIPS*.

Treasury Investment Growth Receipt
A *Treasury stripped* of its *coupons* such that it's effectively a *zero*. Shortened to *TIGER* or *TIGR*.

Treasury note
A *Treasury coupon bond* with a *term* of between two and 10 years.

Treasury shares
Stock bought back but not *retired*. An item in the *equity* section of the *balance sheet*. Also called *treasury stock*.

Treasury stock
Shares bought back but not *retired*. An item in the *equity* section of the *balance sheet*. Also called *treasury shares*.

Treasury STRIPS
Stripped bonds made from *Treasurys*. Short for *Separate Trading of Registered Interest and Principal Securities*. Shortened to *STRIPS*.

Tri-party repo
A *repurchase agreement* that involves an agent like a *custodian bank* in addition to a buyer and a seller.

Trustee
The *fiduciary* financial institution appointed by the *issuer* of a *bond* to manage relationships with *holders*.

Turnover

The degree to which the *securities* in a *fund* or portfolio change. Separately, the sum of sales during a period reported on an *income statement*. Also called *revenue* in that context.

UCITS

A *pooled investment vehicle* that, because it's authorized by a European Union country, is authorized to operate throughout the EU. An acronym for the directive behind it, the *Undertakings for Collective Investments in Transferable Securities*.

U.S. Securities and Exchange Commission

The federal agency that regulates *stock* and *bond* trading in the U.S. Shortened to *Securities and Exchange Commission* or *SEC*.

Unaudited

Not examined by a public accountancy, as with the *financial statements* of some *private* companies. The opposite of *audited*.

Underlier

The *asset* on which the worth of a *derivative* is based.

Underwriter

A financial institution that plays a lead role in an *IPO*. Separately, an insurance company.

Unit

An ownership stake in a *fund* or a *partnership*. Also called *interest*.

Unit holder

An owner of a *fund* or a *partnership*.

Unit trust

A *pooled investment vehicle* common in the UK, comparable to a *mutual fund* in the U.S.

Unlevered free cash flow

A measure of *free cash flow* that does not capture *interest* payments.

Unlisted

Not traded on an exchange, as with *bonds* sold in a *private placement*.

Unrated

Without a *credit rating* from a *credit rating agency*, as with some *fixed income securities*.

Unrealized

Not actualized through a sale or an investment return. The opposite of *realized*.

Unregistered

Not cataloged with an authority, as with *commercial paper* in the U.S. The opposite of *registered*.

Unsecured

The characteristic of *debt* that means it's backed only by *assets* that the issuer hasn't pledged to *collateralize secured* debt. The alternative to *secured*.

Unsubordinated

A characteristic of *debt* set to be *serviced* before *subordinated* debt from the same *issuer* in the event of *distress*. Also called *senior*.

Upgrade

To change from one *credit rating* to a higher one. The opposite of *downgrade*.

Uptick

A just-occurred increase in the price of a *security*. The opposite of *downtick*.

Value investing

An *active* strategy that emphasizes buying *assets* at prices below worth, based on the view that prices gravitate towards worth.

Variable

A characteristic of a *fixed income security* where the *coupon rate* moves with a specified *reference rate*. Also called *floating*. The alternative to *fixed*.

Variance

A measure of the dispersion of a data set, calculated as the *arithmetic mean* of the squared differences from the arithmetic mean. Commonly denoted as σ^2, the lowercase Greek letter sigma raised to the second power.

Volatility

A common proxy for *risk*, broadly defined as the average daily change in the price of a *security* over the last month. A *standard deviation*. Commonly denoted as σ, the lowercase Greek letter sigma.

Volume

The amount of one or more *securities* that changed hands during a period, often used as a measure of *liquidity*. Also called *trading volume*.

WKN

A six-character German *security* identifier number that's been replaced by *ISIN*. Short for *Wertpapierkennnummer*.

Warrant

A *call option* issued by the *issuer* of the *underlier*.

Watch

A *credit rating agency* reassessing a *credit rating* because of an event impacting the *issuer*. Short for *credit watch*.

Waterfall

A tiered payment structure where parties are paid in order of *seniority*.

Weighted average

The *arithmetic mean* resulting from the multiplication of each constituent value by a factor, as *Macaulay Duration* results from the multiplication of each *cash flow* by a time factor.

Wertpapierkennnummer

A six-character German *security* identifier number that's been replaced by *ISIN*. Shortened to *WKN*.

Wrapped

The characteristic of a *bond* that means it has *financial guarantee insurance*.

Write-down

A decrease in the *book value* of an *asset* through the recognition of an irregular expense on the *income statement*.

YTC

Yield to maturity where the *maturity date* is the *call date* and the *issuer* pays the *call price*. Short for *yield to call*.

YTM

The *annualized* return from a *fixed income security* held until the end of its *term*. Short for *yield to maturity*.

YTP

Yield to maturity where the *maturity date* is the *put date* and the *issuer* pays the *put price*. Short for *yield to put*.

YTW

The lowest of *yield to maturity*, *yield to call*, and *yield to put*. Short for *yield to worst*.

Yankee bond

A *fixed income security* denominated in U.S. dollars and issued in the U.S. by a non-U.S entity.

Yield

The return from an *asset* expressed as a percentage and generally *annualized*, of which there are several types. For *fixed income securities* these include *bond-equivalent yield*, *current yield*, *yield to call*, *yield to maturity*, *yield to put*, *yield to worst*, and—with *preferred stock—dividend yield*.

Yield curve

A graph of the prices of *fixed income securities* with the same *credit risk* where the vertical axis is *yield to maturity* and the horizontal axis is time to *maturity*. Also called the *term structure of interest* rates.

Yield curve spread

The difference in *yield* between two *fixed income securities* with different *maturities* that are otherwise similar, often expressed in *basis points*. Also called the *term spread*.

Yield spread

The difference in *yield* between two *fixed income securities* with different *credit risks* that are otherwise similar, often expressed in *basis points*. Also called *credit spread*. Sometimes used to mean *term spread*.

Yield to call

Yield to maturity where the *maturity date* is the *call date* and the *issuer* pays the *call price*. Shortened to *YTC*.

Yield to maturity

The *annualized* return from a *fixed income security* held until the end of its term. Shortened to *YTM*.

Yield to put

Yield to maturity where the maturity date is the put date and the issuer pays the put price. Shortened to YTP.

Yield to worst

The lowest of yield to maturity, yield to call, and yield to put. Shortened to YTW.

Z-bond

The last tranche of a collateralized mortgage obligation.

ZCB

A fixed income security that pays no interest. Short for zero-coupon bond. Also called a pure discount bond or zero.

Zero

A fixed income security that pays no interest. Short for zero-coupon bond. Also called a ZCB or pure discount bond.

Zero-coupon bond

A fixed income security that pays no interest. Shortened to ZCB or zero. Also called a pure discount bond.

BIBLIOGRAPHY

Forbes, Shawn M., John J. Hatem, and Chris Paul. "Yield-to-Maturity and the Reinvestment of Coupon Payments." *Journal of Economics and Finance Education*, vol 5, no. 1, summer 2008, 48-51.

Kahneman, Daniel, and Amos Tversky. "Prospect Theory: An Analysis of Decision Under Risk." *Econometrica* 47, no. 2 (March 1979): 263-92.

Macauley, Frederick R. *Some Theoretical Problems Suggested by the Movements of Interest Rates, Bond Yields and Stock Prices in the United States since 1856*. New York: National Bureau of Economic Research, 1938.

Marshall, Kenneth Jeffrey. *Good Stocks Cheap: Value Investing with Confidence for a Lifetime of Stock Market Outperformance*. New York: McGraw-Hill, 2017.

Swensen, David F. *Pioneering Portfolio Management: An Unconventional Approach to Institutional Investment*. Rev. ed. New York: Free Press, 2009.

NOTES

PREFACE

1. David F. Swensen, *Pioneering Portfolio Management: An Unconventional Approach to Institutional Investment*, Rev. ed. (New York: Free Press, 2009), 269.
2. CFA Institute, "Fixed-Income Markets: Issuance, Trading, and Funding," https://www.cfainstitute.org/en/membership/professional-development/refresher-readings/fixed-income-markets-issuance-trading-funding#:~:text=Fixed%2Dincome%20markets%20include%20not,size%20of%20global%20equity%20markets, accessed August 18, 2024.
3. JPMorgan Chase & Co., "Historical Prime Rate," https://www.jpmorganchase.com/about/our-business/historical-prime-rate, accessed August 18, 2024.
4. Board of Governors of the Federal Reserve System, "Selected Interest Rates (Daily) - H.15," https://www.federalreserve.gov/releases/h15/, accessed August 18, 2024.

CHAPTER 1

1. Connecticut State Department of Revenue Services, "Estate and Gift Tax Information," https://portal.ct.gov/DRS/Individuals/Individual-Income-Tax-Portal/Estate-and-Gift-Taxes/Tax-Information, accessed August 18, 2024.

CHAPTER 2

1. Stiftung für Fachempfehlungen zur Rechnungslegung, "Standards," https://www.fer.ch/en/standards/, accessed August 18, 2024.
2. Tennessee Valley Authority, *2023 Form 10-K*, https://d18rn0p25nwr6d.cloudfront.net/CIK-0001376986/b1d84fa0-fedc-4285-a4c7-cddd3b623ec0.pdf, accessed August 18, 2024.

CHAPTER 3

1. Inter IKEA Systems B.V., "About Our Owner," https://www.inter.ikea.com/en/this-is-inter-ikea-group/about-our-owner, accessed August 18, 2024.
2. Huawei Technologies Co., Ltd., "We Are An Independent Company," https://www.huawei.com/trust-center/trustworthy/we-are, accessed August 18, 2024.
3. London Stock Exchange plc, "Order Book for Retail Bonds," https://www.londonstockexchange.com/equities-trading/asset-classes/debt-trading/order-book-retail-bonds," accessed August 25, 2024.

CHAPTER 4

1. Dooba Finance AB, "About Dooba Finance AB," https://dfabbond.se/, accessed August 19, 2024.
2. Assured Guaranty Ltd., *2023 Form 10-K*, https://d18rn0p25nwr6d.cloudfront.net/CIK-0001273813/26db8d8e-8fec-4219-b73f-7c4274924028.pdf, accessed August 19, 2024.
3. The Hershey Company, *2023 Form 10-K*, https://hershey.gcs-web.com/static-files/31bbd8d5-7789-4664-997e-cb0760321115, accessed August 19, 2024.
4. Berkshire Hathaway Inc., *Prospectus Supplement to Prospectus dated January 28, 2022*, https://www.sec.gov/Archives/edgar/data/1067983/000119312523280631/d532609d424b5.htm, accessed August 18, 2024.
5. Ibid.

CHAPTER 5

1. Latvijas Banka, *Annual Report 2014*, https://datnes.latvijasbanka.lv/ar/AR/LB_AR_2014.pdf, accessed September 5, 2021.
2. European Central Bank, "Governing Council," https://www.ecb.europa.eu/ecb/orga/decisions/govc/html/index.en.html, accessed September 8, 2021.
3. Banco Central del Ecuador, "History," https://www.bce.fin.ec/en/index.php/history, accessed September 5,

2021.

4. Republic of Indonesia, *Prospectus*,
   https://www.sec.gov/Archives/edgar/data/1719614/00011931251736
   0866/d448846d424b1.htm, accessed August 19, 2024.

5. The Toro Company, *2023 Form 10-K*,
   https://www.thetorocompany.com/static-files/782f078e-9840-4db4-
   b102-3b5304358727, accessed August 19, 2024.

6. U.S. Securities and Exchange Commission, *Form 10-Q*,
   https://www.investor.gov/introduction-investing/investing-
   basics/glossary/form-10-q, accessed August 19, 2024.

7. Globe Trade Centre S.A., *Consolidated Financial Statements for the
   Yeaar Ended 31 December 2022*,
   https://www.gtcgroup.com/~/media/Files/G/Globe-Trade-
   Centre/documents/gtc_aurora/2023/22%20YE%20GTC%20IFRS
   %20FS%20Conso%20EUR%20Financial
   %20statements_FINAL.pdf, accessed August 19, 2024.

8. U.S. Bancorp, *Q1 2024 Form 10-Q*,
   https://d18rn0p25nwr6d.cloudfront.net/CIK-0000036104/e139d047-
   f476-413a-8b30-d0f072253e8d.pdf, accessed July 1, 2024.

9. M&T Bank Corporation, *Q3 2023 Form 10-Q*,
   https://ir.mtb.com/static-files/9c226c05-95ad-4fa0-bdbe-
   74abc2672dd4, accessed January 4, 2024.

10. Truist Financial Corporation, *Q1 2024 Form 10-Q*,
    https://app.quotemedia.com/data/downloadFiling?
    webmasterId=101533&ref=318307706&type=PDF&symbol=TFC&
    cdn=510fb029c839b9214cb8c201f91ffe45&companyName=Truist+
    Financial+Corporation&formType=10-Q&dateFiled=2024-05-09,
    accessed July 1, 2024.

11. Walmart Inc., *Q2 2023 Form 10-Q*,
    https://d18rn0p25nwr6d.cloudfront.net/CIK-0000104169/e105f17b-
    360d-4b6b-9c02-9b21bbe4d4d4.pdf, accessed September 30, 2023.

12. Carrefour Group, S.A., *Half Year Financial Report 2023*,
    https://www.carrefour.com/sites/default/files/2023-07/Half-Year
    %20Financial%20Report%202023_0.pdf, accessed September 30,
    2023.

13. BİM Birleşik Mağazalar A.Ş., *Consolidated Financial Statements*

for the Period January 1 - June 30 , 2023, https://english.bim.com.tr/PeriodicalFinancialResults/2023/6%20Mo nth%20Report.pdf, accessed September 30, 2023.

14. National Railroad Passenger Corporation, *FY 2022 Company Profile*, https://www.amtrak.com/content/dam/projects/dotcom/english/publi c/documents/corporate/nationalfactsheets/Amtrak-Company-Profile-FY2022-020823.pdf, accessed January 7, 2024.

15. National Railroad Passenger Corporation, *Management's Discussion and Analysis 2023*, https://www.amtrak.com/content/dam/projects/dotcom/english/publi c/documents/corporate/financial/Amtrak-Management-Discussion-Analysis-Audited-Financial-Statements-FY2023.pdf, accessed June 7, 2024.

16. Axactor ASA, *Report Q4 2023*, https://www.axactor.com/uploads/GROUP-Investor-Relations-assets/Reports-and-presentations/2023/Quarterly-Report-Q4-2023.pdf, accessed August 20, 2024.

17. Axactor ASA, "Main Shareholders," https://www.axactor.com/investor-relations/share-and-debt-information/main-shareholders, accessed August 20, 2024.

18. Standard & Poor's Financial Services LLC., *Norway-Based Debt Collector Axactor ASA 'B' Rating Affirmed Amid Refinancing; Outlook Remains Stable*, https://www.axactor.com/uploads/GROUP-Investor-Relations-assets/Debt-information/RatingsDirect_ResearchUpdateNorwayBasedDebtColle ctorAxactorASABRatingAffirmedAmidRefinancingOutlookRemain sStable_55892465_Aug-28-2023.PDF, accessed August 20, 2024.

19. Axactor ASA, "Debt Information," https://www.axactor.com/investor-relations/share-and-debt-information/debt-information, accessed August 20, 2024.

20. U.S. Securities and Exchange Commission, "Current NRSROs," https://www.sec.gov/about/divisions-offices/office-credit-ratings/current-nrsros, accessed August 20, 2024.

21. European Securities and Markets Authority, "CRA Authorisation," https://www.esma.europa.eu/credit-rating-agencies/cra-authorisation, accessed August 20, 2024.

22. Fitch Ratings, Inc., "Back to Basics," https://www.fitchratings.com; Moody's Corporation, *Rating Scale and Definitions*, https://www.moodys.com/sites/products/productattachments/ap0753 78_1_1408_ki.pdf; and S&P Global Inc., "A Credit Rating is an Informed Opinion," https://www.spglobal.com/ratings/en/about/intro-to-credit-ratings; all accessed August 20, 2024.

23. Banco GNB Sudameris S.A., "Risk Ratings," https://www.gnbsudameris.com.co/investor-relations#risk-raitings, accessed August 20, 2024.

24. Fitch Ratings, Inc., "Fitch Affirms Colombia at 'BB+'; Outlook Stable," https://www.fitchratings.com/research/sovereigns/fitch-affirms-colombia-at-bb-outlook-stable-07-12-2023, accessed August 20, 2024.

25. Moody's Corporation, *Government of Colombia – Baa2 negative: Update following change in outlook to negative*, https://www.moodys.com/research/Government-of-Colombia-Baa2-negative-Update-following-change-in-outlook-Credit-Opinion--PBC_1405268, accessed August 20, 2024.

26. Constellation Software Inc., *Interim Financial Report: Third Quarter Fiscal Year 2023*, https://www.csisoftware.com/docs/default-source/investor-relations/statutory-filings/q3-2023-shareholder-report.pdf?sfvrsn=1e31336_3/%20Q3-2023-Shareholder-Report%20.pdf, accessed February 17, 2024.

27. Constellation Software Inc., *Management's Discussion and Analysis*, https://www.csisoftware.com/docs/default-source/investor-relations/statutory-filings/csi---mda-q3-2023---final.pdf?sfvrsn=8e8985a1_3/%20CSI---MDA-Q3-2023---Final%20.pdf, accessed February 18, 2024.

28. Constellation Software Inc., *Management Information Circular for the Annual Meeting of Shareholders to be Held on May 8, 2023*, https://www.csisoftware.com/docs/default-source/press-releases/constellation-mic-en.pdf?sfvrsn=be37be2e_3/%20Constellation-MIC-EN%20.pdf, accessed February 20, 2024.

29. Yahoo Finance, "Constellation Software Inc. (CNSWF),"
    https://finance.yahoo.com/quote/CNSWF, accessed February 14,
    2024.
30. Standard & Poor's Financial Services LLC, "Constellation Software
    Inc. Rated 'BBB' With A Stable Outlook; Proposed Debt Rated
    'BBB',"
    https://disclosure.spglobal.com/ratings/en/regulatory/article/-/view/ty
    pe/HTML/id/3121116f, accessed February 20, 2024.
31. Fitch Ratings, Inc., "Fitch Rates Constellation Software's New
    Unsecured Notes and Unsecured Revolving Facility 'BBB+',"
    https://www.fitchratings.com/research/corporate-finance/fitch-rates-
    constellation-software-new-unsecured-notes-unsecured-revolving-
    facility-bbb-05-02-2024, accessed February 20, 2024.

CHAPTER 6

1. Standard & Poor's Financial Services LLC, *Heathrow Funding
   Class A 'BBB+' and Class B 'BBB-' Ratings Affirmed on CAA
   Decision; Off Credit Watch; Outlook Stable*,
   https://www.heathrow.com/content/dam/heathrow/web/common/doc
   uments/company/investor/credit-
   ratings/sp/22.03.2023_ratingsaffirmed.pdf, accessed April 30, 2024.
2. Assured Guaranty Ltd., "Assured Guaranty Wraps £140 million
   Fixed Rate Public Bond Issue for Heathrow Airport,"
   https://info.assuredguaranty.com/press-room/all-press-releases/news-
   details/2023/Assured-Guaranty-Wraps-140-million-Fixed-Rate-
   Public-Bond-Issue-for-Heathrow-Airport/default.aspx, accessed
   April 30, 2024.
3. Fitch Ratings, Inc., "Citigroup Inc.,"
   https://www.fitchratings.com/entity/citigroup-inc-
   80089622#securities-and-obligations, accessed April 30, 2024.
4. Sudipto Sarkar and Gwangheon Hong, "Effective Duration of
   Callable Corporate Bonds: Theory and Evidence," *Journal of
   Banking & Finance* 28 (2004) 499–521.
5. Russell Wild, *Bond Investing for Dummies* (Hoboken: Wiley, 2007),
   214.
6. OneMain Finance Corporation, *Prospectus Supplement (To*

Prospectus dated October 13, 2023),
https://d18rn0p25nwr6d.cloudfront.net/CIK-0001584207/951ebf0b-
5ee0-42c2-bd4e-9e96425df345.pdf, accessed July 2, 2024.

7. OneMain Finance Corporation, *2023 Form 10-K*,
https://d18rn0p25nwr6d.cloudfront.net/CIK-0001584207/951ebf0b-
5ee0-42c2-bd4e-9e96425df345.pdf, accessed July 2, 2024.

8. Global Bond Data FZE, "S&P Global Ratings affirms OneMain
Holdings at "BB" (Local Currency LT credit rating); outlook stable,"
https://cbonds.com/news/2726309/, accessed June 28, 2024.

9. FMR LLC, "OneMain Fin Corp Note Call Make Whole 9.00000%
01/15/2029," https://fixedincome.fidelity.com/, accessed July 14,
2024.

10. OneMain, *Prospectus*.

11. Ibid.

CHAPTER 7

1. Shawn M. Forbes, John J. Hatem, and Chris Paul, "Yield-to-
Maturity and the Reinvestment of Coupon Payments," *Journal of
Economics and Finance Education*, vol 5, no. 1 (summer 2008): 48-
51.

2. Frank K. Reilly and Edgar A. Norton, *Investments*, 6th edition
(Mason, Ohio: South-Western, 2003), 659.

3. Frederick R. Macaulay, *Some Theoretical Problems Suggested by
the Movements of Interest Rates, Bond Yields and Stock Prices in the
United States since 1856* (New York: National Bureau of Economic
Research, 1938), 44.

4. Ibid, 45.

5. Ibid, 46.

6. Ibid, 51.

7. Ibid, 52.

8. Santander Issuances, S.A. Unipersonal, *Prospectus Supplement to
Prospectus Dated October 13, 2015*,
https://www.santander.com/content/dam/santander-
com/en/documentos/emisiones/documentos/em-US05971KAA79-
Subordinated%20Note,%20Series%2026,%20November
%202015.pdf, accessed June 28, 2024.

9. Börse Frankfurt, "Banco Santander S.A. 5,179% 15/25,"
    https://www.boerse-frankfurt.de/bond/us05971kaa79-banco-
    santander-s-a-5-179-15-25/charts, accessed June 28, 2024.

CHAPTER 8
1. Amos Tversky and Daniel Kahneman, "Availability: A Heuristic for
    Judging Frequency and Probability," *Cognitive Psychology* 5, no. 2
    (1973): 207–232.
2. Thomas Gilovich, Robert Vallone, and Amos Tversky, "The Hot
    Hand in Basketball: The Misperception of Random Sequences,"
    Cognitive Psychology 17 (1985): 295–314.
3. Aristotle, *Nicomachean Ethics*, trans. C.D.C. Reeve (Indianapolis:
    Hackett Publishing Company, 2014), 123.

CHAPTER 9
1. Tyco International Ltd., *2002 Form 10-K*,
    https://www.sec.gov/Archives/edgar/data/833444/000104746903025
    320/a2113549z10-ka.htm, accessed August 21, 2024.
2. Moody's Corporation, "Moody's Downgrades Tyco's Debt Ratings
    (Long-Term to Baa3, Short-Term to Prime-3); Ratings Remain
    Under Review for Possible Downgrade; Affirms Cit Debt Ratings
    (Long-Term at A2; Short-Term at Prime-1),"
    https://www.moodys.com/credit-ratings-
    tab/IssuerResearch/600042490?orgname=Tyco-International-Group-
    SA-&lang=ko&cy=kor&rdtid=Rating%20Action, accessed August
    21, 2024.
3. U.S. Securities and Exchange Commission, "Complaint dated
    September 11, 2002,"
    https://www.sec.gov/litigation/complaints/complr17722.htm,
    accessed August 21, 2024.
4. Bloomberg News, "Berkshire Hathaway May Profit From Tyco
    Bonds," *New York Times*, May 2, 2003,
    https://www.nytimes.com/2003/05/02/business/company-news-
    berkshire-hathaway-may-profit-from-tyco-bonds.html, accessed
    August 27, 2024.
5. Tyco International Ltd., *Q2 2002 Form 10-Q*,

https://otp.tools.investis.com/clients/us/johnson_controls/SEC/sec-show.aspx?
FilingId=1901098&Cik=0000833444&Type=PDF&hasPdf=1,
accessed August 21, 2024.

6. Bloomberg News, "Berkshire Hathaway."
7. SEC, "Complaint."
8. Tyco International Ltd., *2003 Form 10-K*,
https://www.sec.gov/Archives/edgar/data/833444/000104746903041
163/a2122987z10-k.htm, accessed August 21, 2024.

CHAPTER 10
1. U.S. Department of the Treasury, "Treasury Bills,"
https://www.treasurydirect.gov/indiv/research/indepth/tbills/res_tbill.
htm, accessed August 18, 2024.
2. U.S. Department of the Treasury, "Treasury Notes,"
https://www.treasurydirect.gov/indiv/research/indepth/tnotes/res_tno
te.htm, accessed August 18, 2024.
3. U.S. Department of the Treasury, "Treasury Bonds,"
https://www.treasurydirect.gov/indiv/research/indepth/tbonds/res_tb
ond.htm, accessed August 18, 2024.
4. U.S. Department of the Treasury, "Treasury Inflation Protected
Securities (TIPS),"
https://www.treasurydirect.gov/indiv/research/indepth/tips/res_tips.h
tm, accessed August 18, 2024.
5. U.S. Department of the Treasury, "Floating Rate Notes (FRNs),"
https://www.treasurydirect.gov/marketable-securities/floating-rate-
notes/, accessed August 18, 2024.
6. U.S. Department of the Treasury, "Separate Trading of Registered
Interest and Principal of Securities (STRIPS),"
https://treasurydirect.gov/marketable-securities/strips/, accessed
August 21, 2024.
7. Bundesrepublik Deutschland – Finanzagentur GmbH, "Federal
Securities," https://www.deutsche-finanzagentur.de/en/federal-
securities/types-of-federal-securities/overview-federal-securities,
accessed August 21, 2024.
8. Reserve Bank of India, "Government Securities Market in India – A

Primer,"
https://www.rbi.org.in/commonperson/English/Scripts/FAQs.aspx?
Id=711, accessed August 21, 2024.

9. United Kingdom Debt Management Office, "About Gilts,"
    https://www.dmo.gov.uk/responsibilities/gilt-market/about-gilts,
    accessed August 21, 2024.

10. Agence France Trésor, "About AFT," https://www.aft.gouv.fr/en,
    accessed August 21, 2024.

11. Ministero dell'Economia e delle Finanze, "Public Debt,"
    https://www.dt.mef.gov.it/en/index.html, accessed August 21, 2024.

12. Ministry of Finance, Japan, "Japanese Government Bonds,"
    https://www.mof.go.jp/english/policy/jgbs/index.html, accessed
    August 21, 2024.

CHAPTER 11

1. U.S. Securities and Exchange Commission, "Investor Bulletin:
    Municipal Bonds – An Overview,"
    https://www.investor.gov/introduction-investing/general-
    resources/news-alerts/alerts-bulletins/investor-bulletins-37, accessed
    August 22, 2024.

2. "San Diego Misses $1.6-Million Payment to City Bondholders," *Los
    Angeles Times*, September 7, 1994,
    https://www.latimes.com/archives/la-xpm-1994-09-07-fi-35698-
    story.html, accessed August 22, 2024.

3. Vanguard Group, "VNYUX: Vanguard New York Long-Term Tax-
    Exempt Fund Admiral Shares,"
    https://investor.vanguard.com/investment-products/mutual-
    funds/profile/vnyux, accessed August 25, 2024.

4. Vanguard Group, "VWIUX: Vanguard Intermediate-Term Tax
    Exempt Fund Admiral Shares,"
    https://investor.vanguard.com/investment-products/mutual-
    funds/profile/vwiux, accessed August 25, 2024.

CHAPTER 12

1. Amazon.com, Inc., *Q2 1998 Form 10-Q*,
    https://d18rn0p25nwr6d.cloudfront.net/CIK-0001018724/c9eba28e-

1525-4375-befe-694b90f893a7.pdf, accessed August 22, 2024.

2. Ibid.

3. Amazon.com, Inc., "Amazon.com Announces $275 Million Offering of Senior Discount Notes," https://press.aboutamazon.com/1998/4/amazon-com-announces-275-million-offering-of-senior-discount-notes, accessed August 22, 2024.

4. Amazon, *Q2 1998 Form 10-Q*.

5. Bloomberg L.P., "Buffett Lauds Amazon's 'Courage,' Then Buys Its Junk," https://www.bloomberg.com/news/articles/2003-04-07/buffett-lauds-amazon-s-courage-then-buys-its-junk, accessed August 22, 2024.

6. Amazon.com, Inc., *Q3 2002 Form 10-Q*, https://d18rn0p25nwr6d.cloudfront.net/CIK-0001018724/98bb7182-25dd-4db1-9d6f-3af92d0c39f7.pdf, accessed August 22, 2024.

7. Amazon.com, Inc.. *2001 Form 10-K*, https://d18rn0p25nwr6d.cloudfront.net/CIK-0001018724/96985bfb-79b1-41e9-b552-fd5ad5af6fd3.pdf, accessed August 22, 2024.

8. Amazon.com, Inc., *2002 Proxy Statement*, https://d18rn0p25nwr6d.cloudfront.net/CIK-0001018724/4d1b2a7b-2fe3-4aef-aa0c-7b098bc81768.pdf, accessed August 22, 2024.

9. "Amazon.com's Implied Credit Rating Raised," *Los Angeles Times*, September 5, 2002, https://www.latimes.com/archives/la-xpm-2002-sep-05-fi-techbrfs5.3-story.html, accessed August 22, 2024.

10. Bloomberg L.P., "Amazon's Overall Credit Rating Raised by Moody's," September 5, 2002, https://www.ctinsider.com/business/article/Amazon-s-overall-credit-rating-raised-by-Moody-s-1095283.php, accessed August 22, 2024.

11. Federal Reserve Bank of St. Louis, "Federal Funds Effective Rate," https://alfred.stlouisfed.org/series?seid=FEDFUNDS, accessed August 22, 2024.

12. Amazon.com, Inc., *2002 Form 10-K*, https://d18rn0p25nwr6d.cloudfront.net/CIK-0001018724/fae0d139-777f-489f-8e63-c97285413f9d.pdf p. 67, accessed August 22, 2024.

13. "Amazon.com's Implied Credit Rating," *Los Angeles Times*.

14. Amazon.com, Inc., "Amazon.Com Announces Redemption of Senior Discount Notes," April 24, 2003,

"https://press.aboutamazon.com/2003/4/amazon-com-announces-redemption-of-senior-discount-notes, accessed August 22, 2024.

CHAPTER 13

1. U.S. Department of the Treasury, "Floating Rate Notes (FRNs)," https://www.treasurydirect.gov/marketable-securities/floating-rate-notes/, accessed August 18, 2024.
2. Mutares SE & Co. KGaA, *Bond Terms*, https://ir.mutares.com/wp-content/uploads/2023/05/Bond-Terms-Project-Nova-EV17301590.1.pdf, accessed August 18, 2024.
3. Mutares SE & Co. KGaA, "Bond 2023/2027," https://ir.mutares.com/en/bond/, accessed August 18, 2024.
4. Mutares, *Bond Terms*.
5. Mutares, "Bond 2023/2027."
6. Mutares, *Bond Terms*.
7. The European Money Market Institute, "Rates," https://www.emmi-benchmarks.eu/benchmarks/euribor/, accessed August 18, 2024.
8. Mutares, "Bond 2023/2027."
9. Mutares, *Bond Terms*.
10. Mutares, "Bond 2023/2027."
11. Euronext, "Mutares SE & Co. K 23/27 FRN," https://live.euronext.com/en/product/bonds/NO0012530965-XOAM, accessed August 18, 2024.
12. Börse Frankfurt, "Mutares SE & Co. KGaA 12,222% 23/27," https://www.boerse-frankfurt.de/bond/no0012530965-mutares-se-co-kgaa-12-222-23-27, accessed August 18, 2024.
13. Mutares SE & Co. KGaA, *Earnings Report Q1 2024*, https://ir.mutares.com/wp-content/uploads/2024/05/20240507_Mutares-Earnings-Report-Q1-2024.pdf, accessed August 18, 2024.
14. Mutares SE & Co. KGaA, *Annual Report 2023*, https://ir.mutares.com/wp-content/uploads/2024/04/Mutares_2023_Annual_Report_save.pdf, accessed August 18, 2024.
15. Mutares, *Earnings Report Q1 2024*.
16. Mutares, *Annual Report 2023*.

17. Mutares SE & Co. KGaA, *Annual Report 2022*,
    https://ir.mutares.com/wp-
    content/uploads/2023/04/Mutares_2022_Annual_Report_final.pdf,
    accessed August 18, 2024.
18. Mutares, *Earnings Report Q1 2024*.
19. Mutares, *Annual Report 2023*.
20. Börse Frankfurt, "Mutares SE & Co. KGaA," https://boerse-
    frankfurt.de/equity/mutares-se-co-kgaa, accessed July 26, 2024.
21. Börse Frankfurt, "Mutares SE & Co. KGaA 12,222% 23/27,"
    https://www.boerse-frankfurt.de/bond/no0012530965-mutares-se-co-
    kgaa-12-222-23-27, accessed June 21, 2024.
22. Mutares Investor Relations, e-mail message to author, July 3, 2024.
23. Mutares SE & Co. KGaA, *Press Release*, January 19, 2024,
    https://mutares.com/en/mutares-places-second-tap-issue-of-its-bond-
    issued-in-march-2023-with-a-volume-of-eur-100-million-and-
    strengthens-basis-for-further-development/, accessed August 18,
    2024.

CHAPTER 14
1. Fitch Ratings, Inc., "Short-Term Credit,"
   https://your.fitchratings.com/short-term-credit-2019, accessed
   August 22, 2024.
2. Moody's Corporation, *Rating Scale and Definitions*,
   https://www.moodys.com/sites/products/productattachments/ap0753
   78_1_1408_ki.pdf, accessed August 22, 2024.
3. S&P Global Inc., "Credit Ratings,"
   https://www.spglobal.com/ratings/en/products-
   benefits/products/issue-credit-ratings, accessed August 22, 2024.
4. Federal Reserve Bank of St. Louis, "The Commercial Paper Market:
   Who's Minding the Shop?" April 1, 1998,
   https://www.stlouisfed.org/publications/regional-economist/april-
   1998/the-commercial-paper-market-whos-minding-the-shop,
   accessed August 22, 2024.
5. Reserve Bank of India, "Master Circular - Guidelines for Issue of
   Commercial Paper,"
   https://www.rbi.org.in/commonperson/English/Scripts/Notification.a

spx?Id=798#4, accessed August 22, 2024.

6. Reserve Bank of Australia, "Eligible Securities," https://www.rba.gov.au/mkt-operations/resources/tech-notes/eligible-securities.html#:~:text=Commercial%20paper %20%E2%80%93%20Securities%20issued%20by,that%20are %20not%20government%20guaranteed., accessed August 22, 2024.

7. Marcin Kacperczyk and Philipp Schnabl, "When Safe Proved Risky: Commercial Paper during the Financial Crisis of 2007–2009," *Journal of Economic Perspectives* 24, no. 1 (2010): 29–50, https://pubs.aeaweb.org/doi/pdfplus/10.1257/jep.24.1.29, accessed August 22, 2024.

CHAPTER 15

1. Brødrene A & O Johansen A/S, *Articles of Association*, https://ao.dk/globalassets/download/regnskabsdata/2023/articles-of-association---march-2023.pdf, accessed August 22, 2024.

2. Eniro Group AB, *Årsredovisning 2021*, https://cdn.bequoted.com/media/1/3a3c1691-688d-4233-bb05-eef3a10b9a7c/Eniro-Group-AB_Arsredovisning-2021.pdf, accessed August 22, 2024.

3. Fat Brands Inc., *Form S-1 Registration Statement*, https://d18rn0p25nwr6d.cloudfront.net/CIK-0001705012/8f281a6d-759d-4fd9-95ca-af592fa9755d.pdf, accessed August 22, 2024.

4. Fat Brands Inc., *Q1 2024 Form 10-Q*, https://d18rn0p25nwr6d.cloudfront.net/CIK-0001705012/6ca79184-eb76-4d71-8f10-6aaacb451d90.pdf, August 22, 2024.

5. Fat Brands Inc., *2023 Form 10-K*, https://d18rn0p25nwr6d.cloudfront.net/CIK-0001705012/476041c2-9332-414e-832c-c044d6d381ca.pdf, August 22, 2024.

6. Fat Brands Inc., *2023 Proxy Statement*, https://d18rn0p25nwr6d.cloudfront.net/CIK-0001705012/741b0dc4-7481-4652-8196-c3cbcba98627.pdf, accessed August 22, 2024.

7. Fat Brands, *Q1 2024 Form 10-Q*.

8. Nasdaq, Inc., "Fat Brands Inc. 8.25% Series B Cumulative Preferred Stock (FATBP) Dividend History," https://www.nasdaq.com/market-activity/stocks/fatbp/dividend-

history, accessed August 22, 2024.

9. Yahoo Finance, "Fat Brands Inc. (FATBP),"
    https://finance.yahoo.com/quote/FATBP/, accessed July 23, 2004.

CHAPTER 16

1. Martin Guzman, *An Analysis of Argentina's 2001 Default
    Resolution*, October 2016,
    https://www.cigionline.org/sites/default/files/documents/CIGI
    %20Paper%20No.110WEB_0.pdf, accessed August 22, 2024.

2. Julie Wernau, "How Elliott Earned Billions on Argentine Bonds at
    101% Interest," *The Wall Street Journal*, March 3, 2016,
    https://www.wsj.com/articles/BL-MBB-46981, accessed August 22,
    2024.

3. Guzman, *An Analysis*.

4. Daniel Luna, "Argentina's Crisis Explained," *Time*, December 20,
    2001, https://time.com/archive/6946474/argentinas-crisis-explained/,
    accessed August 22, 2024.

5. Martin Guzman and Joseph E. Stiglitz, "How Hedge Funds Held
    Argentina for Ransom," *The New York Times*, April 1, 2016,
    https://www.nytimes.com/2016/04/01/opinion/how-hedge-funds-
    held-argentina-for-ransom.html, accessed August 24, 2024.

6. The Republic of Argentina, *Prospectus Supplement*, December 27,
    2004,
    https://www.sec.gov/Archives/edgar/data/914021/000095012305000
    302/y04567e424b5.htm, accessed August 24, 2024.

7. Guzman, *An Analysis*.

8. Trading Economics, "Argentina - Credit Rating,"
    https://tradingeconomics.com/argentina/rating, accessed August 24,
    2024.

9. Michael D. Goldhaber, "An Infamous Bet," *The American Lawyer*,
    October 2016.

10. Jérôme Sgard, "Argentina vs. NML Capital, Ltd.," *Global Private
    International Law: Adjudication Without Frontiers* (Cheltenham:
    Edward Elgar Publishing, 2019), 255-270.

11. Goldhaber, "An Infamous Bet."

12. Guzman and Stiglitz, "How Hedge Funds."

13. Goldhaber, "An Infamous Bet."
14. Daniel Luna, "Argentina's Crisis."

CHAPTER 17

1. CPI Property Group S.A., *Final Terms: Issue of €750,000,000 2.750 Percent Senior Notes Due 12 May 2026*, https://ise-prodnr-eu-west-1-data-integration.s3-eu-west-1.amazonaws.com/legacy/Final+Terms_003a6cde-dfc1-428f-8c2e-167235b17186.pdf; and *Final Terms: Issue of £350,000,000 2.750 Percent Senior Notes Due 22 January 2028*, https://cpipg.com/storage/app/uploads/public/611/a4d/455/611a4d45 59871684536771.pdf; both accessed August 24, 2024.

2. CPI Property Group S.A., *Base Prospectus dated 30 May 2019*, https://ise-prodnr-eu-west-1-data-integration.s3-eu-west-1.amazonaws.com/legacy/Base+Prospectus_5d283c18-c9cd-4aee-aea0-43acf7818c06.PDF; and *Base Prospectus dated 27 April 2020*, https://ise-prodnr-eu-west-1-data-integration.s3-eu-west-1.amazonaws.com/legacy/Base+Prospectus_ec821ad7-fe58-4745-80f5-39396b0e1f1f.pdf; both accessed August 24, 2024.

3. Börse Frankfurt, "CPI Property Group S.A. 2,75% 20/26," https://www.boerse-frankfurt.de/bond/xs2171875839-cpi-property-group-s-a-2-75-20-26; and "CPI Property Group S.A. 2,75% 20/28," https://www.boerse-frankfurt.de/bond/xs2106589471-cpi-property-group-s-a-2-75-20-28; both accessed August 24, 2024.

4. Muddy Waters, LLC, "MW is Short the Credit of CPI Property Group S.A. (CPIPGR)," https://muddywatersresearch.com/research/cpipgr/mw-short-credit-cpipgr/, accessed August 24, 2024.

5. Muddy Waters, "MW is Short the Credit of CPI."

6. CPI Property Group S.A., *H1 2023 Management Report*, https://cpipg.com/storage/app/uploads/public/64f/0d1/956/64f0d195 6fce6643030226.pdf, accessed August 24, 2024.

7. CPI Property Group S.A., *Press Release: CPI Property Group Publishes Half-Year Financial Results for 2023*, https://cpipg.com/storage/app/uploads/public/64f/0d2/a5d/64f0d2a5d 046b426219402.pdf, accessed August 24, 2024.

8. CPI Property Group S.A., *Press Release: CPI Property Group Publishes Financial Results for the first quarter of 2023*, https://cpipg.com/storage/app/uploads/public/647/786/a67/647786a6 74e77910206425.pdf, accessed August 24, 2024.

9. Moody's Corporation, *Weekly Market Outlook: A Win for the Doves*, August 31, 2023, https://www.moodys.com/web/en/us/insights/resources/weekly-market-outlook-a-win-for-the-doves.pdf, accessed August 24, 2024.

10. Standard & Poor's Financial Services LLC, "Research Update: CPI Property Group Outlook Revised To Negative On Tightening Credit Metrics Despite Disposal Success; 'BBB-' Affirmed," December 18, 2023, https://disclosure.spglobal.com/ratings/en/regulatory/article/-/view/s ourceId/12948220, accessed August 24, 2024.

11. Börse Frankfurt, "CPI Property Group S.A. 2,75% 20/26."

12. Börse Frankfurt, "CPI Property Group S.A. 2,75% 20/28."

13. Börse Frankfurt, "CPI 20/26."

14. Börse Frankfurt, "CPI 20/28."

15. Standard & Poor's Financial Services LLC., *CPI Property Group Downgraded To 'BB+' On Ongoing Tight Credit Metrics And Financial Policy Deviations; Outlook Negative*, May 31, 2024, https://cpipg.com/storage/app/uploads/public/665/9a1/f90/6659a1f90 ac1c867468104.pdf, accessed August 24, 2024.

16. CPI Property Group S.A., *Press Release: CPI Property Group – Moody's Rating Action*, July 26, 2024, https://cpipg.com/storage/app/uploads/public/66a/3cf/403/66a3cf403 431e362788127.pdf, accessed August 24, 2024.

17. Börse Frankfurt, "CPI 20/26."

18. Börse Frankfurt, "CPI 20/28."

19. Muddy Waters, LLC, "Research," https://muddywatersresearch.com/research/, accessed August 24, 2024.

INDEX

ABOUT THE AUTHOR

Kenneth Jeffrey Marshall is an author, professor, and value investor. He teaches value investing and personal finance at Stanford University; industry analysis in the masters in engineering program at the University of California, Berkeley; and value investing in the masters in finance program at the Stockholm School of Economics in Sweden. He is the author of the books *Good Stocks Cheap: Value Investing with Confidence for a Lifetime of Stock Market Outperformance*, which was also published in Chinese; and *Small Steps to Rich: Personal Finance Made Simple*. He holds a BA in Economics, International Area Studies from the University of California, Los Angeles; and an MBA from Harvard University.

www.kennethjeffreymarshall.com